KU-498-870

# BIG BOOK OF KNOWLEDGE

# CONTENTS

# DK
# BIG BOOK OF
# KNOWLEDGE

## DK

**LONDON, NEW YORK,**
**MELBOURNE, MUNICH, and DELHI**

First published in Great Britain in 1994
by Dorling Kindersley Limited
80 Strand, London, WC2R 0RL

16 18 20 19 17 15
001–194815–07/13

A CIP catalogue record for this
book is available from the British Library.

ISBN 978-1-4093-3325-8

Reproduced by Colourscan, Singapore
Printed and bound in Hong Kong

see our complete product line at

www.dk.com

**General Editor** Sarah Phillips
**General Art Editors** Ruth Shane, Paul Wilkinson
**Subject Editors** Francesca Baines, Val Burton, Deborah Chancellor,
Roz Fishel, Hilary Hockman, Rosemary McCormick, Sarah Miller,
Seán O'Connell, Jean Rustean, Anne de Verteuil
**Subject Art Editors** Flora Awolaja, Liz Black, Amanda Carroll,
Richard Clemson, Ross George, Sarah Goodwin, Sara Nunan,
Ron Stobbart, Andrew Walker, Sonia Whillock
**Designers** Wayne Blades, Alison Greenhalgh, James Hunter,
Marianne Markham, Tuong Nguyen, Alison Verity, Samantha Webb
**Picture Researchers** Lorna Ainger, Caroline Brook, Venetia Bullen,
Anna Lord, Miriam Sharland, Paul Snelgrove
**Subject Consultants** Dr Michael Benton, Nicholas Booth, Martyn Bramwell,
Roger Bridgman, Eryl Davies, Liza Dibble, John Farndon, Adrian Gilbert,
Alan Harris, Paul Hillyard, Dr Malcolm MacGarvin, Diana Maine, Margaret Mulvihill,
Dr Fiona Payne, Chris Pellant, Dr Richard Walker, Shane Winser
**Production Manager** Ian Paton
**Production Assistant** Harriet Maxwell
**Editorial Director** Jonathan Reed
**Design Director** Ed Day

### ACKNOWLEDGEMENTS

**Photographers:** Peter Anderson, Steve Bartholomew, Peter Chadwick, Tina Chambers, Andy Crawford, Colour Company, Geoff Dann, John Downes,
Michael Dunning, John Edwards, Lynton Gardiner, Steve Gorton, Colin Keates, Tim Kelly, Gary Kevin, Chris King, Dave King, Cyril Laubscher,
Kevin Mallett, Ray Moller, David Murray, Tim Ridley, David Rudkin, Karl Shone, James Stevenson, John Swift, Harry Taylor, Andreas von Einsiedel,
Jerry Young. **Illustrators:** Graham Allen, Norman Barber, David Bergen, Roby Braun, Peter Bull, Joanna Cameron, Jim Channell, Bob
Corley, Sandra Doyle, David Fathers, Roy Flooks, Tony Gibbons, Mike Gillah, Tony Graham, Peter Griffiths, Terry Hadler, Edwina
Hannah, Charlotter Hard, Kaye Hodges, Keith Hume, Ray Hutchins, Aziz Khan, Pavel Kostal, Norman Lacey, Stuart Lafford,
Kenneth Lilly, Linden Artists, Steve Lings, Mike Loates, Chris Lyon, Alan Male, Richard Manning, Janos Marffy, Josephine
Martin, Annabel Milne, Sean Milne, Patrick Mulray, Richard Orr, Alex Pang, Darren Pattenden, Liz Pepperell, Jane Pickering,
Gill Platt, Maurice Pledger, Sebastian Quigley, Christine Robins, Eric Rome, Michelle Ross, Simon Roulstone, Colin Salmon,
John Searl, Pete Serjeant, Rob Shone, Clive Spong, Roger Stewart, John Temperton Grose Thurston, Graham Turner, Brian
Watson, Phil Weare, Sonia Whillock, John Woodcock, Michael Woods. **Models:** Celia Allen, Roby Braun, Atlas Models,
Cheltenham Cutaway Exhibits Ltd, Crystal Palace Park, London, Arril Johnson, Donks Models, Centaur Studios, Norrie Carr
Model Agency, Peter Griffiths, John Holmes, Scallywags Model Agency, Truly Scrumptious Child Model Agency.

# How to Use This Book

It's easy to use *The Big Book of Knowledge*. Start by looking at the contents page. There you will see that the book has four chapters, which are divided into different subject areas. Find a subject or a picture that interests you, and turn to that page. If you can't find what you want on the contents page, look it up in the index at the back. This is an alphabetical list of everything covered in the book. After each entry, there is a list of all the pages on which that topic is mentioned.

See how the index works by looking up 'dinosaurs'. Turn to all the pages listed after the entry until you find the section on Enormous Meat-Eaters shown here.

This page uses a picture of that section to tell you about some of the regular features you will find in *The Big Book of Knowledge*.

## ENORMOUS MEAT-EATERS

Like tigers today, Tyrannosaurus rex may have hunted alone, terrorizing its prey with surprise attacks. This fierce dinosaur was a carnivore, which means it lived on a diet of meat. The biggest meat-eater ever to walk on this planet, Tyrannosaurus rex was heavier than an elephant and as tall as a two-storey building. Its name means 'king of the tyrant reptiles'.

Hunters need good eye sight and a strong sense of smell. Large parts of Tyrannosaurus brain controlled its of sight and smell.

*Tyrannosaurus had a massive skull. It took the shock of crashing into prey at speeds of up to 32 kilometres per hour.*

*Tyrannosaurus may have charged with jaws, ready to sink deadly teeth into its prey. Big chunks of flesh swallowed whole.*

*Its short 'arms' weren't long enough to reach its mouth, but they may have been used to grip and kill prey.*

**Duck-Billed Dinner**
Tyrannosaurus probably hunted duck-billed dinosaurs, called hadrosaurs. It may have hidden among the trees, waiting for the right moment to charge at a peaceful herd of grazing ducks.

148

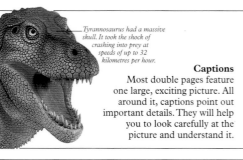

*Tyrannosaurus had a massive skull. It took the shock of crashing into prey at speeds of up to 32 kilometres per hour.*

**Captions**
Most double pages feature one large, exciting picture. All around it, captions point out important details. They will help you to look carefully at the picture and understand it.

Albertosaurus    Tarbosaurus    Dilophosaurus    Ceratosaurus    Allosaurus

**Picture Catalogues**
On some pages, you will find a row of small pictures that are similar to the large one. Try to work out the differences between them.

# ENORMOUS MEAT-EATERS

Like tigers today, Tyrannosaurus rex may have hunted alone, terrorizing its prey with surprise attacks. This fierce dinosaur was a carnivore, which means it

*Hunters need eye sight and sense of smell. parts of Tyras brain controll*

## Title and Introduction
Each double page deals with a different subject. The title tells you exactly what the subject is, and the introduction gives you some basic information about it.

## Step by Step
Occasionally, you will find a series of illustrations that shows you how something works. When you look at these pictures, for instance, you can see that Tyrannosaurus is using its small arms to help it stand up!

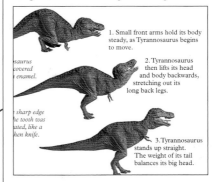

1. Small front arms hold its body steady, as Tyrannosaurus begins to move.

2. Tyrannosaurus then lifts its head and body backwards, stretching out its long back legs.

3. Tyrannosaurus stands up straight. The weight of its tail balances its big head.

**Life-Sized Tooth**
A Tyrannosaurus tooth grew up to 18 centimetres long.

*A Tyrannosaurus tooth was covered with tough enamel.*

*The sharp edge of the tooth was serrated, like a kitchen knife.*

**Stretch Those Legs**
Tyrannosaurus' short 'arms' may also have been used to help the dinosaur up after a rest on the ground.

1. Small front arms hold its body steady, as Tyrannosaurus begins to move.

2. Tyrannosaurus then lifts its head and body backwards, stretching out its long back legs.

3. Tyrannosaurus stands up straight. The weight of its tail balances its big head.

**Cannibal Dinosaurs**
A cannibal is a living thing that eats its own kind. Some meat-eating dinosaurs may have been cannibals. This skeleton of a dinosaur called Coelophysis was found with the tiny bones of a baby Coelophysis inside its stomach.

*ook how small human tooth is!*

*he Family*
*meat-eating dinosaurs to the carnosaur group. me means 'flesh lizard'.*

*saurus*   Tarbosaurus   Dilophosaurus   Ceratosaurus   Allosaurus

## Measurements
In most cases, units of measurement are spelt out, but in some places you will come across the following abbreviations.

| | | |
|---|---|---|
| cm | = | centimetres |
| m | = | metres |
| km | = | kilometres |
| km/h | = | kilometres per hour |
| l | = | litres |

## Stories in a Box
Amazing facts or stories appear in a box. Sometimes boxes suggest experiments to carry out, or things to do that will help you understand the subject better.

**Cannibal Dinosaurs**
A cannibal is a living thing that eats its own kind. Some meat-eating dinosaurs may have been cannibals. This skeleton of a dinosaur called Coelophysis was found with the tiny bones of a baby Coelophysis inside its stomach.

# EARTH AND SPACE

To us, our planet Earth seems enormous, but if we were able to gaze at it across the vastness of space, it would look like a tiny speck. It is one of the eight planets that are constantly hurtling around a star – our Sun – along individual oval paths called orbits.

Together, the Sun and its planets are known as the solar system. This, in turn, is part of a cluster of millions of stars and planets, called a galaxy. Our galaxy, which is shaped like a spiral, is called the Milky Way. It is so huge that a jet would take 100 billion years to fly across it. So far, we have discovered about 6,000 million different galaxies, and together they make up the universe.

Stars are made from layers of burning gas around a dense core. Some planets are mostly gas too, while others are liquid. Our Earth, however, is like a gigantic ball of rock.

**The Earth
Space**

# THE EARTH

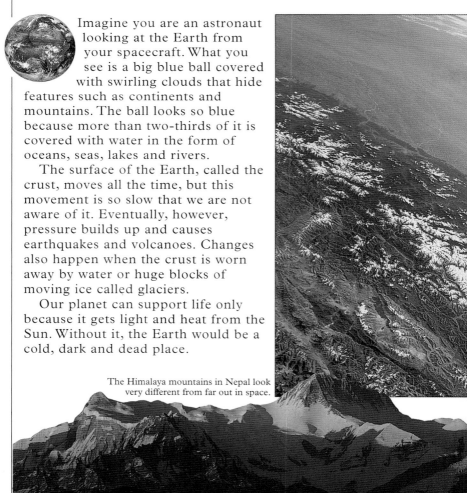

Imagine you are an astronaut looking at the Earth from your spacecraft. What you see is a big blue ball covered with swirling clouds that hide features such as continents and mountains. The ball looks so blue because more than two-thirds of it is covered with water in the form of oceans, seas, lakes and rivers.

The surface of the Earth, called the crust, moves all the time, but this movement is so slow that we are not aware of it. Eventually, however, pressure builds up and causes earthquakes and volcanoes. Changes also happen when the crust is worn away by water or huge blocks of moving ice called glaciers.

Our planet can support life only because it gets light and heat from the Sun. Without it, the Earth would be a cold, dark and dead place.

The Himalaya mountains in Nepal look very different from far out in space.

Stalactites form in caves.

Sandstone

Pumice

Green marble

Uluru (Ayers Rock) in Australia

Earth photographed from a satellite

# THE EARTH'S CRUST

Just like you, the Earth has a very delicate skin. It is so thin that if you compare it to the whole Earth, it is thinner than the skin of an apple.

The Earth's skin, or crust, is made up of rock, built up in layers over millions of years. The layers look like blankets on a bed, with lots of lumps and bumps in them.

*The crust is a thin layer of rock between 6 and 70 kilometres thick.*

*The mantle is the layer below the crust. In parts of it, the rock has melted like treacle.*

*The outer core is made of iron and nickel that have melted to form a liquid.*

*The inner core is a ball of iron and nickel. It is hotter here than at the outer core, but the ball stays solid.*

**How Mountains are Made**

Mountains are made when the Earth's crust is pushed up in big folds or forced up or down in blocks. The different shapes made are given different names.

*Overfold*

*Downfold*

*Upfold*

*The sea lies on top of the oceanic crust. The oceanic crust also runs underneath the continental crust.*

*The land is made out of the continental crust. It is thickest where mountains are found.*

*Under the oceans the crust is as little as 6 kilometres thick, but under the continents it is up to 70 kilometres thick.*

*The mantle*

*Block mountain*

*Fault*

*Rift valley*

## Going Down
This is a rift valley. It was made when a block of land sank down between two long breaks, called faults, in the Earth's crust.

### A Long Way to Go
Did you know that the deepest hole ever drilled into the Earth's crust is only 13 kilometres deep? To reach the centre of the Earth, you would have to drill 500 times deeper.

## Going Up
Here the land has been pushed into giant folds by movements in the Earth's crust. You can see how the crust is made up of lots and lots of layers of rock.

# MOVING PLATES

The Earth's crust is not one unbroken piece. It is made up of many pieces that fit together like a giant jigsaw puzzle. These pieces, called plates, ride on soft, partly melted rock moving underneath them. The pieces push against each other with spectacular effects – earthquakes split the crust, volcanoes form, new land is made and huge mountain ranges are pushed skywards.

### All Scrunched Up
Sometimes, two plates push against each other and then crumple the land to make huge mountain ranges.

### Going Down
Sometimes, one plate slides under another. It is pushed down into the mantle and melts.

### Doing the Splits
Sometimes, two plates split apart and lava bubbles up to fill the gap. It hardens and makes new land.

### Slip, Sliding Away
Sometimes, two plates slip sideways past each other. This kind of movement causes earthquakes.

### On the Move
The plates are never still, they are always moving. In one year they can move about 2.5 centimetres, about as much as your fingernails grow in the same amount of time.

*The red dots show you the places where volcanoes erupt.*

*Continent*

## Past, Present, Future

Have you ever wondered what the Earth looked like in the past? These pictures show you how the continents have moved over the last 300 million years, and how the world may look 50 million years from now.

## The Restless Earth

These houses and roads in Iceland are near a spot where two plates meet and have split the land.

*The green dots show you the places where earthquakes happen.*

*This is where two plates meet.*

300 MILLION YEARS AGO

## Changing Places

The land is coming together to make one gigantic continent.

200 MILLION YEARS AGO

PANGAEA

### All Together

The super continent has come together. It is called Pangaea.

150 MILLION YEARS AGO

LAURASIA

GONDWANALAND

### Worlds Apart

The land is drifting apart again. Pangaea is splitting into two, Laurasia and Gondwanaland.

TODAY

### Familiar Ground

Today, the world looks like this, but the continents are still moving.

50 MILLION YEARS TIME

### Looking Ahead

This is how the world may look in 50 million years time. Can you spot how the land has changed its shape? To start you off, find Africa on the globe and see how it has joined up with Europe.

# VOLCANOES

When you shake up a can of fizzy drink and then pull off the tab, the contents shoot out with a great whoosh! A volcano acts a bit like this. With tremendous force, molten (melted) rock bursts through weak parts in the Earth's crust and is hurled high into the sky.

*Volcanoes can be quiet and not erupt for a long time.*

*Hot springs are often found near volcanoes.*

**Nature's Fireworks**
This volcano is putting on its own spectacular fireworks display. The explosions of red-hot lava and ash from the crater look like gigantic 'Roman Fountains'.

## The Spotter's Guide to Volcano Shapes

**Spreading Out**
Some volcanoes are flat. Their lava is very runny, so it spreads out in a thin sheet.

**Short and Plump**
Some volcanoes are dumpy. They are made of ash, which is lava that has turned to dust.

**Going Up**
Some volcanoes have pointed cones. Their lava is thick and sticky so it does not run far.

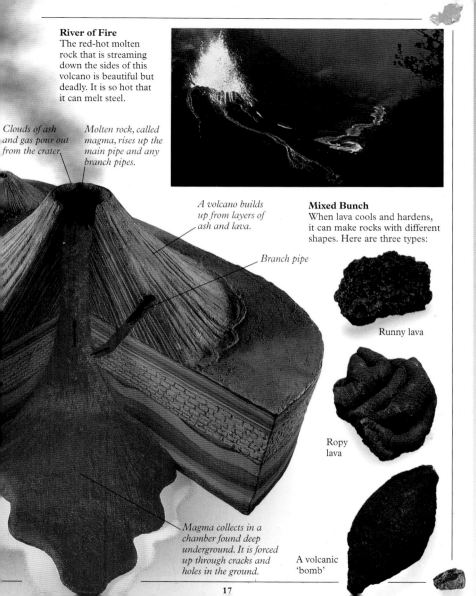

### River of Fire
The red-hot molten rock that is streaming down the sides of this volcano is beautiful but deadly. It is so hot that it can melt steel.

*Clouds of ash and gas pour out from the crater.*

*Molten rock, called magma, rises up the main pipe and any branch pipes.*

*A volcano builds up from layers of ash and lava.*

*Branch pipe*

*Magma collects in a chamber found deep underground. It is forced up through cracks and holes in the ground.*

### Mixed Bunch
When lava cools and hardens, it can make rocks with different shapes. Here are three types:

Runny lava

Ropy lava

A volcanic 'bomb'

# EARTHQUAKES

Our planet is a restless place. Every 30 seconds, the ground suddenly rumbles and trembles. Most of the movements are so slight that they are not felt. Others bring complete disaster. Big cracks appear in the land, streets buckle and buildings crumble. Whole towns and cities can be destroyed. Then everything settles down but is totally changed. The Earth has shaken and an earthquake has happened.

*Fires are started by broken gas pipes and broken electrical cables.*

*Telephone lines brought down*

*Cars are smashed and they settle at crazy angles.*

**Unsafe Ground**
This is the San Andreas Fault in California, USA. Earthquakes regularly happen here.

**Terror from the Sea**
Earthquakes under the sea can cause long, giant, destructive waves called *tsunamis*.

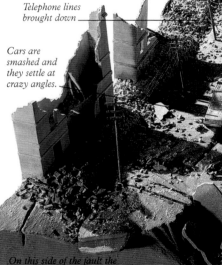

*On this side of the fault the land has moved towards you.*

An earthquake occurs along a fault in the seabed.

*Tsunamis* can travel many kilometres across the ocean.

## Why Earthquakes Happen

You may think that your feet are firmly on the ground, but the Earth's crust is moving all the time. It is made of moving parts called plates. When the plates slide past or into each other, the rocks jolt and send out shock waves.

### Shaken Up

The Mercalli Scale measures how much the surface of the Earth shakes during an earthquake. There are 12 intensities, or grades. At intensity 1, the effects are not felt, but by intensity 12, the shock waves can be seen and there is total destruction.

### What to do in an Earthquake

Indoors, lie down under a bed or heavy table, or stand in a doorway or a corner of a room. After a minute, when the tremors will usually have finished, go outside, away from buildings, to a wide-open space.

### Earthquake Words

The place within the Earth where an earthquake starts is called the focus. The earthquake is usually strongest at the epicentre. This is the point on the Earth's surface directly above the focus. The study of earthquakes and the shock waves they send out is called seismology.

*Fault line*

*On this side of the fault the land has moved away from you.*

### Destructive Force

A *tsunami* piles up and gets very tall before it crashes onto the shore. It is so powerful that it can smash harbours and towns and sweep ships inland.

A tsunami can be more than 60 meters high and can travel as fast as a jet.

# ROCKS

Movements in the Earth's crust are slowly changing the rocks that make up the surface of our planet. Mountains are pushed up and weathered away, and the fragments moved and made into other rocks. These rocks may be dragged down into the mantle and melted by its fierce heat. When a volcano erupts, the melted rock is thrown to the surface as lava, which cools and hardens as rock. This is broken down by weathering, and so the cycle starts again.

**Sedimentary Rocks**
These are made from bits of rock and plant and animal remains. They are broken into fine pieces and carried by rivers into the sea. They pile up in layers and press together to make solid rock. The Painted Desert, in Arizona, USA, is made of sedimentary rocks.

Limestone

Conglomerate

Red sandstone

### In the Beginning
Rocks belong to three basic types. Igneous rocks are made from magma or lava and are also known as 'fiery' rocks. Sedimentary rocks are made in layers from broken rocks. Metamorphic rocks can start off as any type. They are changed by heat and weight and are called 'changed form' rocks.

*In time, material moved by rivers and piled up in the sea will become sedimentary rocks.*

*Rock fragments are carried from one place to another by rivers, glaciers, the wind and the sea.*

*Recently formed sedimentary rocks*

## Igneous Rocks

These are made from magma or lava. It cools and hardens inside the Earth's crust or on the surface when it erupts from a volcano. Sugar Loaf Mountain, Brazil, was once igneous rock under the crust. The rocks above and around it have been worn away.

Marble

## Metamorphic Rocks

These are igneous or sedimentary rocks that are changed by underground heat, underground weight, or both. This marble was once limestone, a sedimentary rock. It was changed into marble by intense heat.

Slate

Obsidian        Granite

*Surface rocks are broken down by the weather and by the scraping effect of tiny pieces of rock carried in the wind or in the ice of glaciers.*

*Some rocks are thrust up as mountain ranges when the crust moves and makes giant folds.*

*Glacier*

*Volcano*

*Lava that erupts from a volcano forms extrusive igneous rock.*

*Molten rock that cools and hardens inside the Earth is called intrusive igneous rock.*

 *Metamorphic rocks*     *Folded rocks*

*Magma*

# CAVES

Caves are hollows beneath the surface of the Earth. The biggest ones are all found in rock called limestone and some are huge. The world's biggest cave, in Sarawak, is so large that you could fit 800 tennis courts in it. Yet these caves began simply as cracks or holes in the rock that, over thousands of years, were made bigger by rainwater trickling into them and eating them away.

### Going Down
Water dripping from the ceiling of a cave leaves behind a mineral called calcite. Very slowly, this grows downwards in an icicle shape that is called a stalactite.

*The stream disappears underground into a pothole.*

*This pothole, or tunnel, leads straight down through the rock. It was made by a stream wearing away the rock.*

*Limestone is a very common rock. It is made from the skeletons and shells of tiny sea creatures that died millions of years ago.*

### Drip . . .
The rainwater that seeps into the ground is very slightly acid and begins to eat away the limestone.

### Drip . . .
The rainwater eats through the rock. It widens the cracks into pits, passages and caves.

### Drip
Over thousands of years, the passages and caves may join up to make a huge underground system.

**Tunnel of Lava**
Caves are found in rocks other than limestone. This one is made of lava and is inside a volcano in Hawaii.

*Cracks in the rock are widened when rainwater seeps along them.*

*Limestone pavements are made when the rock is eaten away along joint lines.*

**Caving In**
Sometimes a cave turns into a gorge. This happens when the roof falls into reveal underground caverns and, far below, the river that carved them.

Cliff

Gallery

Cave mouth

Stream

**Going Up**
Where water drips onto the cave floor, columns of calcite, called stalagmites, grow upwards.

# OCEANS

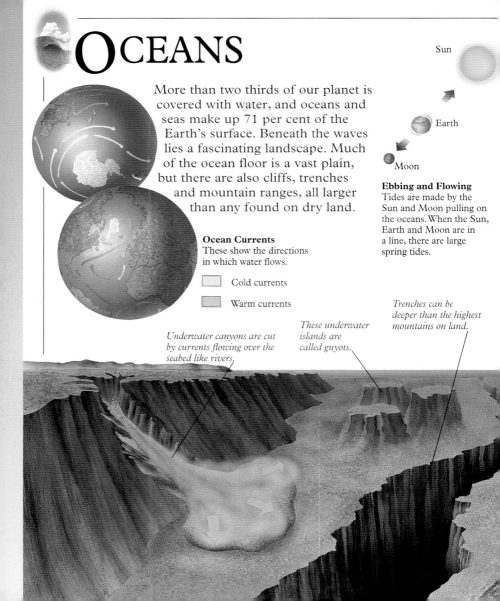

More than two thirds of our planet is covered with water, and oceans and seas make up 71 per cent of the Earth's surface. Beneath the waves lies a fascinating landscape. Much of the ocean floor is a vast plain, but there are also cliffs, trenches and mountain ranges, all larger than any found on dry land.

Sun

Earth

Moon

**Ebbing and Flowing**
Tides are made by the Sun and Moon pulling on the oceans. When the Sun, Earth and Moon are in a line, there are large spring tides.

**Ocean Currents**
These show the directions in which water flows.

Cold currents

Warm currents

*Underwater canyons are cut by currents flowing over the seabed like rivers.*

*These underwater islands are called guyots.*

*Trenches can be deeper than the highest mountains on land.*

**Surface**

Lighted zone
200 metres

Dark zone
6,000 metres

Deepest zone,
a trench of
11,000 metres

**Going . . .**
The water inside a wave moves round and round in a circle. It is the wind that drives the wave forwards.

**Going . . .**
Near the shore, the circular shape of the wave is changed and it becomes squashed.

**Gone**
The top of the wave becomes unstable. When it hits the beach, it topples and spills over.

**The Dark Depths**
Even in clear water, sunlight cannot reach very far. The oceans become darker and darker the farther down you go, until everything turns inky black.

**Ocean Currents**
The direction in which currents move depends on winds and the Earth's spin. Winds blow the top of the oceans forwards, but the Earth's spin makes the water below go in a spiral.

Wind direction

Main current

*This island is a volcano that has erupted from the ocean floor.*

*A long, wide ocean ridge*

*Water, heated by the hot rocks, shoots back into the sea.*

*Molten rock rises up, cools and forms new seabed.*

**Frozen Worlds**
In Antarctica and the Arctic, the oceans freeze. Icebergs break away from glaciers flowing into the water. Only a tiny part of an iceberg is seen above the surface of the ocean.

# COASTLINES

Have you ever built a sand castle and then watched the sea come in, knock it down and flatten it? This is what happens to the coastline, the place where the land and the sea meet. The coastline changes all the time because, every few seconds of every day, waves hit the land and either wear it away or build it up into different shapes.

*Some waves carry sand and pebbles from one part of the coast and leave them at another. This makes a new beach.*

*Headland*

**Going, Going, Gone**
When caves made on both sides of a headland meet, an arch is formed. If the top of the arch falls down, a pillar of rock, called a stack, is left.

*An arch*

*A stack*

*A cave is made when seawater gets into cracks and holes in a cliff and makes them bigger.*

*Some beaches are made in bays between headlands where the water is shallow and the waves are weak.*

**Pounding Away**
Waves pound the coastline like a giant hammer until huge chunks of rock are broken off. The chunks are then carried away by the sea and flung against the coastline somewhere else.

### From Rocks to Sand

Waves roll rocks and boulders backwards and forwards on the shore. The boulders break into pebbles and then into tiny grains of sand. This change takes hundreds or thousands of years.

### Shifting Sands

Dunes are made of sand blown into low hills by the wind.

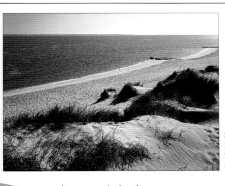

*An estuary is the place where a river flows into the sea.*

*Sea cliffs are one of the best places to see the different layers of rock.*

*Mud flats and marshes*

*Waves can build sand, mud and pebbles into a long strip of new land. It is called a spit.*

### Living Rock

Coral is found in warm, sunny, shallow seas. It is made by tiny sea creatures that look like flowers. Over thousands of years, their skeletons build up into huge coral reefs and islands.

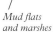

# GLACIERS

A glacier is like a huge river of ice that starts its life as a tiny snowflake. As more and more snow falls and builds up, in time it gets squashed under its own weight and turns to ice.

A glacier moves very slowly downhill. Because it is very heavy, it can push rock along like a bulldozer. It can wear away the sides of mountains, smooth off the jagged bits from rocks and move giant boulders over tens of kilometres.

*Mountains*

*Glaciers begin as huge snowfields.*

*The snow collects in hollows and turns to ice under its own weight.*

*Glaciers usually move downhill very slowly, no more than a few centimetres each day.*

*The ice begins to move and rub away the sides and bottom of the hollow. Little by little, it changes the shape of the land and makes it into a U-shaped valley.*

**Close-Up View**
The pilot in this plane is watching a wall of ice break away from a glacier and begin to crash into the water below.

**Ice Power**
When the water in this bottle freezes and turns to ice, it takes up more room and breaks the bottle. When the water that makes up the ice of a glacier freezes, it takes up more room and pushes away the rock.

*Rubble is carried along by the glacier.*

**Shaping the Land**
When you see a valley like this, you can tell from its U shape that it was once filled with the ice of a glacier.

*Melted ice flows as streams and rivers inside most glaciers.*

*Bumps in the rock can be smoothed out by the ice moving downhill.*

**Out of Place**
This giant boulder of hard rock was moved by a glacier and left on soft limestone. Then, most of the limestone was weathered away, leaving a small block under the boulder.

*Where a glacier flows into water, chunks of ice break off and float away.*

*Rocks carried along by the glacier pile up when the glacier starts to melt and stops pushing them.*

*The lower end of the glacier is called the 'snout'.*

*When the glacier melts, it makes new rivers.*

# RIVERS

Rivers are very powerful, so powerful that the force of the moving water is able to change the shape of the land. As they flow through mountains and over plains, rivers carry away huge amounts of rock, sand and mud. They then dump it somewhere else, usually on riverbanks or in the sea, to make new land.

*A river usually begins in mountains or hills. Its water comes from rain or melted snow.*

*Where the rock is hard, the river makes rapids or waterfalls.*

*Glacier*

**Over the Top**
When a river tumbles over the edge of a steep cliff or over a hard, rocky ledge, it is called a waterfall. This one is in Brazil, South America.

*As the river flows quickly down steep slopes, it wears away the rock to make a V-shaped valley.*

*Oxbow lake*

*Sand, mud and gravel is left by the water as sediment.*

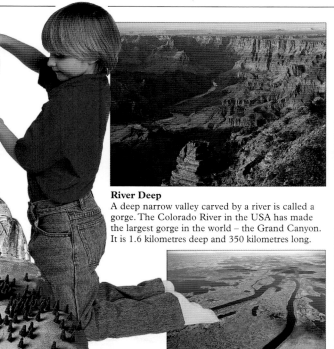

## River Deep
A deep narrow valley carved by a river is called a gorge. The Colorado River in the USA has made the largest gorge in the world – the Grand Canyon. It is 1.6 kilometres deep and 350 kilometres long.

## River's End
This swampy land is part of the Yukon Delta in Alaska, USA.

*A wide bend or meander goes across flat country.*

*As it reaches the sea, the river divides into small streams, leaving a mass of sand, mud, and rock fragments, called a delta.*

## Round the Bend
When a river reaches flat land, it slows down and begins to flow in large loops. It leaves behind sand, gravel and mud, called deposits. This changes the river's shape and course.

The river leaves deposits on the inside bend and eats away the outer bend.

The deposits change the shape of the bend. In time, the neck of the bend narrows and the ends of the neck join up.

The river leaves behind a loop. It is called an oxbow lake because of its shape.

## Record Rivers
The longest river in the world is the Nile, in Africa. It is 6,690 kilometres long. The largest delta in the world covers 77,700 square kilometres. It is made by the Ganges and Brahmaputra rivers, in Bangladesh and India.

# DESERTS

Did you know that deserts come in many different forms? They can be a sea of rolling sand, a huge area of flat and stony ground or mountainous areas of shattered rock. There are hot deserts and cold deserts. So what do these very different areas have in common?

The answer is that they are all very dry and they all get less than 25 centimetres of rain each year. This rain may not fall regularly. Instead, it may all come in a single day and cause a dramatic flash flood.

**Sea of Sand**
A desert may be hard to live in, but it can be stunning to look at. These dunes are in Saudi Arabia.

Tail dune

Wind

Barchan dunes

Seif dunes

Star dunes

**Wind Power**
Wind blows the sand into hills which are called dunes. These have different shapes and names.

*A cuesta is a step of hard rock.*

*A large, steep-sided area with a flat top is called a mesa.*

*Natural rock arch*

*A butte is a small, flat-topped hill.*

*Dunes*

*Hard rock that has been worn into a pinnacle is called a chimney or pipe rock.*

## On the Move

Imagine the hairdryer is the wind. It blows the sand up the gentle slope of the dune. When the sand gets to the top, it tumbles down the steep slope. As more and more sand is moved from one slope to another, the whole dune moves forwards.

*Heavy rain makes flash floods. These rush over the land, loaded with sand and stones, and cut deep channels in the surface of the desert.*

*Broken rocks slide downhill and collect in gullies.*

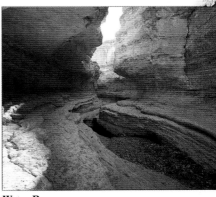

**Water Power**
The tremendous power of water has made this deep ravine near an oasis in Tunisia.

*Where the rock is hard, ridges will stand out in the landscape.*

**Shaping the Land**
Wind-borne sand blows against the rocks and wears them into beautiful and surprising shapes.

*Steep slopes of broken rock*

*Outwash fan*

**Hot and Cold**
This is one of the Devil's Marbles in the Northern Territory, Australia. The rock's outer layers have started to peel off because of the desert's very hot and very cold temperatures.

# SPACE

The universe is made up of galaxies, stars, planets, moons and other bodies scattered throughout space. A galaxy is a group of millions of stars: our galaxy, which is shaped like a spiral, is called the Milky Way.

On a clear night, it is possible to see thousands of stars, which appear as twinkling points of light. Earth's moon is usually clear, and sometimes you can also see five of the planets: Mercury, Venus, Mars, Jupiter, and Saturn. These do not twinkle, but look like small steady discs of light. Earth is the third planet from the Sun, which is about 149 million kilometres away from us.

People have always been curious about the things they could see in the sky. It is only quite recently, though, that science has developed the advanced technology needed to send men and women into space.

Space shuttle

Milky Way

NEPTUNE

URANUS

SATURN

MERCURY

SUN

VENUS

EARTH

MARS

*Asteroid belt*

JUPITER

*Rings*

# ROCKETS

Rockets were invented in China a long time ago. They looked a bit like arrows and worked by burning gunpowder, which burns up very quickly, so the rockets did not travel very far. Since then, people have tried many ways of sending rockets up into space. In modern rockets, two liquid fuels are used. They mix together and burn. Then the hot gas shoots out of the tail, pushing the rocket up and away.

V-2 Rocket 1945    Gemini Titan 1964

**The Fly!**
In 1931 Johannes Winkler launched his HW-1 rocket. It went two metres into the air, turned over and fell back to the ground. A month later he tried again and this time it climbed to 90 metres and landed 200 metres away.

**3,2,1, Fire**
A hundred years ago, soldiers used rockets like this. They were called Congreve rockets.

**Saturn Power**
Saturn 5 is the biggest rocket ever built. It is as tall as a 30-storey building! It was used in the Apollo program, which carried the first American astronauts to the Moon.

*Fuel tank*

**See It Go!**
If you blow up a balloon and let it go without tying a knot in the neck, the air will rush out very quickly. When the air goes out one way it pushes the balloon the other way – just like a rocket!

*The stabilizing fins keep the rocket on course.*

*Five rocket engines*

**Up, Up . . .**
How far can you throw a ball? About 15 or 20 metres? It doesn't go on for ever because the Earth's gravity pulls it back down again.

**Quest for Power**
As rockets have become more powerful their shapes have changed. The latest ones carry shuttles into space.

Soyuz
1967

Space Shuttle
1981

*Rocket engine*

*Launch escape system*

*Service module*

*Lunar module*

*Command module*

*Five rocket engines*

**Overpowering**
See just how enormous Saturn's engines are compared with these people!

**. . . and Away**
To escape from Earth by rocket you have to travel at 40,000 kilometres per hour – more than 40 times faster than a jumbo jet.

**Sky High**
The space shuttle leaves the launch pad in a blaze of bright light. It will circle the Earth over a hundred times in about eight days. Its wings then allow it to glide back to the ground so it can be used again.

# MOON MISSION

*The second stage drops off when its five engines run out of fuel.*

*The command and service modules turn, join onto the lunar module and pull it out of the third stage.*

The Moon is the Earth's nearest neighbour in space but it still takes three days to get there by rocket. It would take 200 days by car! When astronauts first went to the Moon no one knew if it would be safe to land there. But American astronauts have been to the Moon on Apollo missions six times and they all returned safely to Earth. The first Moon trip was in 1969 and the last in 1972.

*Second stage*

*Astronauts who are going to the Moon crawl through a tunnel from the command module to the lunar module.*

**We Have Lift-Off!**
The first stage of the Saturn 5 rocket has five huge engines. When these run out of fuel they fall back to Earth. Then the second stage takes over.

*This air recycling unit keeps the air fresh in the cabin.*

CSM = Command and Service modules
LM = Lunar module
CM = Command module

**Lunar Module**

CSM docks with LM
CSM in orbit
LM back to CSM
LM descends to Moon
Moon

CSM back to Earth
Splash down
Lift - off
Earth
CM splashes down

**Moon Trail**
The Apollo missions to the Moon followed a path in the shape of the figure eight.

The lunar module drops down to the Moon with two astronauts inside. The command module stays in orbit around the Moon.

The top part of the lunar module returns to the command module.

There is not much room in the cabin for three astronauts.

The command module falls to Earth using parachutes, to make a safe landing in the sea.

Command Module

Engine nozzle

Parachute

Fuel tanks

**Service Module**

**Splashdown!**
The command module fell through the Earth's atmosphere so quickly that the bottom got burnt. It splashed down in the sea and was picked up by a helicopter. The balls on the roof are air balloons which helped it to float upright if it turned over in the water.

# LUNAR LANDING

A lunar landing is a Moon landing. If you went to the Moon you would find nothing living at all, no air and no water. If you stayed for a lunar 'day'– about 28 Earth days – you would have two weeks of baking sun followed by two weeks of freezing night. The first men on the Moon went down in the lunar module, nicknamed 'Eagle'.

**The Apollo 11 Crew**
Neil Armstrong and Edwin 'Buzz' Aldrin were the first men to walk on the Moon. Michael Collins stayed in orbit in the command module.

**Hanging Out the Washing?**
No, just setting up a panel to collect dust! The Moon is covered in dusty soil and scattered rocks.

Antenna

Control panel

Television camera

Hand control

Sample collection bags

Seats

**Moon Buggy**
This runabout was taken to the Moon for the first time in Apollo 15. Its proper name is the lunar roving vehicle.

Space for storing equipment

Wire-mesh wheel

**Weather or Not?**
With no wind or rain, the footprints made by the astronauts will remain on the Moon forever. The American flag, left on the Moon by the astronauts, is held out by a metal bar because there is no wind to make it fly.

*Escape tower*

*Command module*

*Service module*

*Lunar module*

*These engines help the astronauts to control the lunar module.*

*Forward hatch door*

*The astronauts carry radio packs. Sound cannot travel without air, so the astronauts use radios to talk to each other.*

*Ladder*

*Foot with rounded pad to stop the leg sinking into the ground.*

**Earthrise**
The lunar module is just leaving the Moon. Behind it you can see what the Earth looks like from the Moon.

*One of the four fold-up 'spider' legs. The first lunar module was nicknamed 'Spider', but that mission didn't land on the Moon.*

**Super Saturn**
The Saturn 5 has three stages. When one stage runs out of fuel it falls off and another part takes over.

*Third stage*

*Second stage*

*First stage*

41

# MERCURY AND VENUS

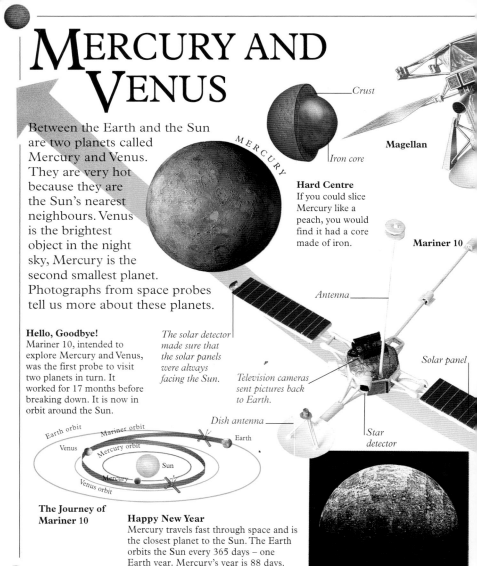

Between the Earth and the Sun are two planets called Mercury and Venus. They are very hot because they are the Sun's nearest neighbours. Venus is the brightest object in the night sky, Mercury is the second smallest planet. Photographs from space probes tell us more about these planets.

MERCURY

*Crust*

**Magellan**

*Iron core*

**Hard Centre**
If you could slice Mercury like a peach, you would find it had a core made of iron.

**Mariner 10**

*Antenna*

### Hello, Goodbye!
Mariner 10, intended to explore Mercury and Venus, was the first probe to visit two planets in turn. It worked for 17 months before breaking down. It is now in orbit around the Sun.

*The solar detector made sure that the solar panels were always facing the Sun.*

*Television cameras sent pictures back to Earth.*

*Solar panel*

*Dish antenna*

*Star detector*

Earth orbit
Mariner orbit
Venus
Mercury orbit
Earth
Sun
Mercury
Venus orbit

### The Journey of Mariner 10

### Happy New Year
Mercury travels fast through space and is the closest planet to the Sun. The Earth orbits the Sun every 365 days – one Earth year. Mercury's year is 88 days.

**Venera 9
Venus
Landing**

*The space probe
was in a capsule on
the Venera spacecraft.*

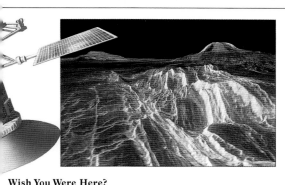

*The capsule fell
through the
atmosphere
of Venus.*

*The heat-shield
covers separated
and fell off.*

### Wish You Were Here?
The Magellan probe used
radar cameras to take pictures
through the thick fog around
Venus. Computers made this
3-D image of the volcanoes.

*The brake is
shaped like a disc
to help slow the
space probe down.*

### Venus Venera
Several Russian missions
have been to Venus; this
program was called
Venera. The spacecraft
sent pictures back to
Earth. This is the part of
Venera 9 that went down
to Venus by parachute.

*Instrument
container*

*The probe
was slowed
down by
a small
parachute.*

*The landing ring
helped to make the
landing soft.*

VENUS

*Three larger
parachutes
were used
for the
final stage.*

### Hot Orange
Venus is the hottest
planet of all – so hot
that it could melt lead!
It has a bright orange
sky with flashes of
lightning. The Earth
spins round once
every 24 hours but
Venus spins very
slowly – once
every 244 days!

*After a safe
landing, the
television cameras
and instruments
were switched on.*

# THE RED PLANET

The Viking lander is folded into a capsule on the spacecraft.

**Viking Spacecraft**

Mars is called the red planet because the soil and rocks are red. Light winds blow dust around, which makes the sky look pink. People once thought there was life on Mars, but nothing living has been found so far.

The Viking spacecraft were sent to Mars to find out what it is like. Two missions, Viking 1 and Viking 2, made the journey.

Perhaps one day people may go to live on Mars because it is the planet most like our own.

It leaves the orbiter and begins its journey down to Mars.

The television camera takes a series of pictures as it moves round.

It moves so fast that it gets very hot.

A parachute is used to slow it down, and then the heat shield drops off.

This remote control arm is used to collect samples of Mars soil.

**Tight Fit**
The Viking lander fits into a capsule on the spacecraft. With its legs folded up, it looks a bit like a tortoise inside its shell.

The legs unfold, and rockets are used as brakes for a soft landing.

**The Viking Lander**

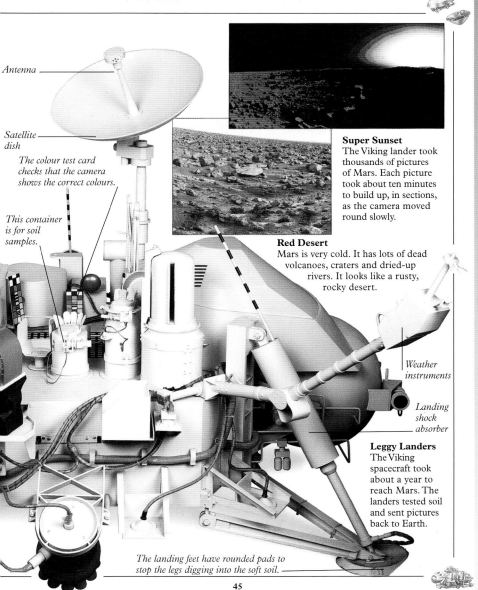

*Antenna*

*Satellite dish*

*The colour test card checks that the camera shows the correct colours.*

*This container is for soil samples.*

### Super Sunset
The Viking lander took thousands of pictures of Mars. Each picture took about ten minutes to build up, in sections, as the camera moved round slowly.

### Red Desert
Mars is very cold. It has lots of dead volcanoes, craters and dried-up rivers. It looks like a rusty, rocky desert.

*Weather instruments*

*Landing shock absorber*

### Leggy Landers
The Viking spacecraft took about a year to reach Mars. The landers tested soil and sent pictures back to Earth.

*The landing feet have rounded pads to stop the legs digging into the soft soil.*

# JUPITER AND SATURN

These two giants are the largest planets in the solar system. Jupiter is made of gas and liquid so it is not solid enough to land on, but if you could drive a car around its equator it would take six months of non-stop travelling. A similar journey around the Earth's equator would take only two weeks. Saturn is a beautiful planet with shining rings around its middle. Both planets spin around very fast, pulling the clouds into stripes.

**Spinning Saturn**
Saturn is a giant spinning ball of gas and liquid held together by gravity This photograph shows a band of clouds and the rings.

SATURN

*A power supply is carried on the probe. It does not use solar power because it is working so far from the Sun.*

*Radio antenna*

*This disc has pictures of the Earth and sounds, such as a baby crying and music. If aliens find the disc it will tell them about Earth.*

*Dish antenna*

**Seven Cold Rings**
Saturn's rings are made up of glittering pieces of ice like trillions of snowballs.

**Voyager Voyages**
The probes sent to explore Jupiter and Saturn were called voyager. Voyager 1 did its job so well that Voyager 2 was re-routed to go on to Uranus and Neptune.

*Television cameras*

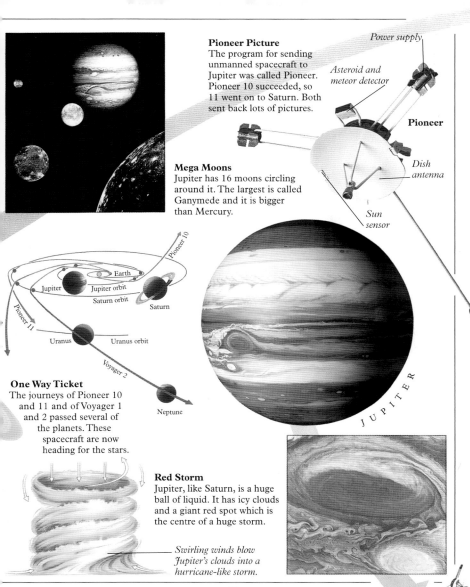

### Pioneer Picture
The program for sending unmanned spacecraft to Jupiter was called Pioneer. Pioneer 10 succeeded, so 11 went on to Saturn. Both sent back lots of pictures.

*Power supply*

*Asteroid and meteor detector*

**Pioneer**

*Dish antenna*

*Sun sensor*

### Mega Moons
Jupiter has 16 moons circling around it. The largest is called Ganymede and it is bigger than Mercury.

Pioneer 10

Earth

Jupiter
Jupiter orbit

Saturn orbit

Saturn

Pioneer 11

Uranus
Uranus orbit

Voyager 2

Neptune

JUPITER

### One Way Ticket
The journeys of Pioneer 10 and 11 and of Voyager 1 and 2 passed several of the planets. These spacecraft are now heading for the stars.

### Red Storm
Jupiter, like Saturn, is a huge ball of liquid. It has icy clouds and a giant red spot which is the centre of a huge storm.

*Swirling winds blow Jupiter's clouds into a hurricane-like storm.*

# THE OUTER PLANETS

Uranus and Neptune are the farthest planets from the Sun so they are called the outer planets. They are very cold. Uranus was the first planet to be discovered using a telescope because you cannot see it from Earth just with your eyes. Pluto orbits outside Neptune and used to be classed as the ninth planet of the solar system until 2006, when it was reclassified as a dwarf planet.

**Sideways Spinner**
Uranus looks as if it is spinning on its side. It is covered in dense fog.

URANUS

1986U1R
Epsilon
Gamma
Delta
Eta
Alpha
Beta
4 5 6

**Outer Solar System**

*The rings of Uranus are made of rocks. They were given these names. The widest ring is 97 kilometres across.*

**Ellipses**
The planets move around the Sun in squashed circles called ellipses. This girl is drawing ellipses.

**Order of Orbits**
The word planet means wanderer. The planets travel around the Sun in paths, called orbits. The ones nearer the Sun have shorter orbits than the ones farther away. One way of remembering the order of the planets in the solar system is to remember the sentence 'My Very Educated Mother Just Served Us Noodles'.

*This diagram shows the orbits of the planets and their places in the solar system. It does not show their sizes.*

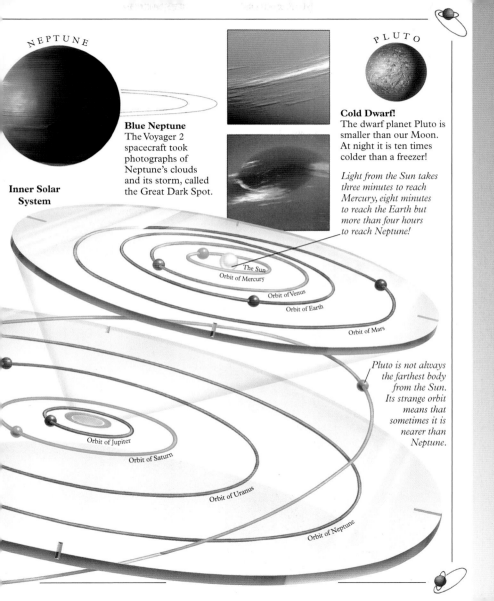

NEPTUNE

**Blue Neptune**
The Voyager 2
spacecraft took
photographs of
Neptune's clouds
and its storm, called
the Great Dark Spot.

**Inner Solar
System**

PLUTO

**Cold Dwarf!**
The dwarf planet Pluto is
smaller than our Moon.
At night it is ten times
colder than a freezer!

*Light from the Sun takes
three minutes to reach
Mercury, eight minutes
to reach the Earth but
more than four hours
to reach Neptune!*

The Sun
Orbit of Mercury
Orbit of Venus
Orbit of Earth
Orbit of Mars

*Pluto is not always
the farthest body
from the Sun.
Its strange orbit
means that
sometimes it is
nearer than
Neptune.*

Orbit of Jupiter
Orbit of Saturn
Orbit of Uranus
Orbit of Neptune

# SKY WANDERERS

Between Mars and Jupiter there is a belt of rocks in orbit called the asteroid belt. The chunks of rock are called asteroids. Sometimes these pieces crash into each other and bits fall down towards Earth.

Also in orbit around the Sun are lumps of rock and ice, called comets. When comets get near the Sun they shine like 'hairy stars' which is what people used to call them long ago. The most famous comet is Halley's comet, named after the man who first studied it.

*Path of Halley's comet*

*Wind from the Sun blows the dust and gas around Halley's comet into an enormous tail. Comets' tails always point away from the Sun and can be millions of kilometres long*

Solar System

**Earth Comets**
Because they are made of rock and ice, comets are often called 'dirty snowballs'. Make your own comet next time it snows!

*The comet's centre is made of ice. As it gets near the Sun the ice melts.*

**A Belt You Cannot Wear**
The asteroids in the asteroid belt are really mini-planets. There are thousands of them. The largest is about 1,000 km across.

*Halley's comet*

**Regular Visitor**
We see Halley's comet from Earth once every 76 years because it takes that long to orbit the Sun. It was shown on a picture, called the Bayeux Tapestry, over 900 years ago!

**Comet Head**
This is a photograph of the head of Halley's comet. Computer colours show the bright centre and the layers round it.

**Meteor Shower**
If a lump of rock or metal burns up before it reaches the ground, it is called a meteor or shooting star. This photograph shows lots of them falling together in a meteor shower.

**Crash! Bang!**
A large meteor that does not burn up as it plunges through the Earth's atmosphere is called a meteorite.

It travels so fast it shatters into pieces as it hits the ground.

It causes shock waves as it lands.

The explosion leaves a big hole, called a crater.

This huge meteorite crater is in Arizona, in the United States of America.

*Dish antenna*

*Solar cells for power*

**Giotto**

**Comet Quest**
In 1986 Giotto, a European spacecraft, passed very close to Halley's comet and took pictures of it. Giotto is now searching for other comets.

*Camera*

*Dust shield*

**Gaspra the Asteroid**
No one had seen a picture of Gaspra until the US spacecraft Galileo took this one in 1991, as it passed the asteroid belt.

# SKY WATCHING

If you look up at the sky on a clear night you can see hundreds of stars and, sometimes, the Moon. But if you use binoculars or a telescope you can see even more – for example, the planets and the craters on the Moon.

When astronomers study the universe they use huge radio telescopes, some with dishes, to help them to see far, far away, and to gather information from space. The Hubble Space Telescope is the largest telescope to be put into space. It can take clear pictures of stars and galaxies because it orbits 600 km above the Earth's murky atmosphere.

**Clearly Venus**
This photograph of Venus was taken by the Pioneer Venus Orbiter. It used radar to get a clear picture through the thick clouds around Venus. The signals were sent back to Earth to a radio telescope where this picture was produced.

*Solar panel*

*Radio telescope*

**Whirligig**
This radio map of the Whirlpool galaxy was taken by a radio telescope. The added colours show the spiral arms of the galaxy.

## Head in the Stars
A nebula is a cloud of dust and gas lit from inside by newly born stars. Through a telescope you can see this picture of the Horsehead nebula. False colours have been added but it looks nearly as bright without them.

## Star Belt
This photograph, taken through a small telescope, shows part of the constellation of Orion – also called 'The Hunter'.

*Small mirror*

*Flap door*

### Star Cluster
This photograph was taken by the Hubble Space Telescope and it shows a star cluster.

*Main mirror*

### Star Light
This natural colour picture was taken from an observatory. It shows the Orion nebula.

## Double Hubble
The Hubble has two mirrors – the largest is 2.4 metres wide and 30 centimetres thick. At one stage, the mirrors were not working quite as well as they should, but astronauts from the Shuttle have now corrected them.

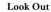
*Antenna*

## Look Out
Observatories are places where astronomers work. These are usually away from big cities where there are no street lights and the air is clear.

# STARS AND GALAXIES

Stars look like tiny points of light from the Earth but really they are huge, hot balls of burning gas deep in space. They are forming, changing and dying all the time. There are big stars called giants, even bigger ones called supergiants, and small ones called dwarf stars. Our Sun is just one of about a hundred thousand million stars that all belong to a galaxy called the Milky Way. A galaxy is a group of millions of stars, held together by a strong force called gravity.

**Starry, Starry Night**
On a clear night do not forget to look up at the sky! You will see hundreds of twinkling stars, like tiny sparkling diamonds, far above you.

*The gas and dust pack tightly together getting smaller and very hot.*

*A group of growing stars is called a cluster.*

*A new star is very bright. It shines steadily for many years.*

*As it cools, the star gets bigger and forms a red giant.*

*A star is born inside a great cloud of dust and gas, called a nebula. The word nebula means mist.*

*Near the end of its life the core of a red giant may cave in and give off layers of gas.*

**Sky Lights**
There are many new stars in the gas and dust of this pink nebula. A new young star on its own shines blue.

Sometimes a giant star explodes and is blown to pieces. This is called a supernova.

A supernova explosion sometimes results in a pulsar. A pulsar is a rapidly spinning star that gives off pulses of radio waves.

A black hole is not really a hole but a very tightly-packed object. It is solid and does not reflect any light, so it looks like a hole! Its gravity pulls things towards it like water down a plughole.

Some dying stars grow into huge red supergiants.

Our solar system

Massive stars shine very brightly but do not live for as long as smaller stars.

If seen through a telescope the star, with its gas shell, now looks like a planet, so it is called a planetary nebula.

Some stars gradually get smaller and whiter until they become white dwarf stars.

**Galaxies**

A spiral galaxy

An elliptical galaxy

A barred spiral galaxy

**Star Spinner**

Our galaxy, called the Milky Way, is a spiral galaxy. Our solar system is about two thirds of the way out from the centre, in one of the spiral arms. There are lots of galaxies in the universe and they have different shapes. Try painting some!

# THE NATURAL WORLD

When Earth was brand-new more than 4,500 million years ago, there were violent storms, lightning bolts and fiery volcanoes on its surface, but there was no life. In time, warm shallow seas formed, and it was here that the first life appeared in the form of simple plants called bacteria and algae. Soon, more complex plants developed and, by about 600 million years ago, tiny soft animals were living in the water too. Later, these became larger and developed spines, and small plants began to grow on the shores.

Insects were the first animals on land, followed by amphibians (which live in water and on land), then dinosaurs, birds, and mammals. It was not until quite recently – about five million years ago – that humans first appeared.

**Plant Life**
**Sea Life**
**Insects and Spiders**
**Dinosaurs**
**Birds**
**Mammals**
**The Human Body**

# PLANT LIFE

Plants grow everywhere, from the icy Arctic to the tropics – any place where there is air, light and water.

In deserts, where it rarely rains, plants have to save moisture. Some, like cacti, have pleated stems that expand to store water when there is a shower. Where the climate is hot and humid, plants grow very quickly all year round to make lush rainforests. In temperate places – where it is not too hot and not too cold, with a medium amount of rain – most plants flower and fruit in summer, but lose their leaves in winter. Plants usually grow in soil, but some absorb what they need directly from the water.

Without plants, our world would be very different; from plants we get food, clothes, paper, and lots of other things. Most important of all, they provide oxygen, which all living creatures need to breathe.

Water hyacinth

The growth of a blackberry from flower to fruit

Stag's horn sumach

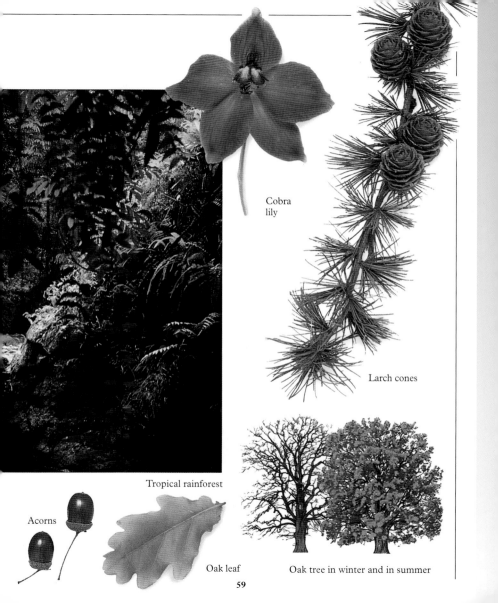

Cobra lily

Larch cones

Tropical rainforest

Acorns

Oak leaf

Oak tree in winter and in summer

59

# WHAT IS A PLANT?

*The leaves are used for making food.*

An apple tree and a cactus do not look much like each other. But they have more in common than you might think. They are both plants. Like all other plants they make their own food, and during the course of their lifetime, they can produce many new plants. To do these things they use their roots, stems, leaves and flowers. You will find that no matter how different one plant may look from another, each one is using these parts in much the same way, in order to live and grow.

**Look, No Hands**
Some plants do not need soil- they prefer to perch in trees. A stag's horn fern gets a good grip by wrapping its large fronds around a branch.

*Apples contain seeds.*

*Trees have a main stem and many branches.*

**Hitching a Lift**
Some plants use other plants for support. This passion flower can travel long distances by twining itself round the trunks and branches of trees.

*The flowers make seeds for new plants.*

*The flexible stems can bend and twine.*

**Fresh Fruit**
Apple trees are not best known for their flowers. But if they did not have flowers first, we would not have apples to eat.

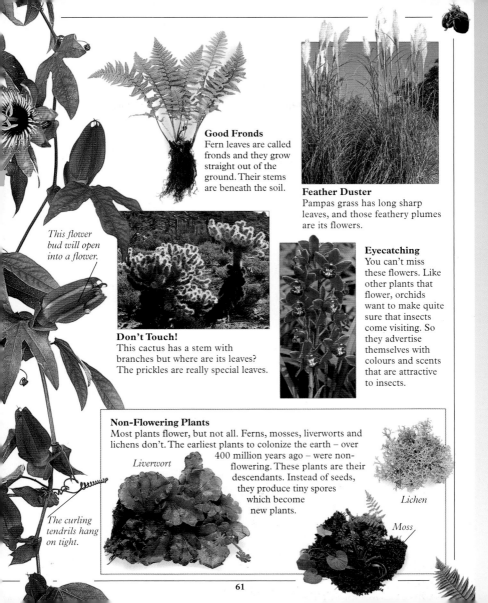

### Good Fronds
Fern leaves are called fronds and they grow straight out of the ground. Their stems are beneath the soil.

### Feather Duster
Pampas grass has long sharp leaves, and those feathery plumes are its flowers.

*This flower bud will open into a flower.*

### Eyecatching
You can't miss these flowers. Like other plants that flower, orchids want to make quite sure that insects come visiting. So they advertise themselves with colours and scents that are attractive to insects.

### Don't Touch!
This cactus has a stem with branches but where are its leaves? The prickles are really special leaves.

### Non-Flowering Plants
Most plants flower, but not all. Ferns, mosses, liverworts and lichens don't. The earliest plants to colonize the earth – over 400 million years ago – were non-flowering. These plants are their descendants. Instead of seeds, they produce tiny spores which become new plants.

*Liverwort*

*Lichen*

*Moss*

*The curling tendrils hang on tight.*

# LEAVES

Leaves work very hard for plants. They make food and they also help plants to cope with serious problems like how to survive the cold, or get enough water. Leaves come in all sorts of shapes and sizes – large and small, thick and thin. In fact, you can tell quite a lot about a plant and where it grows, just by looking at its leaves.

## Weatherproof

Scots pine trees need to be tough to survive long, cold winters. They have thousands of tiny, needle-like leaves. The needles have a waterproof coating to protect them from rain and snow.

## Water Store

Agave plants grow in hot places where it may not rain for weeks on end. They are able to store water in their large thick leaves.

*Wind blows through the needles without damaging them.*

*Their leaves can grow up to two metres long.*

## Open Sesame

Leaves have tiny holes called stomata, which the plant can open and close. When the stomata are open, they let air in and out, and water out. When they are closed, water can't escape from the leaves.

## Shapes and Sizes

Japanese maple    Himalayan birch    Fig    Acacia    Horse chestnut

### Drip-Dry

Life in a tropical forest is hot and damp and there is no shortage of water. Monstera leaves have a special waxy surface, so the water can run off.

*Monstera plants grow in the shade of trees that constantly drip moisture.*

### Prickly Customers

Plants can't run away from hungry animals, so they have to protect themselves. Prickly holly gets left alone!

*Tough, glossy leaves are a good defence against wind and weather.*

### Shady Character

The maidenhair fern lives in damp, shady places, where its fragile leaves won't dry out in the sun.

### Water Signals

Leaves can't talk, but they can sometimes send a message. The leaves of this cyclamen are limp and drooping as if the plant is unhappy. The soil in the pot is dry, and the message is, 'Water me'.

### Do Plants Sweat?

Plants are constantly losing water through their leaves as part of a process called transpiration. Most of the time you can't see it happening. But if you put a plant inside a plastic bag and fasten it, after a while you will see water drops on the inside of the bag. The moisture you can see is coming from the leaves of the plant.

# HOW PLANTS MAKE FOOD

Hungry animals can go out hunting for their food – but plants cannot. Instead, they make their own food in their leaves, using light from the Sun, water from the soil and carbon dioxide from the air. A plant's way of making food is called photosynthesis. It takes place during the day when the leaves are absorbing sunlight.

**Reach for the Sun**
These palms grow in the shade of tall trees. Their leaves are arranged like fans to help them catch all the light they can.

*The leaves of all plants contain a special pigment that gives them their green colour. It is called chlorophyll.*

**Colourful Cover-up**
All leaves contain green chlorophyll. But in some leaves the green is hidden from sight by other, stronger colours.

*The roots take up water from the soil. It is drawn up the stem to the leaves.*

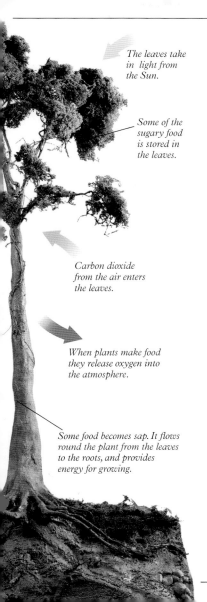

*The leaves take in light from the Sun.*

*Some of the sugary food is stored in the leaves.*

*Carbon dioxide from the air enters the leaves.*

*When plants make food they release oxygen into the atmosphere.*

*Some food becomes sap. It flows round the plant from the leaves to the roots, and provides energy for growing.*

**Rest Time**
Without sunlight, plants cannot make food. When it is dark they shut down for the night by closing their stomata.

**Photosynthesis**
Chlorophyll in the leaves absorbs sunlight. Sunlight provides the plant with energy to turn water and carbon dioxide into food.

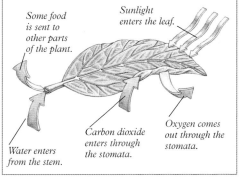

*Some food is sent to other parts of the plant.*

*Sunlight enters the leaf.*

*Water enters from the stem.*

*Carbon dioxide enters through the stomata.*

*Oxygen comes out through the stomata.*

Tree in summer leaf

Bare tree in winter

**Hibernation**
In winter there is less light and the water often freezes in the ground. It is difficult to make food, so plants grow very little at this time of year. Many trees shed their leaves.

# CARNIVOROUS PLANTS

Watch out! These plants are meat-eaters and they have some very cunning devices for trapping their victims. Unlucky insects, attracted by the plant's scent and colour, discover too late that they have been tricked. It is a nasty end for an insect, but a ready-made, nutritious meal for the plant.

**Water Jugs**
A pitcher plant has several pitchers, so it can catch a lot of flies.

*The lid can close to keep rainwater out.*

**Gruesome Gruel**
Flies lose their footing on the slippery rim of the hanging pitcher plant and tumble into the water below. They gradually dissolve into a kind of fly broth.

**Venus Flytrap**
The instant an unsuspecting insect lands, the venus flytrap snaps into action.

*To a fly, this pad looks like a safe landing place.*

*Rim with nectar*

*Pitcher for collecting water*

**Swamped**
Most carnivorous plants, like these cobra lilies, grow in boggy places where the minerals they need are in short supply. The insects they catch make a vital addition to their diet, because they are rich in the missing minerals.

*Remains of flies*

1. A passing damselfly lands on a pad.

The middle of the leaf forms a hinge.

2. It touches the sensitive hairs that trigger the hinge.

An open trap waiting for a visitor.

Sensitive hairs

3. In less than a second, the sides of the trap begin to close.

The trap is closed – there is something inside.

Pointed teeth lock together to make a cage.

4. There is no escape. The teeth close and the damselfly is firmly locked in. It takes two weeks for the venus flytrap to digest its meal.

**Hair-Raising Story**
Any fly that lands on the hairy leaves of the sticky sundew is in for a nasty surprise. In no time at all it finds its legs are hopelessly entangled in the glue produced by the hairs.

**Glued to the Spot**
The glistening, golden leaves of the butterwort are a deadly glue trap. Flies get stuck when they land. But no matter how hard they struggle, the leaf edges curl inwards and the butterwort begins its lunch.

# STEMS

Roots, shoots, leaves and flowers are all connected to the plant's stem. Although it may not always stand as straight, the stem is rather like your backbone, holding all the different parts together. Being in the centre of everything means it is in the perfect position to carry water and food to every part of the plant.

**Clever Creature**
This aphid knows just where to go for food supplies! It takes less than a second to pierce the soft part of the stem which is full of nutritious sap.

*This young tree is two years old.*

**Sun Worshippers**
The stems of sunflowers turn so their flowers can always face the Sun.

*Branches grow out from the stem and hold the leaves out to the light.*

*As the tree gets older and taller, the main stem will thicken to form a trunk.*

**Clinging On**
In its rush to the light, the sweet pea has no time to grow strong stems. Instead it uses twirling tendrils to wrap around other plants. They will support its fast climb to the top.

**The Widest Spread on Earth**
Just one banyan tree can make a forest! Their branches throw down special aerial roots. These grow into the ground and expand into trunks. A single tree in Kolkata, India, has over 1,000 of these trunk lookalikes.

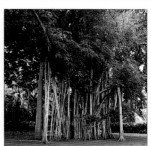

*Water and minerals travel up the stem from the roots.*

### Supporting Role
The strong, hard stems of bamboo are called canes. In some parts of the world they make great thickets seven metres high.

### Weak at the Knees
Gourd stems don't even attempt to stand up to support their fruit, which may weigh several kilos. They just trail gracefully over the ground.

*The branches are slender and not yet very strong.*

*The inside of a bamboo cane is hollow.*

*Food is made in the leaves and travels down to the roots.*

### Keep Off !
It is quite difficult to get near a thistle but any animal that does, won't be back for a second bite.

*Close-up of thistle stem*

*Section through cactus*

### Conservation
Desert cacti hold water reserves in their thick stems. Thirsty animals know that. But the barricade of fierce spines means no free drinks.

### Water Diet
African baobab trees have a special way of surviving. During the rainy season their trunks store so much water that they visibly swell up. These reserves get them through the hot, dry times, when their slimmer shape slowly returns.

# ROOTS

Roots are not pretty or colourful like leaves and flowers, but plants couldn't do without them! Anchored in the soil, they hold plants upright against wind and weather. They also grow out and down in search of water and minerals which are drawn all the way up to the leaves. Think how tall a tree can grow, and you can see it needs strong roots to keep it supported.

*There are little pockets of air in the soil. Without air, roots would wither and die*

*Roots can fit themselves into tiny spaces.*

*When earthworms burrow they help to add air to the soil.*

*The roots of the tree grow outwards to balance the spread of the branches above.*

## Knobbly Knees
Swamp cypresses grow in boggy ground, where there is not enough air. These strange bumps probably supply the roots with the air they need. They are known as cypress knees.

## Strong Intent
Roots don't let much stand in their way. These roots are growing towards the drain in the road, where there is a useful supply of water.

### Rootless Wonder
Draped like strange beards over the branches of trees, the extraordinary Spanish moss plant survives with no roots at all. Spanish moss grows in subtropical climates where the air is very wet. It absorbs all the moisture it needs through its fine, thread-like leaves.

### Rock Climbers
Alpine plants grow against rock faces, to protect themselves from high winds and icy squalls. Their tiny roots wriggle into cracks in the rock.

*Most roots grow in the top 30 centimetres of soil. This part contains most of the important minerals the tree needs.*

### Water Crops
Plants need water, minerals and some support for their roots. But they do not necessarily need soil. Today many food crops are grown entirely in water with special pebbles. They are given liquid minerals to replace those in the soil.

*Every root grows a mass of tiny hairs near its tip to absorb water from the soil.*

# INSIDE A FLOWER

Hibiscus

When you look at flowers you notice many colours, shapes and sizes. Some plants have a single flower, others have so many it is impossible to keep count. But stop and take a closer look – this time inside. However different they may look, flowers all have the same basic parts. This is because all plants produce flowers for the same purpose: to make seeds so another plant can grow.

### New Beginnings
The process of making new seeds is called reproduction. The male and female parts in the centre of this lily are its reproductive parts.

*The male part of a flower is called the anther. Each one of these produces masses of tiny pollen grains.*

*Insects leave pollen on the female part, which is called the stigma.*

Lily

### Mistaken Identity
You could be confused by this poinsettia. What look like bright red petals are actually a kind of leaf, called a bract. The real flowers are the tiny green dots in the centre.

### Grand Finale
Not all plants flower every year, but there is no other plant that is as slow as the puya raimondii from South America. It takes 150 years to produce a massive flower spike, up to 10 metres tall. Exhausted, it then dies, but luckily, not before it has managed to produce a few seeds.

**Mighty Magnolias**
The last of the dinosaurs may have munched on magnolias like these. Magnolia trees are one of the oldest flowering plants. They have been around for one hundred million years, and they are still growing today.

*The petals are brightly coloured, with special markings to attract insects.*

**Is This a Flower?**
Tropical orchids like this one often look more like strange insects than flowers.

*Hundreds of small flowers grow in a single spike.*

*The flowers of the spider orchid can be up to 60 centimetres long.*

**Flower Arrangement**
All these flowers have the same basic parts, but they are arranged on the stem in different ways.

*These bell-shaped flowers hang down.*

*Daisy petals are arranged like the rays of the Sun.*

*Each of these tightly packed flowers is called a floret.*

*Poppy petals open out to the light.*

*Each tiny point is a flower.*

Snake's head fritillary

Allium

Mullein

Transvaal daisy

Poppy

Yarrow

# FLOWERS AND THEIR POLLINATORS

Most plants cannot make seeds without some outside help. The first job is to move pollen from the anther of one flower to the stigma of another. This is called pollination. Plants cannot travel, but their flowers produce sweet nectar, which animals love. As the animal feeds on the nectar, some pollen rubs onto its body. Each time it moves on to another flower, it leaves some pollen behind and picks up a new supply.

**Honey Hunters**
As it feasts on nectar, the Australian honey possum gets pollen on its fur.

**Pollen Stop**
Bees flit from flower to flower all day, feeding on nectar. Each time they stop, they pick up some pollen.

*A flower not a fly!*

*This bee is having a good pollen bath.*

**Clever Tricks**
Fly orchids look and smell like the real thing. Male flies looking for a mate are easily tricked. They buzz off in disgust, taking the orchid's pollen with them.

*Pollen from the anthers of the flower sticks to the butterfly's body.*

**Pollen Galore**
Some flowers are either male or female. A catkin, for example, is a male flower. It produces masses of pollen to make sure some will be blown onto the stigmas of the tiny female flowers.

**Nectar Gatherers**
Brightly coloured flowers attract butterflies looking for nectar.

**Special Collection**
When the hummingbird pushes its long beak deep inside the flower to collect the nectar, some pollen brushes off onto its body.

**Inside Story**
Not many insects would ever find the flowers of the fig tree. They actually grow inside the figs! They are pollinated by special fig wasps that live inside the fig. When the flowers are producing pollen, some of the wasps leave home. They move into another fig, carrying pollen with them on their bodies.

*Pollen is brushed onto the bat's fur as it moves from flower to flower.*

*The bat's long tongue is perfect for whisking out the nectar.*

**Tropical Favourite**
The bird of paradise flower grows in the tropics. It is pollinated by bats as well as by birds.

*On its nightly nectar hunt, one bat can pollinate several flowers.*

*Bats find it easy to pick out the spiky shape of the bird of paradise flower at night.*

# FLOWERS BECOME FRUITS

After they have been pollinated, flowers produce seeds and fruits. The fruits protect the seeds and keep them safe until the time comes for them to grow. Like flowers, fruits come in all sorts of shapes and sizes. Horse chestnuts make conkers, dandelions make parachutes, and plum trees make plums. Every fruit has its own kind of seed. Some are light enough to be blown away on the wind, others are armour-plated so they can be swallowed by animals and pass out in their droppings without being damaged!

**From Rose to Hip**
Bees are attracted to this rose by its sweet smell and the promise of nectar

1. *The swelling beneath the flower is called the receptacle and it will become the fruit.*

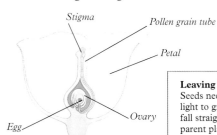

*Stigma*

*Pollen grain tube*

*Petal*

*Ovary*

*Egg*

## Fertilization
An insect leaves some pollen on the stigma of a flower, and fertilization can take place. Each tiny pollen grain grows a long tube. The tube grows down until it reaches the ovary where eggs are produced. Now a male gamete from the pollen tube joins with an egg from the ovary, and a seed is born.

## Leaving Home
Seeds need space and light to grow. If they fall straight off the parent plant, they have to struggle to grow in its shadow. So plants use all sorts of clever devices for making sure their seeds are carried away from them by wind or animals. Some have exploding pods that catapult the seeds into the air.

*Poppy seeds are spread by the wind.*

*Vetch pods explode when they are dry.*

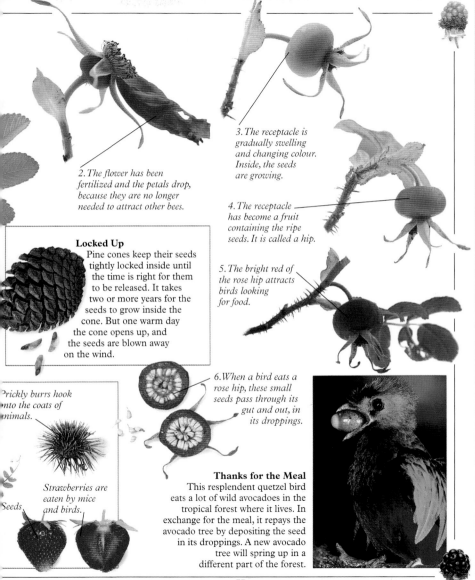

2. The flower has been fertilized and the petals drop, because they are no longer needed to attract other bees.

3. The receptacle is gradually swelling and changing colour. Inside, the seeds are growing.

4. The receptacle has become a fruit containing the ripe seeds. It is called a hip.

5. The bright red of the rose hip attracts birds looking for food.

### Locked Up

Pine cones keep their seeds tightly locked inside until the time is right for them to be released. It takes two or more years for the seeds to grow inside the cone. But one warm day the cone opens up, and the seeds are blown away on the wind.

Prickly burrs hook onto the coats of animals.

Seeds

Strawberries are eaten by mice and birds.

6. When a bird eats a rose hip, these small seeds pass through its gut and out, in its droppings.

### Thanks for the Meal

This resplendent quetzel bird eats a lot of wild avocadoes in the tropical forest where it lives. In exchange for the meal, it repays the avocado tree by depositing the seed in its droppings. A new avocado tree will spring up in a different part of the forest.

# Seeds Become Plants

Below ground, a seed is waiting to start life. But until it gets the right signals, a seed will remain just a seed. As soon as the soil becomes warm and damp the seed can begin to absorb moisture. This makes it swell and the seedcase splits open. Germination has begun – and the seedling starts to grow towards the light.

**Wall Flowers**
Some seeds land in odd places – and there they grow!

*The leaves unfold into a fan shape.*

*Peanuts*

**Peanut bush**

**Coffee bush**

**Seed and Plant**
You may recognize these seeds, but do you know what they grow into?

*Coffee beans*

**Oak tree**

*Lemon pips*

**Lemon tree**

*Acorns*

*Roots grow down through the husk of the coconut.*

**Fast Food**
Mustard and cress seeds are quick and easy to grow. Put some damp cotton wool in clean egg shells and sprinkle a few seeds on top. Look at the seeds each day and keep the cotton wool damp. In about ten days you will have your own home-grown salad!

*Eggshells*

*Seeds*

*Damp cotton wool*

**On the Beach**
A coconut can travel long distances by sea, until it is washed up onto the shore. In the warm sand, it sprouts and starts to grow.

**Some Like it Hot**
Some seeds must literally go through fire and water before they can germinate. In the arid Australian outback, fierce fires can rip across the land. They wake the dormant seeds of these acacia trees.

*The stem is formed from the stalks of the leaves.*

*As the shoot gets longer and thicker, the first leaves open.*

*The coconut contains liquid, so the seedling has its own water supply for a while.*

*Inside the bean, you can see the part that is the future root.*

*A first sign of life – the root pushes through the skin of the bean.*

*The shoot appears above ground. This is the stem.*

**Roots and Shoots**
When the soil gets warm in spring, this broad bean germinates and begins to grow.

# GROWING WITHOUT SEEDS

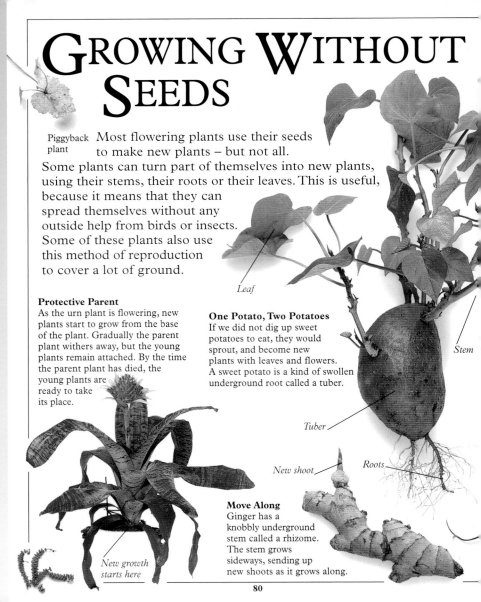

Piggyback plant

Most flowering plants use their seeds to make new plants – but not all. Some plants can turn part of themselves into new plants, using their stems, their roots or their leaves. This is useful, because it means that they can spread themselves without any outside help from birds or insects. Some of these plants also use this method of reproduction to cover a lot of ground.

*Leaf*

## Protective Parent
As the urn plant is flowering, new plants start to grow from the base of the plant. Gradually the parent plant withers away, but the young plants remain attached. By the time the parent plant has died, the young plants are ready to take its place.

## One Potato, Two Potatoes
If we did not dig up sweet potatoes to eat, they would sprout, and become new plants with leaves and flowers. A sweet potato is a kind of swollen underground root called a tuber.

*Stem*

*Tuber*

*New shoot*

*Roots*

## Move Along
Ginger has a knobbly underground stem called a rhizome. The stem grows sideways, sending up new shoots as it grows along.

*New growth starts here*

### Growing Family

Sempervivum plants grow in clusters like spiky cushions. The parent plant produces plantlets all around itself. These in their turn produce more plantlets and so on and on!

### Upside-Down Plants

Papyrus plants grow in damp soil near water. They spread in an unusual way. The stems gradually arch over, until their tips are head down in the damp soil. Now they take root. The old stems wither away, and new stems grow up.

### Clever Arithmetic

A daffodil bulb multiplies below the ground by producing small new bulbs around itself. Once the new bulbs are large enough to flower, there will be several, where once there was only one!

### Turning Over a New Leaf

Crassulas grow in dry places, and their leaves contain water. When leaves drop off they take root. Their private water supply keeps them alive while new roots are growing.

*Leaf bud*

### Long Distance Runners

Strawberry plants can travel a long way by putting out side shoots called runners. Wherever a runner touches the ground, it produces roots and a new plant grows up. It is rather like a large family all holding hands!

### Hats Off!

Small leaf buds grow all around the edges of the Mexican hat plant's fleshy leaves. These drop off onto the ground and take root to make little hats!

*Runner*      *New plant*

# TREES

Monkey puzzle tree

Trees are the longest living of all plants. They grow strong, woody trunks so that they can tower above other plants and get plenty of light. There are trees that lose all their leaves in one go when the weather gets cold. They are known as deciduous trees. Others are evergreen and shed a few leaves at a time throughout the year.

*The heartwood is the oldest part of the tree. It is no longer living but it is very strong.*

*Bark is very important. It protects all the living, working parts of the trunk.*

*This part of the trunk is still alive and busy, carrying water and food to the rest of the tree.*

**Fiery Finale**
Before they fall, the leaves of many deciduous trees change colour. The green chlorophyll disappears, revealing other colours that were hidden. Chemicals in the leaves deepen these colours to fiery golds and reds.

Silver birch

**Bark**
As trees grow, their trunks expand. The bark cracks to make lots of different patterns.

Paperbark maple

Tibetan cherry

**Holding Fast**
Over the years, wind has shaped and battered the branches of this tree. But its trunk and strong roots keep it standing.

**Deciduous trees**

Spanish oak

American mountain ash

Weeping willow

## Cross Section

Every year a tree adds a new layer of growth to its trunk and branches. Look at this slice from a tree's trunk, and you will see lots of rings. Each ring shows the growth made by the tree in one year. By counting the rings you can tell how old a tree is.

*A wide ring shows that the tree grew a lot in this year.*

*A bad year for growth! Thin rings show how slowly trees can sometimes grow.*

Shagbark hickory

Cork oak

Snake-bark maple

## Evergreen trees

Deodar

Mountain gum

Black spruce

### The Incredible Hulk

What size waist do you have? The trunk of this giant redwood in California measures 24 metres all the way round, and stands over 83 metres high. It is so famous it has even been given a name – General Sherman!

# SEA LIFE

Almost three-quarters of the Earth is covered by oceans and seas. These billions of tonnes of salty water are home to silent sharks, playful dolphins, huge whales, spiny orange crabs, giant octopuses with their eight long arms, friendly turtles, and fish of all shapes and sizes. Beautiful underwater gardens of brightly coloured coral provide a home for stinging sea anemones, poisonous sea slugs, and deadly eels.

Leatherback turtle

Many parts of the world's seas and oceans are too deep, dark and cold to support anything except small, simple, forms of life. Other places are so fantastically deep that nobody has ever been able to explore them. Some day, we may discover that even more incredible plants and animals than we imagined inhabit this silent, watery world.

Coral reef

Blue whale

Tropical sundial shells

Flounder with
camouflage
colouring

Female angler fish with males underneath

Edible crab

Harbour seal cub

Common
starfish

# PLANKTON

Seawater is full of billions of very tiny plants and animals called plankton. Most types of plankton are less than one millimetre long, but without them, very little else could live in the sea! They are the most important food for many fish, whales and even birds. Their tiny size means that they are not strong enough to swim against the sea, so they can only drift around helplessly.

*This curved feeler is covered in fine sensory hairs which help the copepod find food.*

*Animal plankton can be over a hundred times bigger than the tiny plants they eat.*

**Bucket Full!**
Copepods are a type of animal plankton. They are so small that over one million could fit into a bucket of seawater.

Plant plankton...eaten by...animal plankton...eaten by...fish...eaten by...seabirds

**Food for Everyone**
Seabirds, turtles and seals all eat other animals, such as fish and shellfish, that eat plankton. They would all starve if there were no plankton in the sea.

**Part-time Plankton**
Some animals begin their lives as tiny plankton, but then they grow much, much bigger.

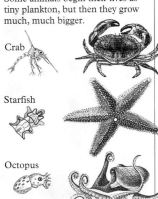

Crab

Starfish

Octopus

*Like all plants, plant plankton use sunlight to make their food.*

**Sun Lovers**
Like all plants, plant plankton use sunlight to make their food.

*There are many different sorts, or species, of copepods. This male is flashing bright blue to attract a female.*

_By waving these bristles, the copepod pushes water over its tiny gills and also traps plant plankton._

**Countless Copepods**
Copepods are the most common animals in the sea.

_Eye_

**Soupy Seas!**
Plant plankton live near the surface of the sea where there is lots of light. They also prefer cooler water because it has more minerals in it. Animal plankton eat plant plankton, so they are found in the same places. This map of the world shows where they both live. The red, yellow and green areas have more plankton than the blue, purple and pink areas. Plankton have not been counted in the grey parts.

_At night, copepods drift nearer to the surface and hunt for food. During the day, they sink deeper down to hide from hungry birds and fish._

_Copepods can't swim against the sea, but they can move around by using their feelers as oars._

**Zooplankton – Animals**

_Tail_

Sea gooseberry

Krill

Arrow worm

**Phytoplankton – Plants**

_Lots of plant plankton, or phytoplankton, have joined together to make this chain. The chain is too big to be eaten by many zooplankton._

87

# SHELLFISH

The shells that you find on a beach are the empty homes of small animals called shellfish. These soft-bodied creatures need hard shells to protect them from starfish, crabs, fish and even birds. The most common types of shellfish are gastropods and bivalves. Gastropods are underwater snails. They grow coiled shells and slide around on a slimy foot. Bivalves have two, flatter shells that cover their whole body.

Eggs    Larva

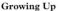

**Growing Up**
Unlike crabs, shellfish never need new shells. Baby shellfish, or larvae, grow a tiny shell that keeps on getting bigger.

*Because their shells are so light, bubble shells can use their mantles as flippers to help them swim.*

Mantle

**The Animal Inside**
Bivalves, gastropods and all other shellfish have soft bodies and no backbones. They are molluscs, just like octopuses!

*Worm*

*These feelers help the shellfish find food.*

*Water in*

*Water out*

*Eye*

**Swimming Scallops**
By taking in water and then shooting it out of its back end, a scallop is able to jump through the sea.

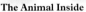

**Buried Alive**
Tusk shells and many bivalves spend most of their life buried in sand. Bivalves dig a hole with their foot, then poke tubes, or siphons, into the sea. The siphons take water into the bivalve's gills and catch food.

*Foot*    *Siphon*

Tusk shell    Tellin

Sand gaper    Razor shell

*Eye on a stalk*

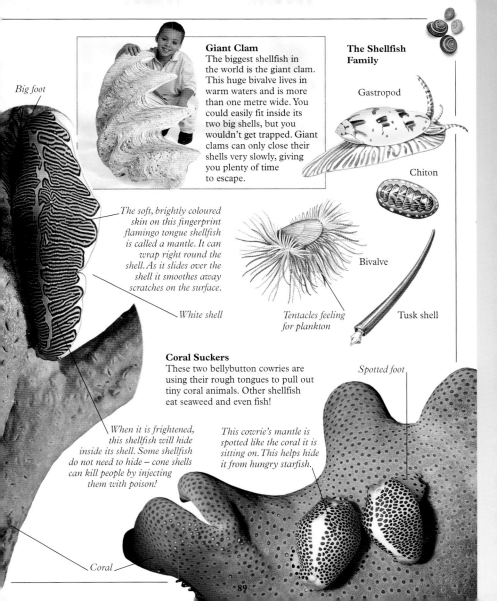

*Big foot*

### Giant Clam
The biggest shellfish in the world is the giant clam. This huge bivalve lives in warm waters and is more than one metre wide. You could easily fit inside its two big shells, but you wouldn't get trapped. Giant clams can only close their shells very slowly, giving you plenty of time to escape.

### The Shellfish Family

Gastropod

Chiton

*The soft, brightly coloured skin on this fingerprint flamingo tongue shellfish is called a mantle. It can wrap right round the shell. As it slides over the shell it smoothes away scratches on the surface.*

*White shell*

*Tentacles feeling for plankton*

Bivalve

Tusk shell

### Coral Suckers
These two bellybutton cowries are using their rough tongues to pull out tiny coral animals. Other shellfish eat seaweed and even fish!

*Spotted foot*

*When it is frightened, this shellfish will hide inside its shell. Some shellfish do not need to hide – cone shells can kill people by injecting them with poison!*

*This cowrie's mantle is spotted like the coral it is sitting on. This helps hide it from hungry starfish.*

*Coral*

# CRABS

What lives in the sea or on land, can be any colour, has its eyes on stalks, swims and walks sideways, and carries its own house? Would you have guessed a crab? Crabs live in all parts of the sea, from the very deepest oceans to wave-swept shores.

Antennae — Eye

Mouth

Crabs use their back four pairs of legs to scuttle sideways.

The strong claws are used for fighting and also for tearing apart fish, shellfish and plants to eat.

Under this spine, there are two feelers, called antennae. The crab uses tiny hairs along the antennae to touch, smell and taste.

The shell is often called the carapace.

When crabs get too big for their shells they split them open and shed them. Underneath the old suit of armour there is a new, soft shell. This can take three days to harden.

This spiny spider crab is protected from most of its enemies by its shell.

Crabs can grow new legs if they are torn off.

Crabs breathe through five pairs of gills. These are inside the shell, near the top of each leg.

**Crab Eaters**
Crabs make a tasty meal for fish, birds, octopuses, seals and people!

Joint

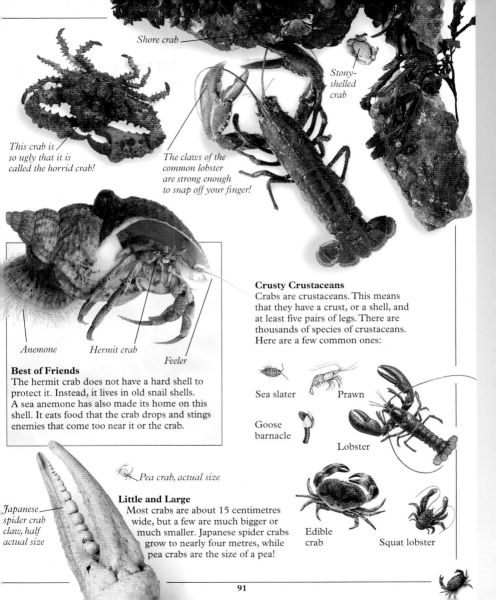

Shore crab

Stony-shelled crab

*This crab is so ugly that it is called the horrid crab!*

*The claws of the common lobster are strong enough to snap off your finger!*

Anemone  Hermit crab

Feeler

## Best of Friends
The hermit crab does not have a hard shell to protect it. Instead, it lives in old snail shells. A sea anemone has also made its home on this shell. It eats food that the crab drops and stings enemies that come too near it or the crab.

## Crusty Crustaceans
Crabs are crustaceans. This means that they have a crust, or a shell, and at least five pairs of legs. There are thousands of species of crustaceans. Here are a few common ones:

Sea slater  Prawn

Goose barnacle

Lobster

*Japanese spider crab claw, half actual size*

*Pea crab, actual size*

## Little and Large
Most crabs are about 15 centimetres wide, but a few are much bigger or much smaller. Japanese spider crabs grow to nearly four metres, while pea crabs are the size of a pea!

Edible crab

Squat lobster

# Starfish

Starfish are star-shaped, but they are not fish – they are echinoderms. This means that they have spiny skin. They cannot swim, but they are very good at crawling! They can walk up strands of seaweed and climb down the sides of rocks. Even in the deepest, darkest parts of the sea, there are starfish creeping around.

*This crimson-knobbed starfish, like most starfish, measures less than 20 centimetres from tip to tip. But some species are as wide as a small car!*

*Starfish don't have any eyes. Instead, they have eyespots on the tips of their arms. These special cells cannot see shapes, but they can tell whether it is light or dark.*

*These bumps are actually spines.*

*Burrowing starfish*

*Starfish's arms are very bendy because their skeleton is made up of lots of tiny spines that can move in any direction.*

*Central disc*

*Cushion star*

*Starfish breathe through their feet and also through tiny tubes that are found all over their body.*

*Common starfish*

**Stomach This**
Starfish eat shellfish. When they find a clam, they pull open its shell with their tiny, tube feet, push their whole stomach inside its shell and slowly digest the clam.

*Common sea urchin*

*Slate-pencil sea urchin*

**Sea Hedgehogs**
Sea urchins are close relatives of starfish. Their long spines, which are sometimes poisonous, make them look like hedgehogs.

*Goosefoot starfish*

*Some starfish have more than five arms. This spiny sun star has twelve!*

**Armless**
This starfish is growing two new arms. The old ones were bitten off by a fish! As long as the central disc and one arm is left, the starfish will survive.

*New arm*

**Spiny Species**
There are more than 6,000 different species of echinoderms, but only five main groups.

Starfish

Brittle stars

*Tube foot*

*Each of these feet has a sucker on the end which helps the starfish stick to rocks and catch food.*

**Flip Side**
It is easy to tell which way up a starfish or a sea urchin is – its mouth is always underneath.

Sea urchin

*Most starfish have five arms.*

Sea cucumber

*If a starfish flips over, it pulls itself the right way up with its arms.*

*Mouth*

Sea lily

93

# OCTOPUSES

Did you know that octopuses are related to snails? But unlike most other molluscs, they don't have shells to protect them. Instead, these eight-armed animals squeeze their soft bodies into small cracks or holes in rocks. Once they are safely hidden, it is very hard for conger eels, sharks, seals and people to find and eat them.

**Bunch of Eggs**
Inside each of these soft-shelled eggs there is a baby octopus.

*With their large eyes, octopuses can see shapes and colours very well.*

*Web*

**Gone Fishing**
Octopuses hunt for their food. They pounce on fish, starfish and crabs. Some have webs between their arms which help them net even more animals.

*Tentacle*

*This common octopus measures only ten centimetres from tip to tip. The largest octopus ever found was over nine metres wide!*

*An octopus can shoot ink, called sepia, out of its siphon. This black cloud hangs in the water and hides the octopus from its enemies.*

*Siphon*

**Jet-propelled**
If an octopus is frightened, it does not crawl slowly away – it jets off! By forcing water out through its siphon, it can shoot through the sea.

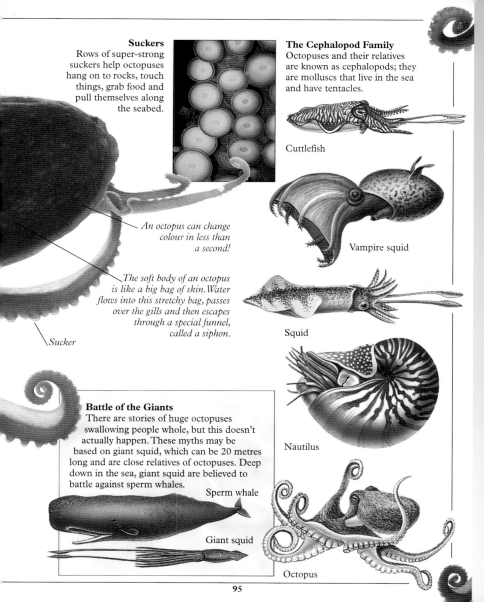

**Suckers**
Rows of super-strong suckers help octopuses hang on to rocks, touch things, grab food and pull themselves along the seabed.

**The Cephalopod Family**
Octopuses and their relatives are known as cephalopods; they are molluscs that live in the sea and have tentacles.

Cuttlefish

Vampire squid

Squid

Nautilus

*An octopus can change colour in less than a second!*

*The soft body of an octopus is like a big bag of skin. Water flows into this stretchy bag, passes over the gills and then escapes through a special funnel, called a siphon.*

Sucker

**Battle of the Giants**
There are stories of huge octopuses swallowing people whole, but this doesn't actually happen. These myths may be based on giant squid, which can be 20 metres long and are close relatives of octopuses. Deep down in the sea, giant squid are believed to battle against sperm whales.

Sperm whale

Giant squid

Octopus

# FISH

All living things need a gas called oxygen to breathe. You cannot see it, but it is found in air and water. You use your lungs to breathe in air. If you swim under water, you either have to hold your breath or use a snorkel. Fish don't have to do this. They can take their oxygen straight out of the water.

**Fish Eggs**
Most fish lay jelly-like eggs. Some guard their eggs until they hatch. Others, like cod, just squirt millions of tiny eggs into the sea. This is called spawning.

*Dorsal fin*

*Fish do not need eyelids – seawater keeps their eyes wet and free of dirt.*

← *Water in*

*Water out* ⎜ *Gills*

*Pectoral fin*

**Breathing Under Water**
Water flows into the fish's mouth, over red flaps called gills and out through the gill openings. The gills take the oxygen out of the water.

*There are four gills behind this opening.*

*Bony fish have a 'balloon' inside them called a swim bladder. It can be filled with air to help them float.*

The pectoral and pelvic fins help the fish move up, down, left or right.

*Pelvic fin*

*Muscle*

*Backbone, or spine*

**Inside Story**
Most of the important parts of a bony fish are in the lower half of its body. The top half is full of muscles, which move the tail.

*Gills*

*Stomach*

*Heart*

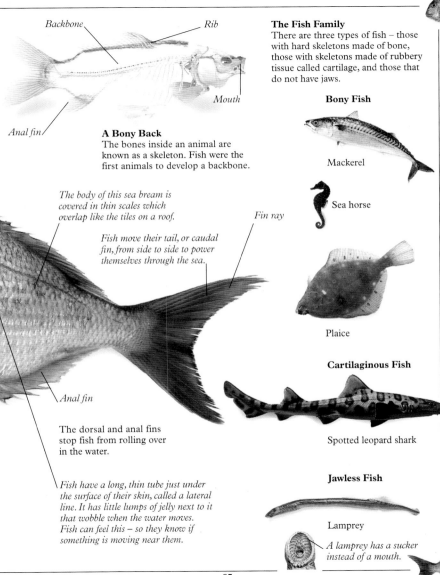

Backbone

Rib

Mouth

Anal fin

**The Fish Family**
There are three types of fish – those with hard skeletons made of bone, those with skeletons made of rubbery tissue called cartilage, and those that do not have jaws.

**Bony Fish**

Mackerel

Sea horse

**A Bony Back**
The bones inside an animal are known as a skeleton. Fish were the first animals to develop a backbone.

*The body of this sea bream is covered in thin scales which overlap like the tiles on a roof.*

Fin ray

*Fish move their tail, or caudal fin, from side to side to power themselves through the sea.*

Plaice

**Cartilaginous Fish**

Anal fin

The dorsal and anal fins stop fish from rolling over in the water.

Spotted leopard shark

**Jawless Fish**

*Fish have a long, thin tube just under the surface of their skin, called a lateral line. It has little lumps of jelly next to it that wobble when the water moves. Fish can feel this – so they know if something is moving near them.*

Lamprey

*A lamprey has a sucker instead of a mouth.*

# SHARKS

Sharks are the best hunters in the sea. With their terrible teeth and huge jaws, they can tear up seals, turtles, fish and even wooden boats! Tiger sharks and great white sharks sometimes bite people, but most sharks are more scared of us and soon swim away.

*See how big this jaw is!*

*Sharks are like a swimming nose. They can smell injured animals and other food that is hundreds of metres away.*

*All living animals produce a small amount of electricity. You cannot sense it, but sharks can. Little dimples on their head work like television aerials to tell them where animals are hiding.*

*Five gill slits on each side of the head let water into the shark's gills.*

### Teeth as Sharp as Knives

Shark teeth can cut through skin and crunch up bones, but they soon get blunt. Each tooth only lasts for a few weeks, then it falls out and is replaced by a new one. Basking sharks eat plankton so they don't need any teeth!

*Dorsal fin*

*Pectoral fin*

### Super Swimmer

A shark swims by bending from side to side. First it moves its head, then its body and last of all its long tail. As this wave travels down its body, it pushes the shark through the sea.

### Shark Attack!

Just before they bite, sharks bend their noses up and move their teeth forwards.

Great white shark

Sandtiger shark

Blue shark

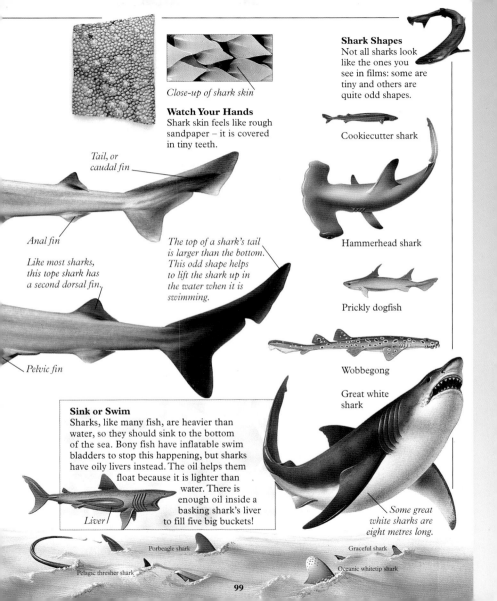

*Close-up of shark skin*

**Watch Your Hands**
Shark skin feels like rough sandpaper – it is covered in tiny teeth.

**Shark Shapes**
Not all sharks look like the ones you see in films: some are tiny and others are quite odd shapes.

Cookiecutter shark

Hammerhead shark

Prickly dogfish

Wobbegong

Great white shark

*Tail, or caudal fin*

*Anal fin*

*Like most sharks, this tope shark has a second dorsal fin.*

*The top of a shark's tail is larger than the bottom. This odd shape helps to lift the shark up in the water when it is swimming.*

*Pelvic fin*

**Sink or Swim**
Sharks, like many fish, are heavier than water, so they should sink to the bottom of the sea. Bony fish have inflatable swim bladders to stop this happening, but sharks have oily livers instead. The oil helps them float because it is lighter than water. There is enough oil inside a basking shark's liver to fill five big buckets!

*Liver*

*Some great white sharks are eight metres long.*

Pelagic thresher shark

Porbeagle shark

Graceful shark

Oceanic whitetip shark

# RAYS

Rays are one of the most common sorts of fish in the sea. A few look like their relatives, the sharks, but most are diamond-shaped and flat. Some of these shy, gentle animals can be glimpsed gliding gracefully through the sea, but others spend most of their time lying on the seabed.

*These sharp spines protect the ray. Stingrays also have one very large poisonous spine which they use to stab their enemies.*

*Thornback ray*

*Like sharks, rays have skeletons made of cartilage.*

*Gill slit*

*Mouth*

**Upside Down**
On the underside of a ray, there are ten gill slits and a mouth that is full of flat teeth.

*Small pelvic fin*

**Mighty Manta**
Most rays are less than two metres wide but a manta ray can grow to over eight metres in width. Luckily for divers, it only eats plankton and small fish.

*When a ray is lying on the sea bottom, its mouth is blocked, so it sucks in water through a tiny hole, called a spiracle, behind each eye.*

*By flapping their fins, rays disturb the sand and uncover crabs – a tasty snack for a ray.*

**Underwater Flying**
A ray is one of the most graceful swimmers in the sea. Flapping its huge fins, it 'flies' like a giant, underwater bird.

### Shocking Ray

Electric rays have special muscles in their bodies that act like batteries. Once they have pounced on a fish, they kill it by using these muscles to produce more than 200 volts of electricity. The shocks are powerful enough to stun people who accidentally step on these rays.

### Ray Shapes

There are more than 350 different types of rays. Half of these are skates.

Sawfish

Guitarfish

Skate

Eagle ray

Stingray

*These swirly patterns help to hide the ray when it lies on sand.*

*Like all rays, this undulate ray's large pectoral fins are joined to its head.*

*Spiracle*

*Eye*

*Rays have a very good sense of smell.*

### Peek-a-boo

When rays hide in the sand, their large, bulging eyes stick out. They have to keep a look out for food and also for sharks that like to eat rays.

# WHALES

Millions of years ago whales used to walk. Since then, they have changed a lot. They have grown bigger and bigger, their back legs have disappeared and their front legs have turned into flippers. They can't live on land any more but they are still mammals. This means that they breathe air and feed their babies milk.

There are two sorts of whales: those that have teeth and those that do not. Whales that have no teeth are called baleen whales.

**Krill for Tea**
Baleen whales eat krill, a kind of plankton. A large whale can eat two tonnes a day – half the weight of an elephant!

*The whale moves its tail up and down to push itself through the sea. The fastest whale is the sei. It can reach speeds of 50 kilometres an hour, ten times faster than a person can swim.*

*No animal has longer flippers than a humpback whale – they are about five metres long, almost as tall as a giraffe.*

**There She Blows!**
When a whale surfaces to fill its lungs with fresh air, warm air escapes from its blowhole. This escaping air mists up, just like your breath on a cold day, and forms a tall spout called a blow.

*Deep throat grooves let a baleen whale's mouth stretch so that it can hold vast amounts of water and krill.*

*Whales have thick fat, called blubber.*

**Jumping for Joy**
Humpback whales love to leap right out of the water. This is called breaching. When they crash back into the sea, they make a huge splash!

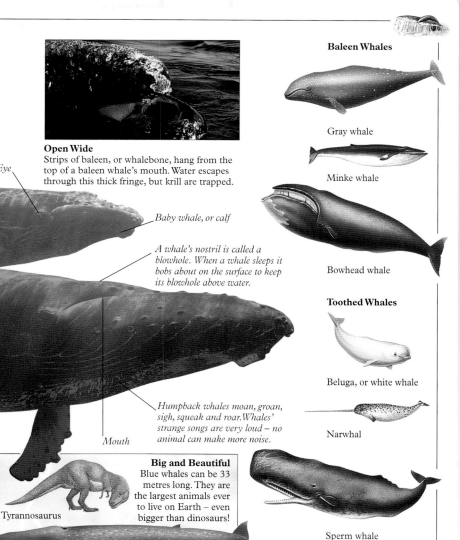

### Baleen Whales

Gray whale

Minke whale

Bowhead whale

### Toothed Whales

Beluga, or white whale

Narwhal

Sperm whale

**Open Wide**
Strips of baleen, or whalebone, hang from the top of a baleen whale's mouth. Water escapes through this thick fringe, but krill are trapped.

*Eye*

*Baby whale, or calf*

*A whale's nostril is called a blowhole. When a whale sleeps it bobs about on the surface to keep its blowhole above water.*

*Humpback whales moan, groan, sigh, squeak and roar. Whales' strange songs are very loud – no animal can make more noise.*

*Mouth*

**Big and Beautiful**
Blue whales can be 33 metres long. They are the largest animals ever to live on Earth – even bigger than dinosaurs!

Tyrannosaurus

Blue whale

# DOLPHINS

Dolphins are small, toothed whales. Some people think that these slim, smooth-skinned mammals are as intelligent as we are. They learn quickly and seem to talk to one another with whistles and clicks. Since ancient times, there has been a special friendship between humans and these playful animals. There are many stories of dolphins saving drowning sailors.

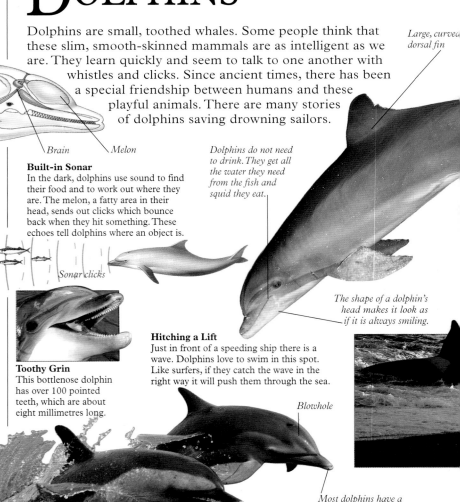

*Large, curved dorsal fin*

*Brain*

*Melon*

**Built-in Sonar**
In the dark, dolphins use sound to find their food and to work out where they are. The melon, a fatty area in their head, sends out clicks which bounce back when they hit something. These echoes tell dolphins where an object is.

*Sonar clicks*

*Dolphins do not need to drink. They get all the water they need from the fish and squid they eat.*

*The shape of a dolphin's head makes it look as if it is always smiling.*

**Toothy Grin**
This bottlenose dolphin has over 100 pointed teeth, which are about eight millimetres long.

**Hitching a Lift**
Just in front of a speeding ship there is a wave. Dolphins love to swim in this spot. Like surfers, if they catch the wave in the right way it will push them through the sea.

*Blowhole*

*Most dolphins have a long snout, called a beak.*

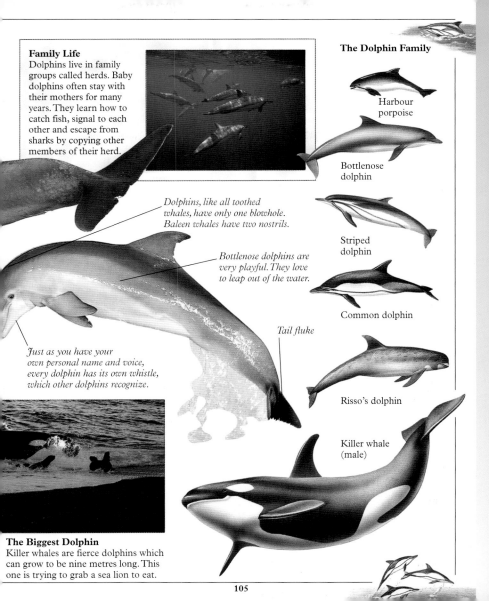

### Family Life

Dolphins live in family groups called herds. Baby dolphins often stay with their mothers for many years. They learn how to catch fish, signal to each other and escape from sharks by copying other members of their herd.

Harbour porpoise

Bottlenose dolphin

*Dolphins, like all toothed whales, have only one blowhole. Baleen whales have two nostrils.*

*Bottlenose dolphins are very playful. They love to leap out of the water.*

Striped dolphin

Common dolphin

*Tail fluke*

*Just as you have your own personal name and voice, every dolphin has its own whistle, which other dolphins recognize.*

Risso's dolphin

Killer whale (male)

### The Biggest Dolphin

Killer whales are fierce dolphins which can grow to be nine metres long. This one is trying to grab a sea lion to eat.

105

# SEALS

Seals are warm-blooded mammals, which means that they can make their own heat. Because they often swim in very cold water, they need to be able to keep this heat inside their bodies. Seals can't put on a winter coat like you to keep warm. Instead, they are covered in short hair or fur and have a layer of fat, called blubber. Sometimes, when seals swim in warmer water, they get too hot and have to fan their flippers in the air to cool down!

**Ball of Fluff**
Baby seals, or pups, are born on land. For a few weeks, many of them have white, fluffy fur.

*All seals have good hearing, but only sea lions and fur seals have ear flaps. All that can be seen of this harbour seal's ears are two tiny holes.*

*When a seal dives under water, it closes its nose, mouth and ears.*

*These whiskers, which are 40 times thicker than your hair, can sense movement in the water. This helps the seal find fish, shellfish, squid and octopus to eat.*

**Pile Up!**
When walruses climb up onto beaches, they often lie right on top of each other to keep warm.

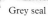

**Flip Flop**
Sea lions, fur seals and walruses use their front flippers to sit up straight and their back flippers can turn forwards. This means that they can walk, and even run, on dry land. Hair seals can only slide around on their bellies when they leave the sea.

**The Seal Family**
There are three different groups of seals.

Grey seal

**Hair seals**

Elephant seal

*Its smooth, streamlined body helps the seal speed away from killer whales and polar bears.*

**Eared seals**

Northern fur seal

*Blubber is between seven and ten centimetres thick.*

**Seal-eating Seals**
Leopard seals are fierce. They leap out of the sea and thump onto the ice to grab penguins and other seals.

California sea lion

*This seal is less than two metres long. An elephant seal can measure six metres from nose to back flippers, which is more than the height of a giraffe!*

**Walrus**

*Male walruses fight each other with their big teeth.*

*Hair seals, like this harbour or common seal, speed through the sea by moving their back flippers up and down.*

# INSECTS AND SPIDERS

Millions of years ago, long before dinosaurs arrived, there were insects on Earth. Scientists have discovered more than a million types of insect, and there are many more waiting to be found.

All insects start as eggs and most go through a larval stage. Their bodies are divided into three parts – head, thorax, and abdomen. Adults have six legs, and most have wings.

Spiders are not insects – they are arachnids. In fact, spiders love to eat insects. Unlike on insect, a spider has eight legs, and its head and thorax are joined.

Both insects and spiders live hidden away, creeping through undergrowth and living in gardens and forests. But occasionally, they come to stay in our homes.

Garden spider

Dragonfly

Honey bee

Peacock butterfly

Peacock butterfly caterpillar

Cactus longhorn beetles

Red ants

Grasshopper

Common house fly

# FLIES

You have probably seen a house fly zooming around your kitchen. Most people think of flies as pests – annoying little creatures that buzz around us, bite us, walk on our food and spread disease. But in other ways, flies are a necessary and useful part of our world. They help to pollinate plants and are eaten by a variety of other animals.

A hoverfly taking off

**Sensitive Flies**
Flies have surprisingly strong senses. This means they have very good eyesight, and a keen sense of taste and smell.

**Nice to See You!**
Our eyes have just one rounded lens. A house fly has thousands of six-sided lenses and each lens sees a part, or piece, of a bigger picture. When a house fly looks at you, it sees you as different pieces.

*Flies have two large compound eyes which see colours and shapes.*

*Many flies, like the house fly, have small antennae*

*When the fly finds liquid food, it simply sucks it up. If it finds solid food, the fly first dissolves it with special juices.*

*At the end of a fly's mouth are two pads that look like lips.*

*When landing, a fly will put its front legs up over its head.*

*Then it grabs hold of the surface and flips its body upside down.*

**Special Feet**

Flies can walk on the ceiling because they have two sharp claws on each foot. These are used to grip hold of the surface. They also have cup-shaped suction pads that stick to smooth surfaces.

**Flittering Flies**

South American mydas fly

Hover fly

Robber fly

Stalk-eyed fly

Horse fly

*True flies don't have back wings. Instead they have little bumps which look like drumsticks. These are called halteres. They help the fly to balance as it flies.*

*A house fly makes a buzzing sound. The buzz is caused by the fly's wings beating amazingly fast – about 200 times per second!*

*Flies have hairy, jointed legs. The hairs sense movement and this helps the fly stay out of danger.*

Claws

Suction pads

Crane fly

*There are about 10,000 known types of crane fly in the world. In England, they are sometimes called daddy-longlegs.*

# BEETLES

There are more species of beetle in the world than any other kind of animal. It is thought there are at least 300,000. Most are plant-eaters but some battling beetles attack and eat other insects and are quite ferocious. Beetles can be pests because they eat valuable crops. But mostly they are helpful to us because they eat dead plants and animals and return them to the earth as important nutrients.

**Ready for Battle**
A beetle's hard outer casing acts like a protective armour.

*Forewing*

**Take That!**
These fighting beetles are stag beetles. They get their name because male stag beetles have large 'horns'. These are really large jaws that are used for fighting like the antlers of a real stag. Males fight to defend their territory.

*The tough, black wing-case protects the delicate hind wings.*

*Hind wing*

*The beetle's claws help it to grip.*

**Special Friend**
Ladybirds are beetles too. Not all beetles can fly but ladybirds can. They use their hind wings to fly.

## Little and Large

The smallest known insect in the world is the feather-winged beetle. It is so small it can sit on a pinhead. The Hercules beetle is thought to be the longest beetle in the world. It can grow up to 17 centimetres long!

*Fighting males lift each other off the ground. They do this by grasping their opponent around the middle.*

## Night Lights

Fireflies are not really flies, they are beetles. At night, the females put on a light show as they flash their tails to attract a mate. They are able to do this because they have a special chemical in their body.

*Hard, antler-like jaws.*

*If it's attacked, it fires off a mixture of burning chemicals.*

**Valiant Beetles**

Rove beetle

Tortoise beetle

Giraffe beetle

Bombardier beetle

*Beetles have palps to help them sense food.*

## Roll Over

Dung beetles go to a lot of trouble to find a safe and nutritious home for their young. They collect animal dung and roll it into large balls. They roll the dung balls all the way to their underground homes. There they lay their eggs in the dung. When the beetle larvae hatch they discover a tasty meal in front of them!

Beetle storing dung

# CATERPILLARS

Caterpillars are like tiny eating machines. They spend most of their time chomping on leaves. Caterpillars are actually the young of butterflies and moths. They hatch from the eggs the adult female has laid on plants. With constant eating they get bigger and bigger, until they are ready to change into butterflies and moths.

**A New Skin**
Caterpillar skin cannot stretch. So as it gets larger, the caterpillar breaks out of its skin. Underneath is a new, larger skin which will last until the caterpillar needs to moult again.

**Hatching Out**
The butterfly's eggs are laid on the underside of a leaf.

The caterpillar bites its way out and then pulls itself free of the eggshell.

The first meal is the eggshell, which is full of good food.

*Caterpillars produce silk from special glands and force it out through a spinneret under the head.*

*Caterpillars have twelve tiny, simple eyes, called ocelli, on their head.*

The egg gets darker as the caterpillar prepares to hatch.

*The front three pairs of legs are called thoracic legs, and are used for walking and clasping.*

*The caterpillar's head is armed with a pair of stout jaws called mandibles.*

*The body is divided into 13 segments.*

*Caterpillars test food and guide it to their mouth with mouthparts called maxillary palps.*

## Wonderful Caterpillars

Caterpillars can be hairy, spiny and have unusual shapes.

Cabbage white caterpillar

Tiger moth caterpillar

Emperor moth caterpillar

Puss moth caterpillar

*Like most insects, caterpillars breathe through openings called spiracles.*

*The five pairs of stumpy, sucker-like legs are called prolegs. The caterpillar uses them for clinging onto plant stalks.*

### Silkworms

Silk is produced by most moth caterpillars. But the finest silk is produced by the large white moth caterpillar, often known as a silkworm. After the caterpillars have spun themselves into a silken cocoon, they are put into boiling water. The silk is removed and spun into threads to create material for clothes.

### Masters of Disguise

To avoid being eaten, some caterpillars have developed crafty disguises. The hawk-moth caterpillar looks like a deadly snake, the lobster moth looks like a raised lobster's claw and the common sailer looks like a shrivelled leaf.

Hawk-moth

Lobster moth

Common sailer

### Excuse Me, I'm Changing

To become adult moths, most moth caterpillars spin themselves a cocoon using silk, which comes out of the spinneret. Inside, they undergo astonishing physical changes.

# BUTTERFLIES

Butterflies are perhaps the most beautiful of all insects. It is amazing to think that a fat, leaf-eating caterpillar can become a brightly coloured, fluttering creature of the air. The change happens in the butterfly chrysalis. The caterpillar's body is broken down and completely changed. After about four weeks, a fully formed butterfly emerges.

**Time to Wake Up**
The butterfly comes out of the chrysalis in three stages. During this time it is very open to attack by hungry birds or spiders.

*1. No longer a caterpillar, a beautiful butterfly comes out of the chrysalis with its wings crumpled up.*

**Monarchs on the Move**
Most butterflies are born, live and die in one place. But when winter comes to the eastern and western coasts of North America, thousands of red monarchs fly south to the warmth of California and Mexico. When warm weather returns to their first home, they fly north again.

## ppy Landings

clouded yellow butterfly comes to land on a thistle. Butterfly ght is more controlled than it ks. The insect is able to ange course instantly and ke sudden landings.

*Butterflies feed through a tube called a proboscis. This is coiled up when not in use.*

*Butterflies have clubbed antennae.*

*Wings open.*

## In the Background

Butterflies make a tasty meal for birds. But if they are able to blend in with their background, they may avoid being eaten. The open wings of the Indian leaf butterfly have a striking orange patterning. But when its wings are closed, the butterfly looks exactly like an old, dry leaf.

*Wings closed, resting on leaf*

**2.** *The butterfly must stay still for some hours, as blood is pumped into the wing veins to stretch the wings. Later it holds its wings apart to let them harden.*

**3.** *When its wings have hardened, the butterfly is ready to fly off to find its first meal of nectar.*

### Brilliant Butterflies

Male bird-wing butterfly

Glass swallowtail butterfly

88 butterfly

Cramer's blue morpho butterfly

## Scaly Wings

The wings of both butterflies and moths are made up of tiny scales, which overlap like the tiles on a roof. Bright colours can either be used to attract a mate, or to warn predators that the butterfly, or moth, is not good to eat.

# MOTHS

Most moths are night-fliers and their strong sense of smell and hearing make them well suited to a night-time existence. They can easily find their way through darkness and although attracted to light, they are dazed by it. Moths rest by day, and many are coloured to look like tree bark or leaves so that they cannot be spotted by natural enemies such as birds and lizards.

*Moths' antennae are straight or fernlike. They are used for smelling out nectar, or other moths at night.*

*The South American ghost moth has the biggest wingspan of any moth. Wingtip to wingtip, it can measure up to 30 cm.*

**Wings At Rest**
One way to tell a moth from a butterfly is to see how the insect folds its wings. Most moths rest with their wings folded over their backs. But butterflies close their wings upright.

Nymphalid butterfly

White ermine moth

*A moth's body is thick and strong.*

*A moth's wings are joined together.*

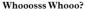

## Whooosss Whooo?

To scare off enemies, like birds, the wing patterns of some moths mimic the appearance of fierce animals. The great peacock moth has big eyespots on its wings which look like an owl's eyes. With these staring back at them, birds think twice before attacking!

### Day-Flying Moths

Colombian blue wing moth

Madagascan red-tailed moth

Verdant hawk-moth

Sloan's uraniid moth

### A Real Eyeful!

Pyraustine moths have strange feeding habits. With their long proboscises, they drink the tears of animals such as cows and buffaloes. They are so gentle, that the animal's eye does not become irritated.

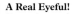

*The veins of the moth's wing help to warm or cool the insect.*

### Spot the Moth!

This geometrid moth from the jungles of Borneo looks like lichen on a tree trunk. The secret of its camouflage is not just colour, but ragged outlines and broken patterns.

# ANTS

Ants live together in nests that are like underground towns. There may be up to half a million ants in one nest. Most of these are female and are called workers. Some workers build and repair the nest, while some are 'soldiers' and guard the entrance. Others gather food for the larvae and the huge queen. Her life is spent laying millions of eggs, and the survival of the nest depends upon her wellbeing.

**Weaving Away**
Weaver ants make their nests in trees. They sew leaves together using a sticky silk thread produced by their larvae. The queen lives inside the leaf envelope.

*Ants have powerful jaws, or mandibles, for chopping food. Their mouth is just below the mandibles.*

*Some ants will spray a nasty chemical from their rear end if they sense danger!*

*When ants meet they 'tap' antennae. The antennae contain chemical 'messages' which can be passed on by touching.*

*Ants can run very fast because they have long legs.*

**Farming Fungus**
Leaf cutter ants are the farmers of the ant world. They cut up bits of leaf and take them back to the nest. Fungus grows on the rotting leaf – and then the ants feed on the fungus!

### Left, Right!
Driver ants from South America are very fierce insects. They are nomadic, which means they are always on the move. They march in columns through the forest, killing and eating everything in their path. Here they are raiding a wasp's nest.

**Bustling Ants**

Red ant

Black ant

Harvester ant

Wood ant

Dinoponera – the largest ant

### Living Larders
Some honeypot ant workers spend their whole lives feeding on nectar. Their abdomens swell and when food is hard to find, other workers use them as a food supply.

### Inside an Ant's Nest
The success of an ant's nest relies on the hardworking and organized inhabitants.

*The queen lays her eggs in the royal chamber.*

*Seed crusher ant*

*Wingless workers take care of the ant larvae.*

*A network of tunnels joins the chambers in the ant's nest.*

*Soldier ant guarding the entrance.*

# GRASSHOPPERS

Grasshoppers are known for the 'ticking' sounds they make and for their ability to leap high into the air. There are more than 20,000 different kinds of grasshopper in the world. Grasshoppers are plant-eaters, feeding on leaves and stems. Normally, they prefer to be alone. But under special conditions, they undergo a series of physical changes. They increase in size, become more brightly coloured and gather in their millions to become a swarm of hungry locusts.

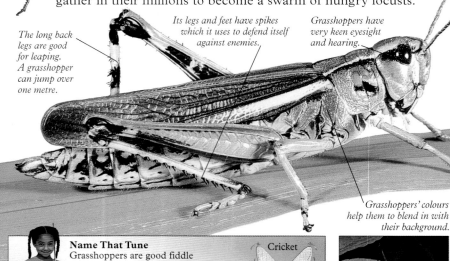

*The long back legs are good for leaping. A grasshopper can jump over one metre.*

*Its legs and feet have spikes which it uses to defend itself against enemies.*

*Grasshoppers have very keen eyesight and hearing.*

*Grasshoppers' colours help them to blend in with their background.*

## Name That Tune

Grasshoppers are good fiddle players. They make music the same way a violin produces sound. The grasshopper's leg is its bow and the tough wing vein is the string. Crickets are also known for their musical ability. They use their wings to make sound. One wing has a thick vein with bumps on it. This is called the file. The cricket rubs the file over a rough ridge on the other wing to make cricket music.

Cricket

Grasshopper

## Chirping Cousins

Crickets belong to the same insect group as grasshoppers. But crickets have longer antennae and like eating other insects.

## Growing Up

Female locusts lay their eggs in the sand. The babies, called nymphs, hatch and dig their way out. When they appear, they are tiny versions of their parents. In order to become fully grown adults, the nymphs moult between three and five times. After each moult the nymphs are bigger than before. When they moult for the final time, they emerge with full-sized wings.

*Nymph crawling out of nest*

*Adult pulling itself free of skin*

*Adult resting while its wings harden*

## The Trouble with Locusts

When heavy rains fall in hot, dry regions, lush plant life begins to grow. With lots of food, large numbers of grasshoppers get together to mate. After mating, they eat all the plant life around them and grow much larger. In search of more food they take to the air in huge swarms, devouring fields of valuable crops.

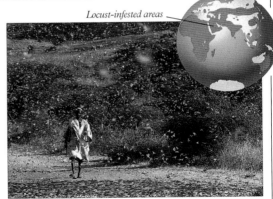

*Locust-infested areas*

## Extended Family

All of these insects are related to grasshoppers but they have quite different features – and very clever disguises.

Leaf insect

Stick insect

Praying mantis

123

# BEES

Bumble bee

You have probably heard the buzz of a honeybee as it flies from flower to flower. During the spring and summer months, bees spend their time collecting food. There are thousands of different types of bees and many of them live alone. But social bees, like honeybees, live in large nests or hives. They gather nectar to be stored in the hive and turned into honey.

**Nest Making**
Some bees make their hives out of chewed leaves, mud and animal hairs.

**Working Hives**
Man-made hives are specially made to house thousands of bees. Farmers place these hives in their orchards so the bees will pollinate the trees.

*As the honeybee moves from flower to flower, bright yellow pollen sticks to its body. The bee combs the pollen into pollen baskets on its back legs and carries it back to the hive where it is turned into food.*

*This honeybee is feeding on nectar, a sweet liquid found in flowers. It sucks out the nectar with its long, tube-like mouthparts.*

*Bees help to pollinate flowers by carrying pollen from flower to flower.*

*The bee's sting is in its tail.*

African killer bee

Orchid bee

Parasitic bee

Asian carpenter bee

**Sweet Drink**
Worker honeybees look after the young and turn nectar into another sweet liquid we call honey.

*A large hive can hold up to 50,000 bees.*

*Inside the hive, the bees store honey in a comb, which is made up of thousands of little six-sided cells. The bees feed on the honey during the cold winter months.*

**Shall we Dance?**
Worker bees scout for food. When they find a good supply they do a dance – in a figure of eight pattern – to tell the other bees where the food is. The bees in the hive then know where the food is by the angle of the 'figure of eight' and the position of the Sun in the sky.

**Queen Bee**
Every hive needs a queen. The queen bee mates with the male, called a drone. She then lays all the eggs. New hives are formed in summer when a young queen leads lots of workers out of the old hive to a new one.

**Royal Jelly**
Royal jelly is actually bees' milk. It is filled with good things like sugar, protein and vitamins. The worker bee larvae do not get to eat the royal food – they are fed on pollen and honey. Only the honeybee larvae that are destined to become queens eat royal jelly. Because it is so rich in vitamins and proteins, people now use it to make face creams, soap and vitamin tablets.

Royal jelly products

# DRAGONFLIES

Many insects are good fliers but dragonflies are truly the champions of flight. Millions of years ago, man-sized dragonflies patrolled the skies. Even today's finger-length dragonflies are quite large compared to other insects. Once dragonflies have emerged from their water-based nymph stage, they take to the air, flying at speeds of up to 56 kilometres per hour.

**Wing Power**
Dragonflies have strong muscles which control the base of the wings. In flight, the wings look like a rapidly changing X shape.

**Dancing Dragonflies**
To attract a mate, swarms of male dragonflies perform dances in the air.

Mating dragonflies

**Baby Dragonflies**
When the female is ready to lay her eggs, she dips her abdomen into the water. The eggs sink below the surface.

*Each pair of clear, veined wings can beat separately. This means that dragonflies can hover.*

*Dragonflies have excellent eyesight. They have two huge compound eyes. Each eye can have up to 30,000 lenses.*

*The bristles on the dragonfly's front legs help it to trap prey in the air.*

**Growing up**
Once the fully developed dragonfly nymph has climbed up out of the water, it begins its last and most spectacular change. The nymph's skin cracks open and an adult dragonfly pulls itself free.

## Beautiful Friends

The delicately beautiful damselfly and mayfly are related to the powerful dragonfly. They also spend most of their lives under water, as nymphs. When they become adults, they have a short time to live. In that time they must mate and lay eggs so that the next generation can develop.

Mayfly

Damselfly

*When dragonflies are at rest, their wings are fully open.*

**Mighty Dragonflies**

Flat-bodied 'darter' dragonfly

Emperor dragonfly

Club tail dragonfly

Common darter dragonfly

*Dragonflies are usually very brightly coloured. Their bodies are long and slender.*

# WEB SPIDERS

Spiders are afraid of us, so the only signs we tend to see of them are the silken webs they spin to catch their prey. Not all spiders make webs, but the ones that do, like this funnel web spider, are good at recycling. When its web gets damaged, the spider eats it, digests the silk, then uses it to spin another one.

**I'll Eat You Later**
If a web spider catches a tasty insect, but is not hungry, it poisons it but does not kill it. Then it wraps it in silk and keeps it for later.

**Up, Up and Away**
When baby spiders – called spiderlings – want to travel long distances they take to the air. They do not have wings but they are still able to fly. They produce a piece of silk and use it like a balloon.

*Spiders do not have bones. Their head and thorax are covered by a hardened shield.*

*The spiderling suspends itself from a long line.*

*It makes a loop, which is slowly drawn up by the breeze.*

*When it's ready to take off, it cuts itself free.*

*Silk is produced through the spinnerets on the end of the spider's abdomen. Spiders use their legs to pull the silk out.*

*The sac-like abdomen contains the heart, lung, silk glands and the reproductive parts.*

**Garden Surprise**
Scientists think that insects are attracted to spiders' webs because the webs reflect ultraviolet light. Insects use ultraviolet light to find their way and to find food.

## Ready to Attack

This Australian funnel web spider is one of the world's deadliest. Here it is poised, ready to attack! When spiders catch their prey, usually insects, they use their 'fangs' to poison and kill them. The funnel web spider, like most spiders, uses its strong digestive juices to dissolve the insect's insides so the spider can suck it dry.

## Spiders and Webs

The net-casting spider lives in trees, mostly in jungle areas. To catch prey, it spins a sticky net and throws it over passing insects.

*Most web spiders have eight simple eyes, called ocelli. But even so, they cannot see very well.*

## Making a Web

Making a web takes time and special care. Spiders only spin new webs when the old ones become untidy or damaged.

The water spider spins a web in the shape of a bell under the water. It fills the bell with a bubble of air and moves in.

*Spiders have a pair of graspers, called palps, on each side of their mouthparts. They are used to seize prey.*

The web of the orb web spider looks like a target. It takes about an hour to spin a complete web.

*Spiders have eight legs.*

*Even though spiders do not have ears, they can 'listen' to the world around them through their webs. The webs are very sensitive to vibrations in the air.*

The female purse web spider lives in a silken pouch. When an unsuspecting insect lands on top, the spider bites through the pouch and grabs it.

# HUNTING SPIDERS

Many spiders catch their prey without the use of silk. They are called hunting spiders. Some patrol their territory looking for insects to pounce on. Others crouch in burrows and wait for prey to wander past. Unlike web spiders, hunting spiders have strong jumping legs and keen eyesight so that they can easily spot their victims.

*This Chilean red-leg spider is one of the world's largest hunting spiders. It is about thirteen centimetres from leg to leg. It hunts at night and feeds on small birds and mice.*

*A hunting spider has eight simple eyes on the front of its head. It hardly has to move its head to be able to see in all directions.*

**Hide and Seek**
Tree-trunk trapdoor spiders are tricky creatures. After they have made a safe, secure burrow with their powerful jaws, they construct a trapdoor at the entrance. Unseen, they lie in wait behind the trapdoor, ready to leap upon any unsuspecting insects that might crawl by.

*The hairs on the spider's body are very sensitive to vibrations made by moving prey.*

*It has strong legs for digging burrows.*

Brazilian wandering spider

Crab spider

## Long Jumpers
Hunting spiders need good eyesight because they have to see and chase after their next meal. Many can measure exactly the leap they must make onto their victim, as they run along after it.

Raft spider

### Full Speed Ahead
Wolf spiders hunt during the day. This Australian wolf spider lurks at the entrance of its silk-lined tunnel ready to race full speed after prey.

Woodlouse spider

## Take Aim, Fire!
Spitting spiders spit when they are hungry. When they spot an insect, they spit streams of sticky gum from each fang. This glues the insect to the ground until the spider can arrive to eat it.

# DINOSAURS

The only dinosaur you will ever see is a dead dinosaur! No human being has ever seen a real, live dinosaur because the last of these incredible creatures died about 65 million years ago, long before the first humans appeared. Dinosaur skeletons and life-like models can help us imagine what these fantastic animals were like. We know that dinosaurs hatched out of eggs and grew up in just a few years. Scientists believe that some lived like we do, in families where the adults took care of their young. Some dinosaurs had large brains, and were smart enough to hunt in packs. Others had tiny brains and were not very intelligent.

Dinosaurs were the biggest land animals of all time, and different to anything that is alive today.

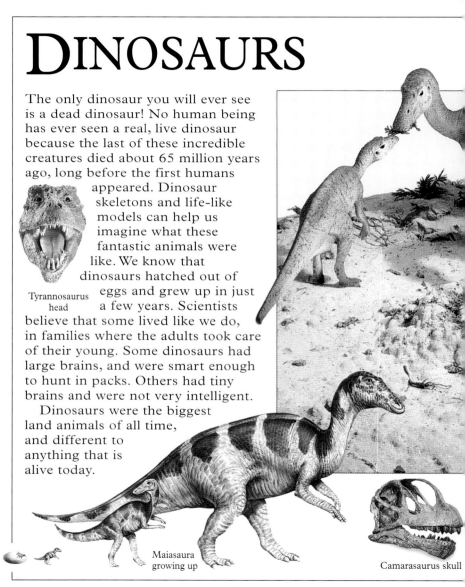

Tyrannosaurus head

Maiasaura growing up

Camarasaurus skull

Maiasaura family

Barosaurus

Triceratops

Deinonychus's
foot bones

# DIFFERENT DINOSAURS

Dinosaurs were first named nearly 200 years ago. There has been an explosion of excitement about them ever since. The huge number of different dinosaur species makes the study of dinosaurs fascinating for everyone. Thousands of bones belonging to hundreds of different dinosaurs have now been discovered. Today, dinosaurs are big business, with millions of dinosaur books and toys on sale in the shops.

## First and Last
Herrerasaurus was one of the first dinosaurs. It lived about 230 million years ago. Tyrannosaurus was one of the last dinosaurs and became extinct about 65 million years ago. Today, we are closer in time to Tyrannosaurus, than Tyrannosaurus was to Herrerasaurus!

## Classic Jurassic
The middle part of the dinosaur age is called the Jurassic Period. It started about 200 million years ago and lasted for 60 million years.

## Dinosaur Ancestor
Scientists think that over millions of years, all the different dinosaurs may have developed from one single reptile, called Lagosuchus. The hips and long legs of this primitive reptile are similar to those of the earliest dinosaurs.

## The Age of the Dinosaurs
Dinosaurs didn't all live at the same time. When one species died out, another rose up to take its place. The dinosaur age is split into the Triassic, Jurassic and Cretaceous Periods. The first dinosaurs appeared during the Triassic Period, about 230 million years ago.

*Plateosaurus*

*Dilophosaurus*

*Heterodontosaurus*

*Ornitholestes*

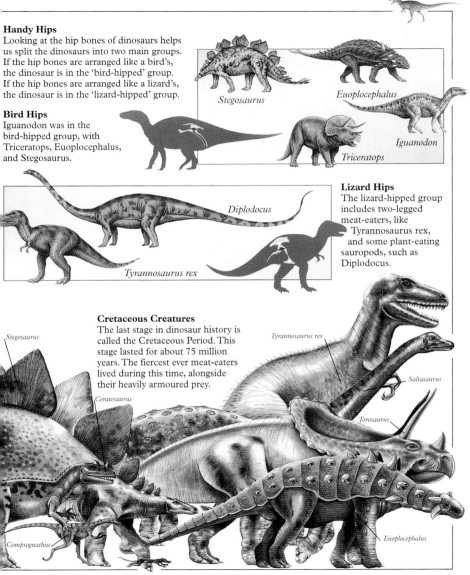

## Handy Hips

Looking at the hip bones of dinosaurs helps us split the dinosaurs into two main groups. If the hip bones are arranged like a bird's, the dinosaur is in the 'bird-hipped' group. If the hip bones are arranged like a lizard's, the dinosaur is in the 'lizard-hipped' group.

## Bird Hips

Iguanodon was in the bird-hipped group, with Triceratops, Euoplocephalus, and Stegosaurus.

*Stegosaurus*

*Euoplocephalus*

*Iguanodon*

*Triceratops*

*Diplodocus*

## Lizard Hips

The lizard-hipped group includes two-legged meat-eaters, like Tyrannosaurus rex, and some plant-eating sauropods, such as Diplodocus.

*Tyrannosaurus rex*

## Cretaceous Creatures

The last stage in dinosaur history is called the Cretaceous Period. This stage lasted for about 75 million years. The fiercest ever meat-eaters lived during this time, alongside their heavily armoured prey.

*Stegosaurus*

*Ceratosaurus*

*Compsognathus*

*Tyrannosaurus rex*

*Saltasaurus*

*Torosaurus*

*Euoplocephalus*

# DIGGING UP A DINOSAUR

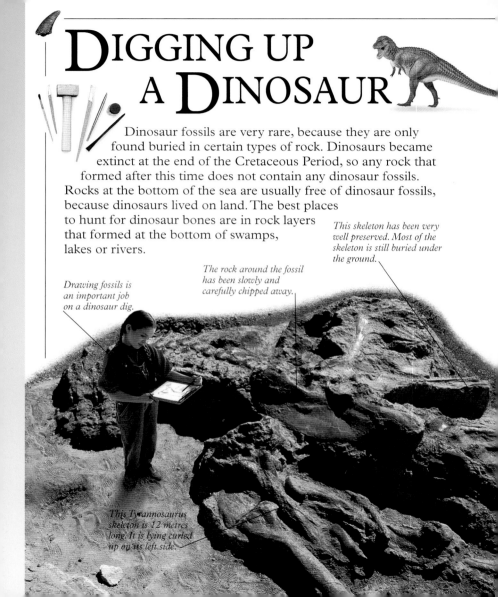

Dinosaur fossils are very rare, because they are only found buried in certain types of rock. Dinosaurs became extinct at the end of the Cretaceous Period, so any rock that formed after this time does not contain any dinosaur fossils. Rocks at the bottom of the sea are usually free of dinosaur fossils, because dinosaurs lived on land. The best places to hunt for dinosaur bones are in rock layers that formed at the bottom of swamps, lakes or rivers.

*This skeleton has been very well preserved. Most of the skeleton is still buried under the ground.*

*The rock around the fossil has been slowly and carefully chipped away.*

*Drawing fossils is an important job on a dinosaur dig.*

*This Tyrannosaurus skeleton is 12 metres long. It is lying curled up on its left side.*

## Old Bones, New Technology

Modern technology, like this ground-penetrating radar, can be used to find bones below the rock surface. In the 1980s, a dinosaur named Seismosaurus was found in this way, in New Mexico.

### Dinosaur Trap

The Dinosaur National Monument in America is one of the world's richest dinosaur treasure troves. It was once a sandy riverbed, which trapped many dying dinosaurs and preserved their bones.

## Handle with Care

Although dinosaurs were strong when they were alive, their fossils are very fragile now. Digging up a dinosaur is a slow and very delicate process.

1. The thick layers of rock above the dinosaur are often cleared away with mechanical diggers, and sometimes blasted away with explosives.

2. The last 20 centimetres or so of rock above the dinosaur are removed very carefully with tools.

3. The exact positions of the bones are then mapped out and recorded with drawings and photographs.

### Fossil Collection

Dinosaur bones are not the only kind of fossils found at dinosaur sites.

Footprints

Skin

Stomach stones

Eggs

Droppings

Teeth

4. The fragile bones must be covered with plaster for protection, before they can be moved away from the site.

5. At last, the strengthened bones are loaded up in a van and driven to a laboratory for further study.

# REBUILDING A DINOSAUR

*Thick bones in the neck held up the heavy weight of Tyrannosaurus' head.*

Jigsaws can be tricky, especially if some pieces are missing and pieces from different jigsaws are mixed in. People who rebuild dinosaur skeletons are faced with a similar puzzle. Fossil bones must be put together in the right order to form a skeleton. Bones belonging to different dinosaurs may have found their way into the collection by mistake. Missing bones are modelled by looking at the bones of similar dinosaurs. Broken bones must be cleaned and mended before they can be assembled.

## Back at the Lab

Dinosaur bones are taken from the fossil site to a laboratory. Experts clean and mend them, ready for rebuilding into a skeleton. Sometimes, fossils may be prepared for study, but are never displayed in museums.

## Belly Ache

Early this century, scientists argued over how to rebuild the skeleton of Diplodocus. Some believed Diplodocus was built like a lizard, with long legs sprawling out from its body. This was an impossible pose. Diplodocus would have needed to drag its belly through a trench to walk!

1. First, hard protective plaster must be removed from the bone with special tools.

2. Next, the bones must be carefully cleaned. This stage can take a very long time.

3. The bones are then treated with resin to make them stronger. They must also be repaired if necessary.

4. Finally, copies are made of the bones using a light material, like fibre glass. The copies, called casts, can be put together to make a museum display.

**Super Skull**
Some fossils are almost perfectly preserved. After millions of years buried under rock, this Tyrannosaurus skull did not need much patching up in the fossil laboratory!

**Model Making**
This model of a Maiasaura nest was sculpted by a scientific artist.

1. The basic Maiasaura shapes are made up with wood and wire.

2. The nest site is built up around the models. The wire skeletons are covered with paper and clay.

3. The clay models are carefully painted a sandy colour. In life, Maiasaura was probably well camouflaged.

**Building Tyrannosaurus**
This skeleton of Tyrannosaurus rex has been on display in an American museum since 1915. Today, scientists think that a big mistake was made in the way the skeleton was put up. They now think Tyrannosaurus held its tail up high above the ground.

*A strong ribcage protected its heart, liver, stomach and lungs.*

*Huge hips supported the thigh, shin and foot bones.*

*Strips of steel run underneath each bone, fitting snugly into the bone's shape.*

*The metal framework supporting the skeleton is called an armature.*

*A strong metal pillar holds up the metal strips, supporting the full weight of the skeleton.*

*The tail bones were an extension of Tyrannosaurus' spine.*

# LOOKING CLOSER

Staring up at the towering skeletons of dinosaurs can make you feel tiny. But bones alone do not give the whole picture of a living, breathing dinosaur. What colour was the dinosaur when it was alive? How strong were its muscles, and how big were its heart and lungs? Looking closely at animals alive today gives us useful clues about features, such as the skin colour of dinosaurs. We can even imagine what their insides may have looked like!

*Brachiosaurus' heart nestled underneath its lungs. It must have had very high blood pressure for the heart to be able to pump blood all around its body.*

**Weight Watcher**
Barosaurus was a very heavy sauropod, like Brachiosaurus. Sauropod means 'reptile foot'. Both dinosaurs had hollow bones in their spines. This was a useful weight-saving device.

*Brachiosaurus finished digesting its food in the longest part of its gut, called the small intestine.*

*Two massive lungs fitted snugly inside its ribcage.*

*Tough food was broken down inside the thick walls of the stomach.*

*Moisture was taken out of digested plants in this part of the intestine.*

*Powerful tail muscles made it possible to swing this bulky tail.*

*Sturdy leg bones supported the 77-tonne bulk of Brachiosaurus.*

*Strong neck muscles held up its long neck.*

*Brachiosaurus had nostrils on top of its head.*

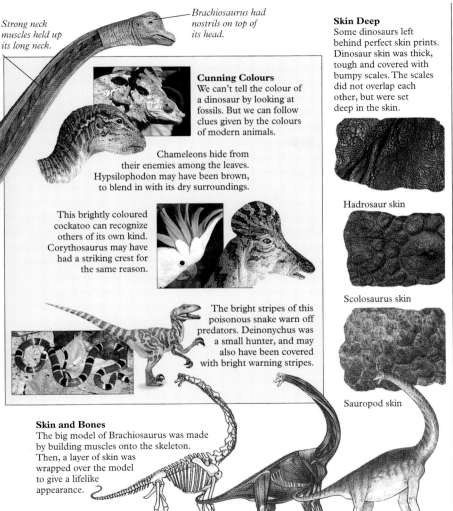

## Skin Deep
Some dinosaurs left behind perfect skin prints. Dinosaur skin was thick, tough and covered with bumpy scales. The scales did not overlap each other, but were set deep in the skin.

Hadrosaur skin

Scolosaurus skin

Sauropod skin

### Cunning Colours
We can't tell the colour of a dinosaur by looking at fossils. But we can follow clues given by the colours of modern animals.

Chameleons hide from their enemies among the leaves. Hypsilophodon may have been brown, to blend in with its dry surroundings.

This brightly coloured cockatoo can recognize others of its own kind. Corythosaurus may have had a striking crest for the same reason.

The bright stripes of this poisonous snake warn off predators. Deinonychus was a small hunter, and may also have been covered with bright warning stripes.

### Skin and Bones
The big model of Brachiosaurus was made by building muscles onto the skeleton. Then, a layer of skin was wrapped over the model to give a lifelike appearance.

# BIG VEGETARIANS

Plant-eating dinosaurs were some of the biggest animals that ever roamed the Earth. Imagine stepping into the footprint of a Barosaurus – it would be big enough to have a bath in! The big vegetarian dinosaurs called sauropods were peaceful creatures. They grew to their huge sizes on a diet of plants alone.

**Gentle Giants**
Sauropods had small heads, bulky bodies and long necks and tails.

Brachiosaurus

Camarasaurus

Mamenchisaurus

Apatosaurus

*A long tail could come in useful for whacking an enemy, but most of the time it was used to help Barosaurus balance.*

Teeth

Stones

**Weedy Teeth**
Many big vegetarian sauropods had weak teeth. This meant they did not chew plants, but often swallowed them whole. Gulping down stones may have helped grind up food in their stomachs. These stones, called gastroliths, churned tough plants into a pulp.

*Its feet were flat and padded, just like an elephant's.*

**So Long?**
The reason why sauropods had such long necks isn't certain. There are three main theories.

1. While Barosaurus stayed in one spot, its neck stretched out for food on land or in the water.

2. Did Barosaurus use its neck as an underwater snorkel, breathing through the nostrils on top of its head? Probably not, as water pressure on its body would have meant it couldn't breathe at all.

3. Barosaurus fed in the treetops. But if it lifted its neck for too long, the blood would have stopped flowing to its brain, making it faint.

**Plant Binge**
No plant was safe from a sauropod's mouth unless it stood more than 15 metres above the ground!

*Conifers are plants with cones. Barosaurus and many other vegetarian dinosaurs ate conifers.*

*Ferns varied in height, from small to tree-sized plants. No fern was too tall for Barosaurus!*

*Barosaurus ate cycads. These plants still grow in hot climates.*

*Huge legs supported the crushing weight of Barosaurus.*

# FEEDING ON PLANTS

Nearly all the huge treetop-munching dinosaurs died by the end of the Jurassic Period, about 140 million years ago. The very tall plants disappeared with them. Smaller dinosaurs then arrived on the scene. Iguanodon was well adapted to chewing and chomping. Its jaws were packed with rows of ridged teeth. These grinders pounded away at leaves Iguanodon nipped off with a sharp, beaky snout.

**Chewy Chops**
Your cheeks keep food inside your mouth as you chew. Unlike the big sauropods, Iguanodon had cheeks to hold in plant food while it chewed with its teeth.

*Big, fleshy cheeks kept food in Iguanodon's mouth as it ate.*

*A sharp beak nipped off the leaves, and strong teeth at the back of its mouth chewed them into a pulp.*

*Iguanodon ate plants, but no meat, like all the bird-hipped dinosaurs.*

*Iguanodon browsed on ferns and horsetails.*

**Snatch a Snack**
Iguanodon had a sharp thumb claw, which may have ripped down tough leaves. A bendy finger grasped plants tightly.

## Vegetarian Mouths

The mouths of these dinosaurs were well adapted for eating plants. Heterodontosaurus had three types of teeth, for cutting, puncturing and grinding. Edmontosaurus had a broad snout for gathering up big leafy mouthfuls. Hypsilophodon had a bony beak, with short teeth farther back in its mouth for chopping up its food.

Heterodontosaurus    Edmontosaurus    Hypsilophodon

Jaw bone of Edmontosaurus

*Rows of teeth for grinding down plants*

### Captain Beaky

Just like a turtle, Iguanodon had a beak, which it used for nipping plants. This horny beak never stopped growing, but was ground down by a constant diet of tough leaves. Behind the beak was a solid set of teeth, grinding up and down and from side to side.

### Fighting Back

Dinosaurs were the biggest plant-eaters of all time. Plants had to find ways of fighting back to survive. Some were so successful, they outlived the dinosaurs, and are still around.

*The spikes of a monkey puzzle tree put off most dinosaurs. Today, no animal will touch them.*

### Battle of the Flowers

The first flowering plants bloomed about 100 million years ago. They were successful because they could spread their seeds and reproduce more quickly than plant-eaters could gobble them up.

*Waxy pine needles taste as bad today as they did in the dinosaur age.*

# HUNTING IN PACKS

Not all dinosaurs were plant-eaters. Packs of hungry meat-eating dinosaurs roamed all over the land, looking for their next meal. Deinonychus was a small dinosaur that hunted in a pack. It could outrun its prey and pounce to the kill with frightening accuracy. Dinosaurs much bigger than Deinonychus lived in fear of this clever hunter. Deinonychus was named after its most deadly weapon – its name means 'terrible claw'.

**Running Reptiles**
Deinonychus was in a family of meat-eating dinosaurs called the dromaeosaurids, which means 'running reptiles'.

**Compsognathus**

Compsognathus fossil

Bavarisaurus

Velociraptor

**Lizard Lunch**
Many pack-hunting dinosaurs chased other dinosaurs, but the smaller hunters enjoyed a diet of lizards or shrew-like mammals. This fossil of the hen-sized Compsognathus has the bones of its last meal inside its stomach. It was a Bavarisaurus lizard.

Dromaeosaurus

*The body of Deinonychus was light and speedy. This was ideal for chasing after prey.*

Stenonychosaurus

**Deadly Claw**
Deinonychus had a claw on the tip of each of its toes, but one claw was much bigger than the rest. This huge, sharp talon could swipe round in a semi-circle, slashing a deadly wound into the flesh of the dinosaur's prey.

*The claw was 13 centimetres long.*

**Brain Box**
Each member of a pack of hunting dinosaurs had to time its movements and communicate with the rest of the group. Deinonychus had a big skull, which held a large brain, shown here in red. This means that Deinonychus would have been intelligent enough to hunt in a pack.

**Why Hunt in Packs?**
One wolf cannot attack a deer on its own, but a pack of wolves can easily pull one down. The reason for hunting in packs is the same now as it was at the time of the dinosaurs. Small, meat-eating dinosaurs joined together to overpower much bigger dinosaurs.

*Sharp, jagged teeth pointed backwards, for a strong, tearing bite.*

*Sharp eyesight was very useful for spotting prey.*

*Often just a quarter of the size of its prey, Deinonychus was about 3 metres long and 1.8 metres tall.*

*This plant-eating Tenontosaurus bled to death from the gashes made by the Deinonychus pack.*

# ENORMOUS MEAT-EATERS

Like tigers today, Tyrannosaurus rex may have hunted alone, terrorizing its prey with surprise attacks. This fierce dinosaur was a carnivore, which means it lived on a diet of meat. The biggest meat-eater ever to walk on this planet, Tyrannosaurus rex was heavier than an elephant and as tall as a two-storey building. Its name means 'king of the tyrant reptiles'.

*Hunters need good eye sight and a strong sense of smell. Large parts of Tyrannosaurus' brain controlled its senses of sight and smell.*

*Tyrannosaurus had a massive skull. It took the shock of crashing into prey at speeds of up to 32 kilometres per hour.*

*Tyrannosaurus may have charged with open jaws, ready to sink its deadly teeth into its prey. Big chunks of flesh were swallowed whole.*

*Its short 'arms' weren't long enough to reach its mouth, but they may have been used to grip and kill prey.*

**Duck-Billed Dinner**
Tyrannosaurus probably hunted duck-billed dinosaurs, called hadrosaurs. It may have hidden among the trees, waiting for the right moment to charge at a peaceful herd of grazing duckbills.

### Life-Sized Tooth
A Tyrannosaurus tooth grew up to 18 centimetres long.

*A Tyrannosaurus tooth was covered with tough enamel.*

*The sharp edge of the tooth was serrated, like a kitchen knife.*

*Look how small a human tooth is!*

### Meet the Family
The big meat-eating dinosaurs belong to the carnosaur group. This name means 'flesh lizard'.

### Stretch Those Legs
Tyrannosaurus' short 'arms' may also have been used to help the dinosaur up after a rest on the ground.

1. Small front arms hold its body steady, as Tyrannosaurus begins to move.

2. Tyrannosaurus then lifts its head and body backwards, stretching out its long back legs.

3. Tyrannosaurus stands up straight. The weight of its tail balances its big head.

### Cannibal Dinosaurs
A cannibal is a living thing that eats its own kind. Some meat-eating dinosaurs may have been cannibals. This skeleton of a dinosaur called Coelophysis was found with the tiny bones of a baby Coelophysis inside its stomach.

Albertosaurus   Tarbosaurus   Dilophosaurus   Ceratosaurus   Allosaurus

# DEATH OF THE DINOSAURS

We can tell how old dinosaur fossils are by looking at the age of the rock they were found in. From this, we know that the last of the dinosaurs died out about 65 million years ago. But we can only guess why this happened. Perhaps a huge disaster wiped out all the dinosaurs in one go, or they may have become extinct over a very long time.

**Rock Solid Proof**
The rock on the Earth's surface is formed in layers. The deeper the layer, the older the rock. No dinosaur fossil has been found above the layer that formed 65 million years ago. This proves the last dinosaurs died this long ago.

**From Outer Space**
Some scientists believe that an enormous asteroid crashed into the Earth at the end of the Cretaceous Period. The huge impact of the asteroid could have spelled doom for the dinosaurs.

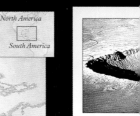

North America

South America

Yucatán

*The asteroid may have hurtled towards Earth at about 241,350 kilometres per hour.*

### Slow Change
Dinosaurs may not have disappeared overnight. The world's climate could have cooled over millions of years, slowly killing off the dinosaurs. New plants grew in this colder climate. The warm jungles that covered most of the dinosaurs' world slowly turned into cooler forests.

### Wild Guesses
Many theories try to explain the death of the dinosaurs. Some are more unlikely than others! Perhaps peckish mammals ate their eggs.

Or perhaps the dinosaurs were poisoned by new, nasty plants. But no single theory can explain what really happened.

### The Survivors
Life on Earth did not end with the death of the dinosaurs. Birds, mammals, reptiles and amphibians are some of the animal groups that survived, and are still around today.

Bird

Mammal

Reptile

Amphibian

### What a Hole
A crater 180 kilometres wide has been found in Yucatán, Central America. It may provide evidence for the asteroid theory. This photo shows a similar crater that was made by an asteroid in Arizona.

*Shocked quartz*

### Finding Proof

*Iridium*

The asteroid crushed rock in the Earth's surface as it hit Yucatan. Shocked quartz has been found at the crater site. Iridium is a rare metal, found in asteroids. There are high levels of iridium in the rock that contains the last dinosaur fossils.

*The disaster would have set off a chain reaction. 400 million, million tonnes of rock and dust blocked out the Sun's light and the temperature dropped to -10°C. Acid rain fell on the dinosaurs.*

# BIRDS

Any animal that grows feathers is a bird. Some are bigger than people; others are almost as small as bees. Birds hatch out of eggs, which are kept in a nest. All birds have feathers and wings, even the ones that do not fly. Because they have no teeth, birds cannot chew. Instead, they grind food in a gizzard. Some food stays in a storage bag called a crop so it can be coughed up later for chicks to eat! Birds are like us in the way they breathe oxygen into their lungs. But they are a little like aeroplanes too, because their smooth bodies allow them to slip through the air, soaring above snowy mountains, darting through steamy jungles, and skimming over ocean waves. More than 100,000 million birds live here with us on Earth.

Blue-tit nest

Parrot feathers

Budgerigar feathers

Owl feather

Green-winged parrot skeleton

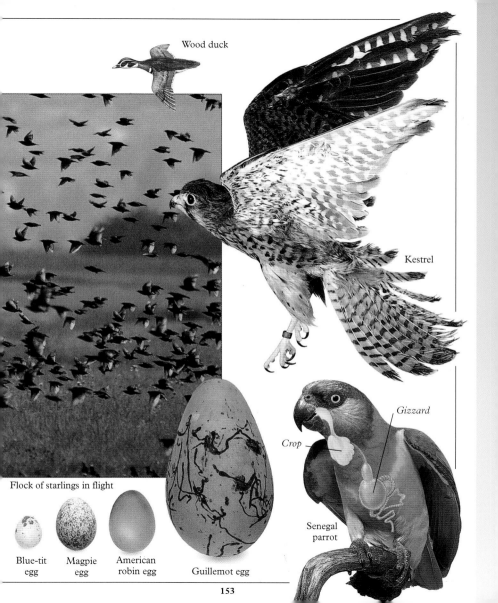

Wood duck

Kestrel

Flock of starlings in flight

Blue-tit egg

Magpie egg

American robin egg

Guillemot egg

*Gizzard*

*Crop*

Senegal parrot

# FEATHERS AND FLYING

*Feathers are made of keratin, like your hair and nails!*

Three types of animal can fly – birds, bats and insects. Birds are the best fliers because they have a coat of feathers. Long, light feathers or small, soft feathers cover almost every part of a bird's body. Usually, only a bird's beak, eyes, legs and feet are bare. Feathers do much more than cover a bird's naked body: they keep birds warm and dry and enable them to stay up in the air.

*Ducks fly in a straight line.*

*Flapping*   *Resting*   *Scarlet tanagers bob up and down as they flap, then rest, then flap again.*

**Flight Patterns**
Flying can be hard work. Not all birds flap their wings all the time. Some birds save energy by resting between short bursts of flapping.

**Wind Power**
If you blow hard across the top of a piece of paper, the air on top moves faster than the air underneath. This difference in air speed creates lift and the paper rises. In a similar way, the air moving over the top of a bird's wing moves faster than the air going underneath it. This lifts the bird up in the sky.

Waterproof body feathers keep the bird dry.

Underneath its body feathers, the bird wears a warm vest of fluffy down feathers.

This rosella has about 4,000 feathers.

Adult birds lose old feathers and grow new ones. This is called moulting.

Primary feathers can twist like propellers to power the bird through the air.

**Flapping Flight**
As this pigeon flaps its wings down, its feathers close so that they can push against the air. On the way up, the feathers open to let the air slip through.

These secondary flight feathers help lift the bird up in the air.

Vane

Barbule

Barb

**Hooked Up**
Each flight feather has about a million fine strands, called barbules. These hook around each other and hold the feather in shape, even in very windy weather.

Strong shaft

Tail feathers are used for steering and stopping.

Quill

**Wash and Brush-Up**
Birds keep their feathers clean and tidy by preening. They nibble each feather to zip the barbules back together and to get rid of insects. Most birds also waterproof their feathers by rubbing oil into them. This oil comes from a preen gland which is just above their tail.

# SETTING UP HOME

A nest is a cradle in which eggs and baby birds are kept safe from enemies such as snakes and rats. Nests can be holes in trees, mounds of earth or piles of branches. Greenfinches tuck their cup-shaped nests into bushes where they cannot be seen, whereas eagles' lofty nests are easy to see but hard to get at. Each species tries to give its chicks the best chance of survival.

**Courting**
Before starting a family, male birds have to attract a mate. Peacocks do this by showing off!

**Nesting Material**
Birds, just like people, build their homes out of all sorts of things. Most nests are made with twigs and leaves, but a few use much stranger ingredients, such as string.

Cattle hair

Seeds

String

Silver foil

*Many songbirds glue their nest together with sticky cobwebs!*

*Birds may make thousands of trips to collect all their nesting material.*

**Building a Nursery**
In many species of bird, both parents build the nest. These long-legged great blue herons are trampling on twigs to make a huge, cup-shaped nest.

**Spot the Eggs**
Ringed plovers don't build a nest. They lay their pebble-like eggs on the beach.

**No Teacher Needed**

Weavers are brilliant builders, but they don't have lessons or copy other birds. They just know how to weave their nest. This 'knowing without learning' is called instinct.

**Knitted Nest**

The weaver uses his beak and feet to tie the grass into knots!

*Cup-shaped nests have walls to stop eggs from rolling out.*

*Baby birds don't need pillows – they have soft feathers to lie on.*

Grass is sewn into the nest to form a ring.

After weaving the walls, roof and door, he hangs upside down from his home and invites a female to move in.

*Nests in trees and bushes are kept dry by the leaves – they form little umbrellas!*

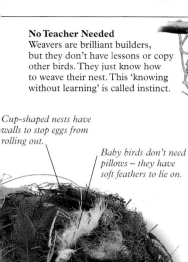

*Lichen is used to camouflage the nest.*

*Dried moss helps to keep the eggs warm.*

*This cup-nest was built by squashing! The greenfinch pressed the material into place with its breast as it spun round in a circle.*

**Burrowing Bee-Eater**

Carmine bee-eaters nest underground! The male chooses a sandy riverbank and pecks at the earth. When the dent is big enough to cling to, he starts to dig with his beak and feet. The female moves in when all the work is done!

# FAMILY LIFE

Family life for most birds is brief, but busy. After the female bird has mated she lays her eggs, usually in a nest. The baby birds, or chicks, do not grow inside her because this would make her far too heavy to fly. When they hatch, the chicks eat a lot, grow bigger and bigger, and then, as soon as they can fly, they leave home for ever.

**Baby Sitting**
Eggs must be incubated, or kept warm, otherwise the baby birds inside will die. The parents do this by sitting on them.

**What's Inside an Egg?**
All bird eggs have the same things inside them: a growing baby bird which feeds on a yellow yolk, and a watery egg white that cushions the chick from knocks. Woodpeckers and warblers are ready to hatch in 11 days but Royal albatrosses take more than 11 weeks!

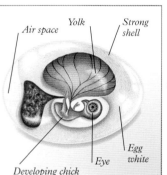

*Air space*　*Yolk*　*Strong shell*

*Developing chick*　*Eye*　*Egg white*

*Ostrich egg (actual size)*　*Hummingbird egg (actual size)*

**Peck, Peck, Peck . . .**
Getting out of an egg is called hatching. The chick taps at the tough shell until it is free. This can take hours or even days!

*The blunt end of the egg is pecked off by the chick with a horny spike called an egg-tooth.*

*First crack*

*The chick cheeps to tell its parents it is hatching.*

*Empty shell*

**Nearly Grown Up**
After baby birds have left home they are called fledglings. Many are eaten by cats and hawks, but some from each nest survive and have families of their own.

**Feed Me!**
Nestlings are helpless when they hatch: they are blind and naked. All they can do is eat and grow.

*The parents push food into their chicks' bright, begging beaks.*

**Fast Food**
Blue tits bring back more than 1,000 juicy caterpillars and aphids to the nest each day for their hungry chicks.

*Caterpillar*

*Ducks' eyes are open when they are born.*

*The wet, sticky fluff, or down, soon dries out.*

*After the chick has pushed itself head-first out of the egg it is very tired.*

*This egg-tooth drops off after a few days.*

**Follow the Leader**
Baby ducks follow the first big, moving thing that they see – usually one of their parents. This instinct is called imprinting.

*Like most water birds, just one hour after hatching this duckling can walk, see, swim and feed itself.*

# THE FROZEN NORTH

The North Pole lies in the middle of a frozen ocean, which is surrounded by a cold, flat, treeless, snowy wasteland, called the tundra. Few birds can survive the long, dark winters of the tundra. But in the summer, when the Sun never sets, millions of birds arrive to raise their families. Flowers bloom and the air is full of buzzing insects, but in just a few short weeks the summer holiday is over and they all fly south again.

**The Big Melt**
During the summer, the ice melts. But this water can't sink into the frozen ground, so it forms lots of lakes – ideal for ducks!

## Bird's Eye View
Hunting birds have eyes on the front of their head so that the sight from both eyes overlaps and they can see exactly how far away their victims are. Birds which are eaten by other animals, have eyes on the side of their head, so they can look around for danger.

Snowy owl

*Blind area*

Ptarmigan

*Both eyes can see this dark area.*

*Only one eye can see this light area.*

## Tundra Residents

Snowy owl

Snow bunting

Gyr falcon

Raven

*Tough ptarmigans survive the winter by eating dwarf willow twigs.*

*Birds have a third eyelid that is see-through and helps keep their eyes moist.*

*Ptarmigans shiver to keep warm.*

*Snow-coloured feathers camouflage ptarmigans.*

### Causing a Stir

Red phalaropes reach the insects that live at the bottom of lakes by swimming in circles! This stirs up the water and makes the insects float upwards. You can try this too – put some buttons in a bowl of water, give it a stir and watch!

### Duck Down

Eider ducks pluck soft feathers, called down, from their breast to line their nest. People collect this down to make soft pillows.

*Eider down*

### Summer Coat

Willow ptarmigans don't need thick, white coats in the warm summer, so they moult, and grow dark red feathers.

*Just like big, woolly socks, these feathers keep the ptarmigan's legs, feet and toes warm.*

**Willow ptarmigans** are about 35 centimetres tall and live in the Arctic.

**Summer Visitors**

Ruff

Red phalarope

Red-breasted goose

King eider

# COLD FORESTS

One-tenth of the land on Earth is covered in conifers. These tall trees, such as pines, and firs, have needles instead of broad leaves and woody cones instead of flowers. The cold forests are home to many birds, from seed-eating siskins to big birds of prey. But conifer forests planted by people, where the trees are all the same type, height and age, are home to fewer birds.

*This Japanese waxwing has a bunch of little feathers, called a crest, on its head.*

*The siskin's tail spreads out and acts as a brake.*

*These feather are called the alula – they are joined to the bird's thumb.*

*The feet are stretched out to grab the branch.*

**Sleeping Safely**
When birds bend their legs to sit down, or perch, muscles in their legs make their toes curl. Now the bird can't fall off its perch, even if it falls asleep!

*Waxwings are named after these red dots – which look like drops of wax.*

**Ant Antics**
A Steller's jay gets rid of mites or feather lice by making ants crawl all over its body. The ants get annoyed and squirt out formic acid, which kills the tiny insects!

*Angry ants*

### Cone-Opener
Crossbills' beaks can snip open cones a bit like a tin-opener. Red crossbills eat spruce seeds, but bigger species can open up large pine cones.

*Crossed beak*

Larch cone

*This greenish-brown bird is a female red crossbill – only the males are red!*

Spruce cone

### Inside a Cone

*Woody scale*

*Tasty seed*

Pine cone

### Starved Out
Every few years, winter is even colder than usual. When this happens, the crossbills and waxwings leave the cold forest to feed in warmer woods.

*By opening up its feathers, the siskin can reduce its speed.*

### Touchdown
Birds have to slow down to land, but, just like planes, if they go too slowly they can stall and fall out of the sky. By sticking out their alula, they can change the flow of the wind over their body and avoid crash-landings!

### Up and Over
Like a little feathered mouse, the tree creeper creeps up tree runks looking for spiders and earwigs to eat. It starts at the bottom of the tree, swirls round and round the trunk, walks along the first big branch and then drops down to the bottom of the next tree.

163

# IN THE WOODS

Europe and large parts of America were once covered by a green carpet of trees. Most of these maple, beech and oak woods have been cut down to make room for farms and cities. But if you go into the woods that are left, you may still find some of the beautiful birds that live there. Even if you don't spot them through the layers of leaves, you will hear them. Songbirds, such as nightingales, sing flute-like songs, both day and night.

**First-Class Flier**
Woodland birds, such as this cheeky blue tit, have short wings. This allows them to twist and turn between the trees.

*Woodpeckers' feet are designed for climbing trees – two toes point backwards.*

*Pied flycatcher chasing flies*

*Tough beak*

*Tawny owls sleep during the day. This one is being woken up by birds who think it is roosting too near their nests.*

*This greater spotted woodpecker has a 'shock absorber' around its brain to stop it from getting hurt when the bird hammers.*

**Who's There?**
Knock, knock – this is the sound a woodpecker makes when it hammers its beak onto a tree to dig out insects!

*By placing their long, stiff tail-feathers against the tree trunk, woodpeckers are able to keep steady while they feed.*

*Song thrushes open up snails by hitting them against rocks.*

*Robins sing to claim their territory.*

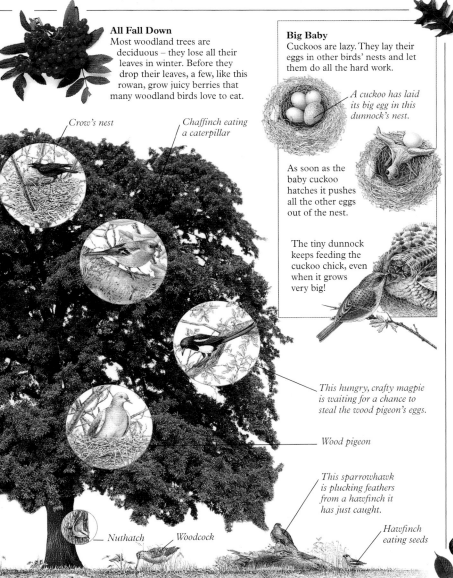

## All Fall Down

Most woodland trees are deciduous – they lose all their leaves in winter. Before they drop their leaves, a few, like this rowan, grow juicy berries that many woodland birds love to eat.

## Big Baby

Cuckoos are lazy. They lay their eggs in other birds' nests and let them do all the hard work.

*A cuckoo has laid its big egg in this dunnock's nest.*

As soon as the baby cuckoo hatches it pushes all the other eggs out of the nest.

The tiny dunnock keeps feeding the cuckoo chick, even when it grows very big!

*Crow's nest*

*Chaffinch eating a caterpillar*

*This hungry, crafty magpie is waiting for a chance to steal the wood pigeon's eggs.*

*Wood pigeon*

*This sparrowhawk is plucking feathers from a hawfinch it has just caught.*

*Hawfinch eating seeds*

*Nuthatch*    *Woodcock*

# SWAMPS AND MARSHES

Half water, half land, swamps and marshes are strange places to live. But to thousands of birds, the shallow water and soggy soil is an ideal home – it is full of food. Birds that live in these tree-filled swamps or murky marshes can either walk through the water or swim. Those that walk, are called waders. Wading birds have long, thin legs, sometimes thinner than a pencil!

*To keep their eggs and chicks dry, reed warblers build their nests high up in the reeds, well above the water.*

*Young scarlet ibises have grey feathers. They only grow red feathers when they are several years old.*

*Black tip to the long, red wing*

*This is not a knee, but an ankle!*

**Scarlet ibises** are about 46 centimetres tall and live in swamps in South America.

**Highly Strung**
Foxes, and other egg-thieves, can't walk on marshy ground. So, to keep their family safe, reed warblers build their homes in tall marsh-plants, called reeds. The nest is tied tightly onto the reeds and won't fall down, even on a windy day.

### Up in the Air

Walking on stilts makes your legs longer. Now you can splash through puddles and your clothes still won't get wet. A little wading bird, called the black-winged stilt, likes to keep its feathers dry, so it has very, very long legs, which work like stilts.

### Fitting the Bill

Storks stab, shoebills dig, flamingos sieve and spoonbills trap – these amazing beaks, or bills, are all shaped to catch food.

Spoonbill

Saddle-billed stork

Shoebill

Greater flamingo

*Nostril*

*All birds' legs are covered in small scales.*

*This long, curved beak can poke deep down into the sticky mud and water at the bottom of the swamp to find frogs and fish.*

*These big feet stop the ibis sinking into the mud by spreading its weight over a larger area.*

### A Shady Bird

Sunlight, shining on water, makes it hard to see the fish below. Black herons solve this problem by shading the water with their wings.

# LAKES AND RIVERS

Still lakes and flowing rivers provide a well-stocked larder for flocks of ducks, geese, swans and many more unusual birds. Wherever you live in the world you can spot these wonderful water birds bobbing about on the surface or paddling in the shallows, for they are not shy of people and live on lakes and rivers in cities too.

**Flipper Feet**
Water birds have webbed feet. They use these webs of skin like flippers, to push through the water.

**Splash!**
Brilliant blue kingfishers plunge into rivers to catch minnows that are half the length of their body. With its wings folded and its eyes and nostrils tightly shut, the kingfisher flies into the water. It has to struggle to free itself from the pull of the water, but it soon succeeds and flies away with its fish.

**Treading Water**
These western grebes are dancing. When the birds have paired up, they dance across the lake together. Often a male bird tries to steal another's partner!

*Water skiing*  *Gathering speed*  *Lift-off*
*Touchdown*

**Water-Runways**
Heavy water birds can't land or take off on the spot; they need runways like aeroplanes!

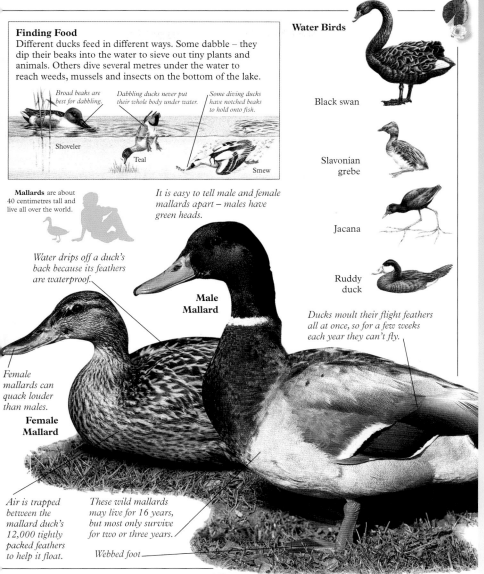

## Finding Food

Different ducks feed in different ways. Some dabble – they dip their beaks into the water to sieve out tiny plants and animals. Others dive several metres under the water to reach weeds, mussels and insects on the bottom of the lake.

*Broad beaks are best for dabbling.*

*Dabbling ducks never put their whole body under water.*

*Some diving ducks have notched beaks to hold onto fish.*

Shoveler

Teal

Smew

**Water Birds**

Black swan

Slavonian grebe

Jacana

Ruddy duck

**Mallards** are about 40 centimetres tall and live all over the world.

*It is easy to tell male and female mallards apart – males have green heads.*

*Water drips off a duck's back because its feathers are waterproof.*

**Male Mallard**

*Ducks moult their flight feathers all at once, so for a few weeks each year they can't fly.*

*Female mallards can quack louder than males.*

**Female Mallard**

*Air is trapped between the mallard duck's 12,000 tightly packed feathers to help it float.*

*These wild mallards may live for 16 years, but most only survive for two or three years.*

*Webbed foot*

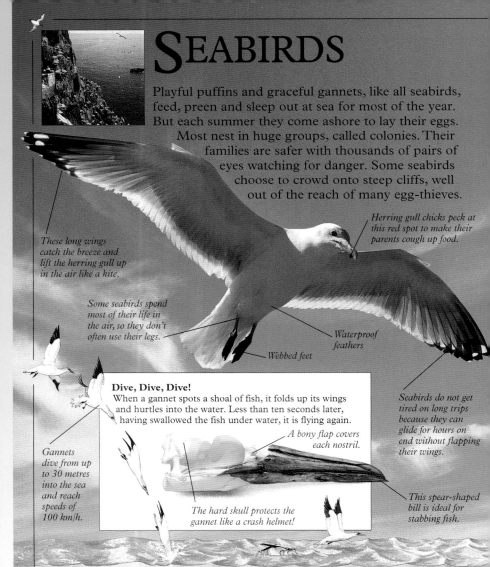

# SEABIRDS

Playful puffins and graceful gannets, like all seabirds, feed, preen and sleep out at sea for most of the year. But each summer they come ashore to lay their eggs. Most nest in huge groups, called colonies. Their families are safer with thousands of pairs of eyes watching for danger. Some seabirds choose to crowd onto steep cliffs, well out of the reach of many egg-thieves.

*These long wings catch the breeze and lift the herring gull up in the air like a kite.*

*Herring gull chicks peck at this red spot to make their parents cough up food.*

*Some seabirds spend most of their life in the air, so they don't often use their legs.*

*Waterproof feathers*

*Webbed feet*

*Seabirds do not get tired on long trips because they can glide for hours on end without flapping their wings.*

### Dive, Dive, Dive!
When a gannet spots a shoal of fish, it folds up its wings and hurtles into the water. Less than ten seconds later, having swallowed the fish under water, it is flying again.

*A bony flap covers each nostril.*

*Gannets dive from up to 30 metres into the sea and reach speeds of 100 km/h.*

*The hard skull protects the gannet like a crash helmet!*

*This spear-shaped bill is ideal for stabbing fish.*

170

**Floating on Air**
When the wind hits a cliff,
it shoots up towards the sky.
By stretching out their wings,
seabirds, such as puffins, can
use this breeze to lift them up
to their lofty nests.

**Beaky Bird**
A puffin's big, bright
beak is hinged so that
it can snap up fish
and still keep a
grip on those it
has already caught.

Puffin

Herring gull

Gannet

Guillemot

**Spinning Eggs**
Guillemots do not build
nests. Their eggs are pointed
at one end, so if they are
moved they just roll in a
circle and not off the cliff.

**Going Up!**
A cliff is like a high-rise
block of flats. Shags
nest on the ground
floor, in caves near to
the bottom of the cliff.

**Pebbles that Move**
Ringed plovers live on the beach.
They are so well camouflaged
that they are hard to see.

Shag

# TROPICAL FORESTS

Giant trees, which seem to stretch to the sky, form a huge umbrella over the top of a tropical forest. In the shade beneath this green canopy live thousands of weird and wonderful birds. The hot, wet jungles are home to over half of the world's 9,000 species of birds. Noisy parrots gather fruit and nuts, colourful sunbirds sip the juice out of flowers and harpy eagles swoop down on chattering monkeys.

*When a toucan goes to sleep, it rests its big, brightly coloured beak on its back.*

**Toco toucans** are about 35 centimetres tall and live in South America.

*This beak is not as heavy as it looks. It is hollow, and has thin rods of bone inside for strength and support.*

*The toucan uses the jagged edge of its beak like a saw to cut through large fruit.*

**Big Stretch**
With its long, clumsy-looking beak, the toucan can reach fruit and berries that are further away. It picks them up and tosses them into its throat.

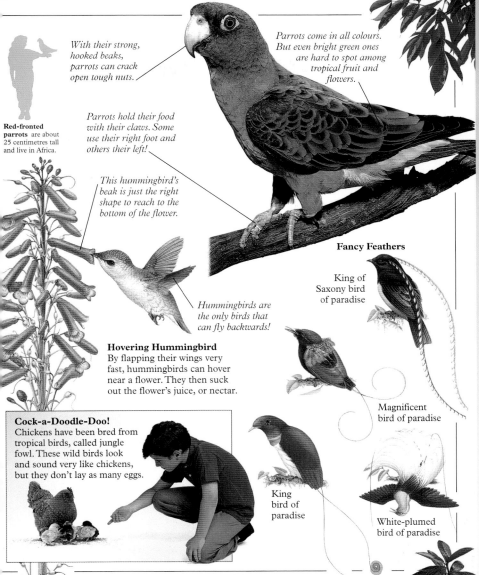

With their strong, hooked beaks, parrots can crack open tough nuts.

Parrots come in all colours. But even bright green ones are hard to spot among tropical fruit and flowers.

**Red-fronted parrots** are about 25 centimetres tall and live in Africa.

Parrots hold their food with their claws. Some use their right foot and others their left!

This hummingbird's beak is just the right shape to reach to the bottom of the flower.

Hummingbirds are the only birds that can fly backwards!

**Hovering Hummingbird**
By flapping their wings very fast, hummingbirds can hover near a flower. They then suck out the flower's juice, or nectar.

**Fancy Feathers**

King of Saxony bird of paradise

Magnificent bird of paradise

**Cock-a-Doodle-Doo!**
Chickens have been bred from tropical birds, called jungle fowl. These wild birds look and sound very like chickens, but they don't lay as many eggs.

King bird of paradise

White-plumed bird of paradise

173

# GRASSLANDS

Grass grows in the vast spaces between wet forests and dry deserts. These rolling seas of grass have several names: the tropical African plains are known as savanna and the colder grasslands are called prairies, pampas or steppes. These green lands are important to people because they make good farmland. To birds they are just a perfect place to live. There is tall grass to hide in, and seeds, grasshoppers, beetles and worms are waiting to be eaten.

Crowned crane

**Two for Dinner**
Honeyguides love beeswax but they can't open a bees' nest. They have to find a big-clawed badger to rip open the nest for them.

*The honeyguide leads the way.*

*The badger leaves plenty for the patient bird.*

Bees

*If an oxpecker sees a lion it calls very loudly and warns the buffalo of danger.*

*Oxpeckers have strong, sharp claws for clinging to thick skin.*

**Oxpeckers** are about 12 centimetres tall and live in Africa.

**Doctor Oxpecker!**
Oxpeckers peck juicy insects, called ticks, out of the skin of buffalo and zebra. This 'surgery' helps to keep the animals healthy.

*The buffalo ignores the oxpecker, unless it pecks inside its ears!*

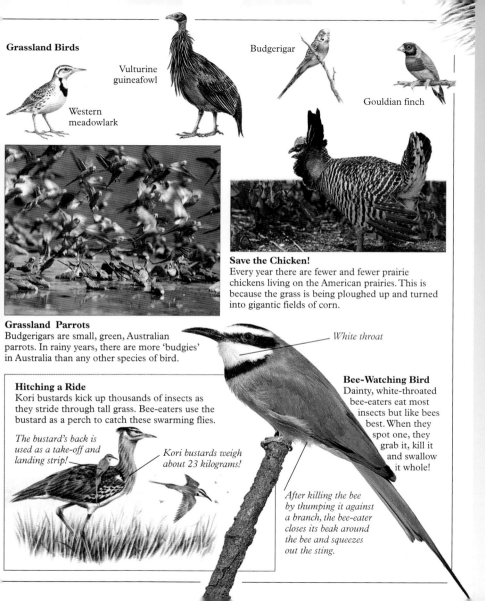

## Grassland Birds

Western meadowlark

Vulturine guineafowl

Budgerigar

Gouldian finch

### Save the Chicken!
Every year there are fewer and fewer prairie chickens living on the American prairies. This is because the grass is being ploughed up and turned into gigantic fields of corn.

### Grassland Parrots
Budgerigars are small, green, Australian parrots. In rainy years, there are more 'budgies' in Australia than any other species of bird.

### Hitching a Ride
Kori bustards kick up thousands of insects as they stride through tall grass. Bee-eaters use the bustard as a perch to catch these swarming flies.

*The bustard's back is used as a take-off and landing strip!*

*Kori bustards weigh about 23 kilograms!*

*White throat*

### Bee-Watching Bird
Dainty, white-throated bee-eaters eat most insects but like bees best. When they spot one, they grab it, kill it and swallow it whole!

*After killing the bee by thumping it against a branch, the bee-eater closes its beak around the bee and squeezes out the sting.*

# DRY LANDS

At midday, hot, dusty, dry lands are quiet and appear to be empty. Only at sunrise and sunset, when the air and ground are cooler, do birds come out of the shade to feed and find water. Elf owls are lucky – they eat juicy meat and do not need to drink. Sandgrouse eat dry seeds and have to fly up to 50 kilometres every day to get a drink of water.

**Sandgrouse Suck**
Most birds have to tip their head back to make water trickle down their throat. Sandgrouse are unusual – like you, they can suck.

*Shaggy crest*

*In cartoons, roadrunners say 'beep beep'! In real life, they rattle their beak to make a 'clack'.*

*Roadrunners run, but they can also fly.*

**Take-Away Water**
Male sandgrouse sit in puddles! Their belly-feathers soak up water like sponges. When they return to their nests, the chicks drink from the soggy coat.

*After the cold desert night, roadrunners warm up by standing with their backs to the sun and sunbathing.*

**Roadrunners** are about 30 centimetres tall and live in Mexico and North America.

*Roadrunners swallow rattlesnakes that are up to 50 centimetres long.*

*Roadrunners can run as fast as an Olympic sprinter!*

*Like most ground-feeding birds, roadrunners have long legs and toes.*

*Roadrunners use their tail to balance as they zig-zag across the desert.*

### Building a Sand Castle!

A mallee fowl doesn't build a nest, it makes a massive mound. It piles leaves into a pit and covers them with sand. The rotting leaves give out heat and incubate the eggs.

*The chicks will dig their way out.*

*Sand is scraped away if the eggs overheat.*

### Sandy Birds

Pale-coloured feathers reflect the Sun's heat and are good desert camouflage.

*This little elf owl is sheltering from the scorching sun in a hole made by a gila woodpecker.*

*Tiny verdin hang upside down from cactus branches to look for insects.*

*Cactus wrens have scaly legs and tough feathers to protect them from the cactus spines.*

*Gila woodpeckers peck away dead bits of cactus as they hunt for insects.*

*This Western bluebird is keeping cool in a shady bush.*

*Gambel's quail search under stones for seeds and scorpions.*

# THE FROZEN SOUTH

**Chinstrap Penguin**

Antarctica, the land that surrounds the South Pole, is almost empty. The blanket of two-kilometre-thick ice, howling winds and freezing temperatures stop plants and land-living animals from surviving. But the ocean around this frozen land is full of fish and krill, so the coasts are home to millions of birds. Penguins are the best known residents of the snowy south but there are also seabirds such as skuas, petrels and terns.

*Australia*
*Antarctica*
*South Africa*
*South America*

## Belly Flop
The quickest way to get about on slippery ice is to slide. Penguins can't use a sledge like you, so they scoot along on their big bellies!

*They push themselves along with their strong feet and wings.*

*These Adélie penguins have to slip and slide over 100 kilometres from their nesting colonies to the sea.*

## Egg-Thief
Skuas rarely go hungry because there are plenty of penguin eggs and chicks for them to steal. While one skua distracts the parent penguins, the other one grabs a meal.

*They can't fly, but penguins are excellent swimmers.*

*Adélies eat small animals called krill.*

178

### The Longest Night
Once the Antarctic winter sun sets, it is dark for more than two months.

*Male and female penguins cough up food from their stomachs to feed their chicks.*

**Emperor penguins** are the biggest birds in Antarctica. They can be 1.2 metres tall.

*Baby penguins keep warm by sitting on their parents' feet!*

*This feathery jacket keeps warm air in and cold water out.*

### On Ice
Female emperor penguins lay an egg at the start of winter. For the next 64 cold, dark days and nights, the male incubates this egg by standing still and balancing it on his feet.

### Safety in Numbers
When their parents are fishing, the fat, fluffy chicks form groups called crèches. This helps keep them warm and protects them from skuas.

*Thick fat, called blubber, keeps penguins warm.*

*Penguins come to the surface to gulp down air about every 15 seconds.*

*Adélie penguins can swim at up to 32 kilometres per hour.*

*By building up speed, they can shoot themselves out of the sea.*

*Leopard seals eat penguins.*

# BIRDS OF PREY

Eagles, hawks and falcons are birds of prey, or raptors. These strong, fast, fearless birds, kill and eat other birds and animals – their prey. Whether they are the size of a sparrow or have a wingspan of three metres, like the condor, they all have three things in common: hooked beaks, sharp claws and 'eagle' eyes that can spot rabbits over five kilometres away!

**Dressed for Dinner**
Vultures poke their heads into dead animals to eat. Their heads are bare as feathers would get messy!

**Steep Stoop**
Peregrines have been timed diving at speeds up to 280 kilometres per hour. At the last moment, they thrust out their feet and stab their victim with their claws.

*Wings are swept back and the tail closes like a fan.*

*The wings are strong enough to lift the falcon into the air even if it is carrying a dead duck.*

*Its pointed wings help the peregrine falcon fly faster than any other bird.*

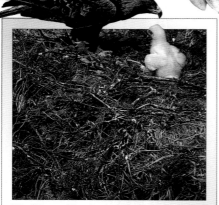

*Pigeon dies and falls to the ground*

*The tail is used for steering.*

**The Biggest Nest in the World**
Golden eagles' nests, often called eyries, can be over four metres wide – bigger than some cars! They do not build a new nest every year but fly back to an old nest and just add a few twigs. Some nests are hundreds of years old.

**Peregrine falcons** are about 32 centimetres tall and live all over the world.

**Bendy Legs!**
African harrier hawks have long legs which they use to reach eggs, chicks and bats inside holes in trees. To make it easier to snatch a meal, they bend their legs backwards, forwards and even sideways.

**Working Together**
Raptors do not hurt humans and for many hundreds of years, they have been trained to hunt with people. In the Middle Ages, this lanner falcon would have been flown by a squire, a boy who worked for a knight.

*The glove stops the bird's claws scratching you.*

*Birds of prey have brilliant colour vision.*

*Nostril*

*This powerful, hooked beak is used to pull apart animals that are too big to be swallowed whole.*

*Like all birds of prey, peregrines spend most of the day resting or preening, not hunting.*

*Many birds of prey have bare legs, but others wear feathered 'trousers'.*

*This needle-sharp claw, or talon, is used to grab prey.*

**All-American Eagle**
This US army badge has a bald eagle on it because it is the national bird of the United States.

**Meat-Eating Birds**

American kestrel

Goshawk

Harpy eagle

# FLIGHTLESS BIRDS

Emu

Kagu

**Eye-to-Eye**
Ostriches' round eyes are nearly as big as tennis balls!

Flying is hard work – it takes a lot of energy to flap wings and lift off the ground. For most birds it is worth the effort because it helps them escape from danger or search for things to eat. But some birds, like kiwis and kagus, live on islands where there are no enemies and others have found that they can run or swim after food.

Over millions of years, birds such as ostriches, emus and penguins have gradually lost the ability to fly.

*Its tiny wings are hidden under brown fur-like feathers.*

*The kiwi's nostrils are on the tip of its long beak.*

**Super Egg**
Ostriches lay bigger eggs than any other bird: they are 24 times bigger than a chicken's egg! The shell is so strong that even if you stand on top of an ostrich egg, it will not break.

*The shell is about two millimetres thick.*

**Sniff Sniff**
The national bird of New Zealand, the kiwi, is one of only a few birds to have a good sense of smell. It sniffs out worms that are in the soil.

**Ready, Steady, Go!**
Ostriches live on the African grasslands. They cannot fly away from lions and hyenas, but they can run very fast. They sprint at speeds of 70 kilometres per hour – much faster than a galloping horse.

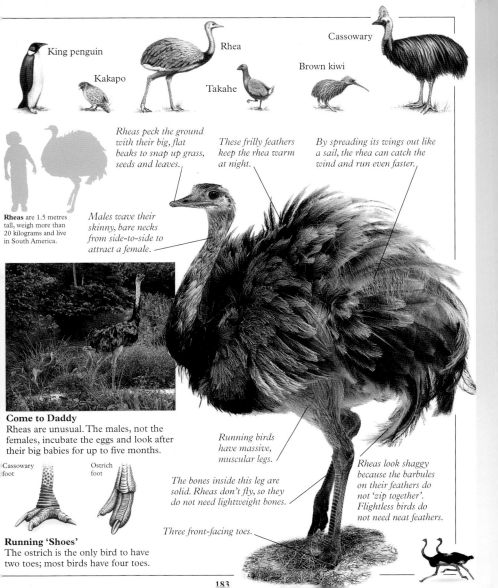

King penguin

Kakapo

Rhea

Takahe

Brown kiwi

Cassowary

**Rheas** are 1.5 metres tall, weigh more than 20 kilograms and live in South America.

Rheas peck the ground with their big, flat beaks to snap up grass, seeds and leaves.

These frilly feathers keep the rhea warm at night.

By spreading its wings out like a sail, the rhea can catch the wind and run even faster.

Males wave their skinny, bare necks from side-to-side to attract a female.

**Come to Daddy**
Rheas are unusual. The males, not the females, incubate the eggs and look after their big babies for up to five months.

Cassowary foot

Ostrich foot

**Running 'Shoes'**
The ostrich is the only bird to have two toes; most birds have four toes.

Running birds have massive, muscular legs.

The bones inside this leg are solid. Rheas don't fly, so they do not need lightweight bones.

Three front-facing toes.

Rheas look shaggy because the barbules on their feathers do not 'zip together'. Flightless birds do not need neat feathers.

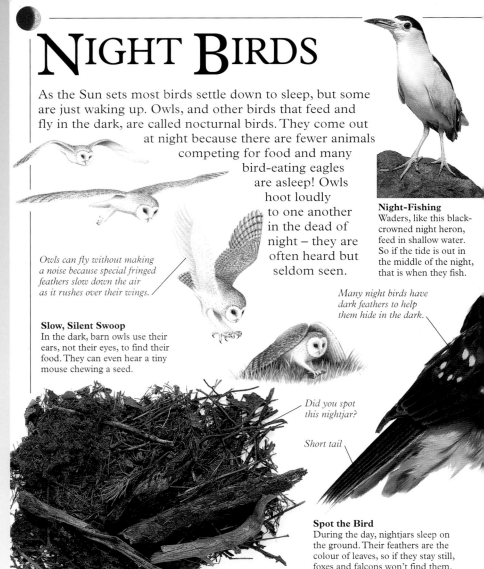

# NIGHT BIRDS

As the Sun sets most birds settle down to sleep, but some are just waking up. Owls, and other birds that feed and fly in the dark, are called nocturnal birds. They come out at night because there are fewer animals competing for food and many bird-eating eagles are asleep! Owls hoot loudly to one another in the dead of night – they are often heard but seldom seen.

*Owls can fly without making a noise because special fringed feathers slow down the air as it rushes over their wings.*

**Slow, Silent Swoop**
In the dark, barn owls use their ears, not their eyes, to find their food. They can even hear a tiny mouse chewing a seed.

**Night-Fishing**
Waders, like this black-crowned night heron, feed in shallow water. So if the tide is out in the middle of the night, that is when they fish.

*Many night birds have dark feathers to help them hide in the dark.*

*Did you spot this nightjar?*

*Short tail*

**Spot the Bird**
During the day, nightjars sleep on the ground. Their feathers are the colour of leaves, so if they stay still, foxes and falcons won't find them.

**Face to Face**

Long-eared owl

Elf owl

Barn owl

Eagle owl

**Wooden Actor**
If a frogmouth sees you it will point its head up at the sky and pretend to be a broken branch. It leaves one eye slightly open though, just in case you're not fooled.

*Owls see ten times better than you in the dark!*

*Owls cannot move their eyes, but they can turn their necks right round to look backwards.*

*Like all birds, the ears are small slits hidden under the feathers.*

*Boobook owls are often called 'morepork' owls – this is what they shout!*

**Boobook owls** are about 20 centimetres tall and live in Australia and New Zealand.

*Soft feathers*

*This curved claw kills rats, mice, lizards and spiders.*

**Cough it Up**
Owls don't have teeth, so they can't chew their food – mice and birds are swallowed whole! Bones, feathers and fur cannot be digested so they are made into pellets and coughed up.

*Vole rib*

*Mouse leg bone*

*Vole fur*

Skull    Hip bones    Jaw    Leg bones    Shoulder blades

# MAMMALS

Pale kangaroo-mouse

Mammals are amazing animals. Some climb trees, others race across the ground, burrow, or even fly. Seals and otters are examples of mammals that live in the water. Mammals come in many shapes and sizes – a giraffe is tall, a mouse is small and a platypus looks like an otter with a duck's beak. So what makes them all mammals? They are hairy, they breathe air into lungs and they feed their babies milk.

Mammals are warm blooded, which means their temperature is controlled by their bodies. Most are born live, not hatched from eggs, although platypuses lay eggs. Marsupials are a special kind of mammal because they give birth to babies that are only half formed. These tiny creatures grow into adults nestled in a warm safe pouch on their mother's body. Many mammals eat only plants, while others eat meat or insects. You are a mammal too.

Platypus

Black-tailed jack rabbit

Golden mice

Giant panda

Gelada

186

Snow-leopard cub

Little brown bats

Giraffe

Asian elephant

Tiger

Giant otter

Koala

Royal antelope

Desert hedgehog

# MARSUPIALS

A marsupial is an animal that has a pocket, called a pouch, on its tummy for carrying its babies. Inside this nursery the baby is safe and has milk to drink. Today, most mammals with pouches live in Australia, but 50 million years ago they lived in the Americas and the Antarctic. Most marsupials died out when the more modern mammals, such as horses, cats and rats developed. Marsupials survived in Australia because the 'new' mammals could not reach this island. Kangaroos are the most famous marsupials but there are also marsupial 'mice' and 'dogs'.

Australia

*Like deer, kangaroos have long faces to make room for their big, flat, grass-grinding teeth.*

**Female red kangaroos** are one metre tall. Males are twice as big. They live in Australia.

*Kangaroos can't walk backwards!*

*Female red kangaroos are called blue fliers because they have blue-grey fur and bounce faster than the red males.*

*The tail helps it to balance as it bounds along.*

*Kangaroos lick a bald spot on their arms to cool down! As the saliva dries it takes heat away.*

*Only females have pouches – males don't need them because they don't have babies!*

*The baby, or joey, hops into the pouch if it sees an eagle or dingo.*

**Jump to It!**
A kangaroo's back legs are so big that it would fall over if it ran. But they are good for jumping – a red kangaroo can bounce along at 65 kilometres per hour.

*Huge leg muscles*

188

### Missing Marsupial

The last Tasmanian wolf is thought to have died in a zoo in 1936. It was striped like a tiger and had a thick tail like a kangaroo. Farmers shot them all because they ate sheep.

*Birth*

### Jumping Bean?

A newborn wallaby looks like a red bean! It is less than two centimetres long and has no legs, hair or eyes. Like all marsupials, it carries on growing in a pouch, not inside the mother's body.

*The 'bean' squirms through the forest of hair by waving its stumpy arms.*

*Three minutes later it reaches the pouch.*

*It hooks onto a nipple and starts to suck milk.*

### Acting Star

Opossums are the only living American marsupials. When a Virginia opossum is attacked it sticks out its tongue, lies very still and pretends to be dead – it plays possum!

### Hold on Tight

This baby koala is too big to fit inside its mother's pouch, so it clings to her fur as she clambers through the eucalyptus leaves!

### Mammals with Pouches

Tasmanian devil

Honey possum

Numbat

Ring-tailed rock wallaby

# INSECTIVORES

Insectivores are sharp-toothed, long-nosed animals that munch insects and juicy worms, slugs and snails! Their busy little bodies lose heat easily, so they need to eat frequently. The food they eat produces the energy needed to keep them warm. But how do insectivores survive winters, when there are fewer insects to eat? Shrews search through rotting leaves and most manage to find enough food. Moles stay underground and hedgehogs spend cold winters in a deep sleep, called hibernation.

**A Bite for Lunch**
The water shrew is one of the few poisonous mammals. Its saliva can kill frogs, but not people!

**How Hungry?**
Imagine having to eat a pile of food that weighs twice as much you – shrews have to do this every day!

*The tiny eyes are covered by fur. A mole can only just tell the difference between light and dark.*

*Little bumps on its tail and its nose help this European mole sense where it is going.*

*A mole's wide front feet are shaped like spades – ideal for digging.*

*Molehill*

*The grass nest is the size of a football.*

*Worms burrow into the tunnel and are caught by the mole.*

*Moles turn round by doing forward rolls. If the tunnel is too narrow, they run backwards.*

*Moles eat more than 50 worms a day! Live ones are stored in a larder.*

*Moles live alone. This worm-thief will soon be chased away.*

**Greedy Guts**

Shrews often eat animals that are bigger than themselves. This long, juicy worm will fill its tummy for two or three hours!

**Worms in a Week**

Streaked tenrecs grow up faster than any other mammals. They stop drinking milk and start to eat worms when they are only six days old.

**Insect-Eaters**

Golden mole

*A hedgehog can stay rolled up for hours.*

**Roll Up, Roll Up!**

Fearless hedgehogs don't run away from danger – they stick out their spines and roll into a ball. No one wants to eat a mouthful of needles!

*Head*

Desman

*Some foxes and badgers have learned to push hedgehogs into puddles to make them unroll!*

Star-nosed mole

*The hedgehog's skin is larger than its body. When it curls up, it can pull its prickly skin over its head!*

Solenodon

*Spines are just stiff, hollow hairs.*

*One-week-old baby shrews hold on to one another so that they don't get lost.*

White-tailed shrews

*Adult European hedgehogs have more than 5,000 needle-sharp spines.*

# CATS

*A cheetah can accelerate as quickly as a Ferrari car*

Cats are carnivores. Most creep up on their prey by sneaking slowly and silently through the undergrowth. Then, suddenly, they will hurl themselves onto their surprised victim. The sharp canine teeth quickly deal the deadly blow. The biggest cat of all, the stripy tiger, can eat 25 kilograms of meat in a meal! But this terrifying animal never meets the lion, the king of the cats, because lions live in Africa and tigers in Asia.

Tigers

**Bright Eyes**
When light shines on a cat's eyes, they glow like the reflectors on the back of a bike. This happens because the light bounces back off a special layer in the cat's eyes. This layer collects light. It helps cats see six times better than you in dim light.

**Aerial Ambush**
All cats climb trees. This spotty jaguar is waiting to drop down on a passing peccary or tapir. It will even tackle giant alligators.

**Grassland Queens**
Lions are the odd-cats-out because they live in groups called prides. The male lions are often called the 'Kings of the Jungle', but in fact they do not live in jungles and the females, or lionesses, are in charge.

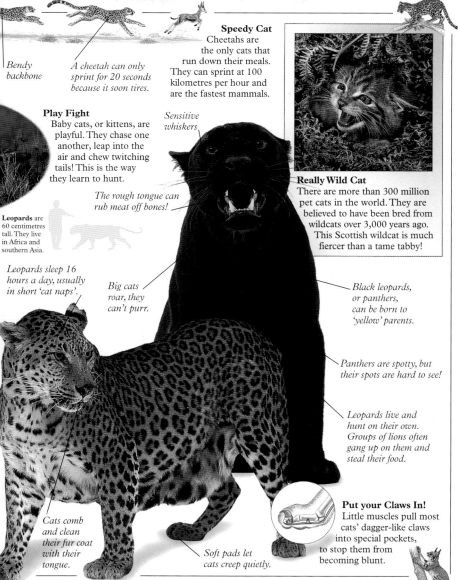

*Bendy backbone*

*A cheetah can only sprint for 20 seconds because it soon tires.*

**Speedy Cat**
Cheetahs are the only cats that run down their meals. They can sprint at 100 kilometres per hour and are the fastest mammals.

**Play Fight**
Baby cats, or kittens, are playful. They chase one another, leap into the air and chew twitching tails! This is the way they learn to hunt.

*Sensitive whiskers*

*The rough tongue can rub meat off bones!*

**Leopards** are 60 centimetres tall. They live in Africa and southern Asia.

*Leopards sleep 16 hours a day, usually in short 'cat naps'.*

*Big cats roar, they can't purr.*

**Really Wild Cat**
There are more than 300 million pet cats in the world. They are believed to have been bred from wildcats over 3,000 years ago. This Scottish wildcat is much fiercer than a tame tabby!

*Black leopards, or panthers, can be born to 'yellow' parents.*

*Panthers are spotty, but their spots are hard to see!*

*Leopards live and hunt on their own. Groups of lions often gang up on them and steal their food.*

*Cats comb and clean their fur coat with their tongue.*

*Soft pads let cats creep quietly.*

**Put your Claws In!**
Little muscles pull most cats' dagger-like claws into special pockets, to stop them from becoming blunt.

193

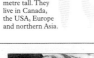

# DOGS

Like all carnivores, dogs eat meat. On its own a dog can only trap animals that are smaller than itself, but 20 African hunting dogs, working together, can easily catch and kill a zebra. Most dogs have learned this lesson and prefer to hunt in family groups, called packs. The 35 types of wild dogs have often been treated as enemies, not loved like pet dogs. Wolves have been wiped out in many places. Foxes only survive because they are smaller and more cunning.

*All pet dogs have been bred from grey, or timber, wolves. The first dogs were tamed more than 12,000 years ago!*

**Hoooooowl!**
In the dead of night, the wolves in a pack get together, throw back their heads and howl. This warns other wolves to keep out of their territory.

*A wolf can hear a watch ticking over ten metres away.*

**Grey wolves** are about one metre tall. They live in Canada, the USA, Europe and northern Asia.

*Dogs cool down by panting.*

*Pointed canine teeth stab the prey. Cheek teeth slice the meat into pieces that are small enough to swallow.*

*Grey wolves trot more than 60 kilometres a day when they are hunting a moose or an ox.*

**Pack Property**
Female African hunting dogs can have as many as 16 babies. These puppies belong to the whole pack, not just the mother. They are even suckled by other females.

*This pup is eight weeks old. It already eats meat but will not go hunting with the pack until it is six months old.*

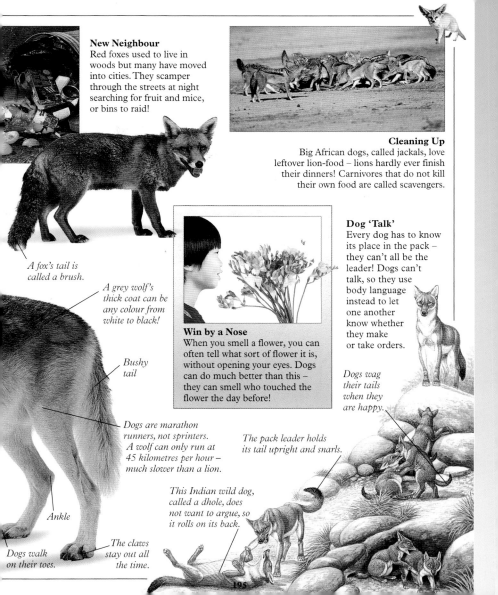

**New Neighbour**
Red foxes used to live in woods but many have moved into cities. They scamper through the streets at night searching for fruit and mice, or bins to raid!

**Cleaning Up**
Big African dogs, called jackals, love leftover lion-food – lions hardly ever finish their dinners! Carnivores that do not kill their own food are called scavengers.

*A fox's tail is called a brush.*

*A grey wolf's thick coat can be any colour from white to black!*

*Bushy tail*

**Win by a Nose**
When you smell a flower, you can often tell what sort of flower it is, without opening your eyes. Dogs can do much better than this – they can smell who touched the flower the day before!

**Dog 'Talk'**
Every dog has to know its place in the pack – they can't all be the leader! Dogs can't talk, so they use body language instead to let one another know whether they make or take orders.

*Dogs wag their tails when they are happy.*

*Dogs are marathon runners, not sprinters. A wolf can only run at 45 kilometres per hour – much slower than a lion.*

*The pack leader holds its tail upright and snarls.*

*This Indian wild dog, called a dhole, does not want to argue, so it rolls on its back.*

*Ankle*

*Dogs walk on their toes.*

*The claws stay out all the time.*

# BEARS

Bears are big and usually have thick, shaggy coats. Brown bears are the most common but giant pandas are more famous. People have argued for years about whether giant pandas are bears or not. Scientists now think, as any child can see, that they are black-and-white bears! Bears look cuddly, but they are fierce. People have shot so many of these big beasts that today bears only survive in hilly hideaways.

## The Big Sleep
Bears that live in cold places spend the winter inside warm caves. The females give birth to their tiny cubs, usually twins, while they are asleep.

*Polar bear pawprint*

## Honey and Grass for Tea?
Most bears eat all sorts of things – they are omnivores. These are a few of their favourite foods.

Honey

Grass

Berries

## Open Wide!
A grizzly bear has a simple way of fishing. It stands in a river and waits for fish to leap right into its mouth.

## Masters of Disguise
Polar bears live in the icy Arctic and are the only carnivorous bears. Seal skin is their favourite food.

*The polar bear hides its black nose with its white paw.*

*It sneaks up on the seal by pretending to be an iceberg!*

*The cunning bear springs out of the icy water to kill the surprised seal with one swipe of its huge paw.*

*Half-webbed toes*

*Ringed seal pup*

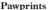

**Pawprints**
Unlike cats and dogs, bears have flat feet. Their heels touch the ground when they walk.

*A special pad on a panda's paw is used as a sort of thumb – useful for grasping bamboo shoots.*

*This big brown bear is over twice the size of a tiger!*

*All bears have small, round ears.*

*A bear's face always looks the same – you can't tell whether it is angry or happy!*

**Save the Giant Panda!**
There are less than 1,000 giant pandas left. It is not going to be easy to save them – females are only fertile for three days a year. They also need to eat 20 kilograms of one special type of bamboo a day.

*Many bears have rotten teeth. This is because they love sweet foods – especially honey!*

*With their big, strong arms, bears can hug a person to death!*

*Grizzly bears are a type of brown bear. They are called grizzly bears because the tips of their brown hairs are grey, or grizzled.*

**Grizzly bears** stand up to 3 metres tall. They live in Canada and the USA.

*The front paws can be used as clubs to hit other large animals.*

197

# APES

Playful       Begging for food

There are four sorts of ape: chimpanzees, orangutans, gibbons and gorillas. They all live for many years, have big brains, no tails and can walk upright. Apes are the closest relatives of people.

Orangutan (male)

Gorillas are the biggest and strongest apes but they are gentle giants. Chattering chimps are cheeky and cute but much more dangerous – they even kill deer and monkeys to eat! Family life is important to all these intelligent animals: chimps cuddle and shake hands when they meet.

**Playtime**
Baby chimps take a long time to grow up. Their mothers feed them milk for five or six years – so they have plenty of time to play.

**Brainy Beast**
Chimps are one of the few animals to use tools. They use leaves as sponges! First they soften handfuls of leaves by chewing them and then they use them to soak up water.

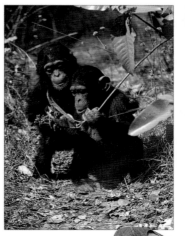

**Go Bananas**
Gorillas really do eat bananas. They also like nettles, giant celery and banana leaves.

**Walk Like an Ape**
All apes can stand on just two feet, but they usually walk on all fours like this.

*Apes walk on their knuckles.*

**Frightened**    **Angry**

**Not a Word**
The chimp is one of the few mammals that can pull faces to show its feelings.

**Holding Hands**
You can pick things up because you are able to fold your thumb across your hand. Apes and monkeys have these useful, 'opposable' thumbs too.

*Like you, apes have sensitive hands.*

**Male gorillas** stand 1.7 metres tall. They live in Africa.

*An orangutan's big toes can grip things too!*

*Gorillas have about the same number of hairs as you. They look more hairy because their hair is long and thick.*

*Big brain*

*Gorillas can climb trees but they spend most of the day lazing on the ground.*

**Is it a Bird?**
Every night, orangs build a cosy nest to sleep in. It takes just five minutes to build a mattress of branches and a blanket of leaves.

*Apes see things in colour – just like you.*

*Baby gorillas learn to crawl at ten weeks, climb at five months and walk at eight months. They may live to be forty.*

*All apes can sit and stand up straight.*

# MONKEYS

Monkeys are primates. It is easy to tell them apart from the cleverer primates, people and apes, because they have tails. Some, such as mandrills, live on the ground but most monkeys are light enough to jump or swing through the trees.

**Squirrel monkey**

They always look before they leap though, because there is danger all around. Large eagles may swoop down from above and leopards lurk below. If they miss their footing, monkeys may plunge up to 60 metres to the ground – like falling from the 13th floor of a building!

**Built to Balance**
If you start to lose your balance, you can use your arms to steady yourself. Monkeys use their tails instead – leaving their arms free for climbing.

**Keep it Clean!**
These rhesus monkeys are queuing up to have insects and dirt picked out of their fur. They even pick one another's teeth clean! This grooming helps to keep them tidy and also good friends.

*Groups of monkeys are called troops.*

**Face to Face**

**Telltale Tail**
Ring-tailed lemurs are primitive primates and live in troops like monkeys. They keep together in tall grass by pointing their tails upwards.

*This lemur is looking for a tail to follow!*

Mandrill (male)     Proboscis monkey (male)

Bald uakari     Cotton-top tamarin

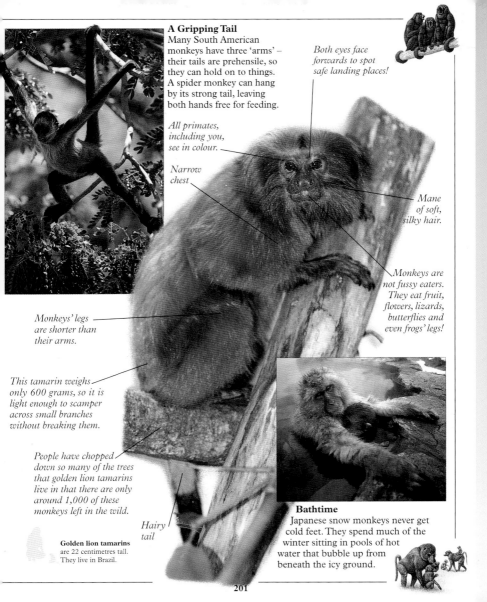

**A Gripping Tail**
Many South American monkeys have three 'arms' – their tails are prehensile, so they can hold on to things. A spider monkey can hang by its strong tail, leaving both hands free for feeding.

*Both eyes face forwards to spot safe landing places!*

*All primates, including you, see in colour.*

*Narrow chest*

*Mane of soft, silky hair.*

*Monkeys are not fussy eaters. They eat fruit, flowers, lizards, butterflies and even frogs' legs!*

*Monkeys' legs are shorter than their arms.*

*This tamarin weighs only 600 grams, so it is light enough to scamper across small branches without breaking them.*

*People have chopped down so many of the trees that golden lion tamarins live in that there are only around 1,000 of these monkeys left in the wild.*

*Hairy tail*

**Golden lion tamarins** are 22 centimetres tall. They live in Brazil.

**Bathtime**
Japanese snow monkeys never get cold feet. They spend much of the winter sitting in pools of hot water that bubble up from beneath the icy ground.

# BATS

Bats are furry, flying mammals. Their wings are made of thin, leathery skin, which is stretched across their fingers like material over the spokes of an umbrella. Bats live all over the world but you will not often see them flying. Most bats hang upside down and sleep during the day. They hunt at night. Small bats eat mice and mosquitoes. Larger, vegetarian bats, often called flying foxes because they have fox-like faces, feed on bananas and nectar.

*The ears of this long-eared bat are almost as big as its body. It tucks them under its wings when it sleeps.*

*Bats hear better than most other mammals.*

*Mouse-like, furry body*

*Wrist*

*Acrobatic bats swoop through the sky at up to 55 kilometres per hour – fast enough to escape from owls.*

*Moth*

*Bats squeak to find one another in the dark. This bat's mouth is full, so it will have to squeak through its big nose!*

## Fruity Bat
Jungles might not exist without bats! Fruit-eating bats pollinate plants and the seeds they spit out or pass in their droppings can grow into trees.

## The Bat Cave
Nearly all bats are awake at night – they are nocturnal. Sleepy days are spent inside caves or holes in trees. As the Sun sets, millions of bats stream out of their caves to go hunting.

## Camping Bats
Imagine having to build a new house every night – tent bats do! These small, white bats nibble through the middle rib of a palm leaf until it droops down to form a tiny tent. The bats hang underneath, out of the wind and rain.

**The Smallest Mammal**
The hog-nosed bat can fit in the palm of your hand. Its body is three centimetres long and it has a wingspan of just 15 centimetres. It weighs less than one grape.

*This is a thumb. Bats use their thumbs as combs to groom their fur and as hooks to hold on to things.*

*The wing can be used as a scoop to catch flying insects.*

*Long finger*

**Fangs for Dinner!**
Vampire bats love the taste of blood. This one has sliced open the foot of a sleeping chicken with its sharp teeth. It will lap up about one tablespoonful of blood.

**Long-eared bats**
have a wingspan of 28 centimetres. They live in northern Europe.

## Sounds Tasty
Many bats don't use their eyes to see, they use their voice and ears instead! American fishing bats make clicking noises as they fly over ponds. When these sounds bounce back off ripples, they know that a fish is near to the surface.

*The bat hears the tiny echo and swiftly swoops down to grab the fish.*

# Small Rodents

A rodent is an animal that gnaws with sharp, chisel-shaped teeth. Most are mouse-like and vegetarian: they nibble plant stems, seeds and roots. Forty per cent of all mammals are rodents. They live all over the world, from African jungles where crested rats clamber up trees, to scorching deserts where jerboas hop across the sand. House mice have even hitched lifts on ships to reach huts in Antarctica.

*Dormouse*

*These newborn, rubbery, wriggling mice can only squeak, sleep and suckle.*

## Moving House

Every three or four years, thousands of lemmings dash from their overcrowded homes. Many die in the frantic search for new places to live and feed.

## A Plague of Rats

Every year, millions of nibbling rats wreck one fifth of the world's crops!

*The greasy fur leaves dirty marks on things it touches.*

*Many brown rats live in sewers. They use their feet as paddles when they swim and can tread water for three days!*

*Flat teeth at the back of a rat's mouth grind up grass and grain.*

*Scaly tail*

*After walking through dirt, rats walk over food. This is how they spread diseases.*

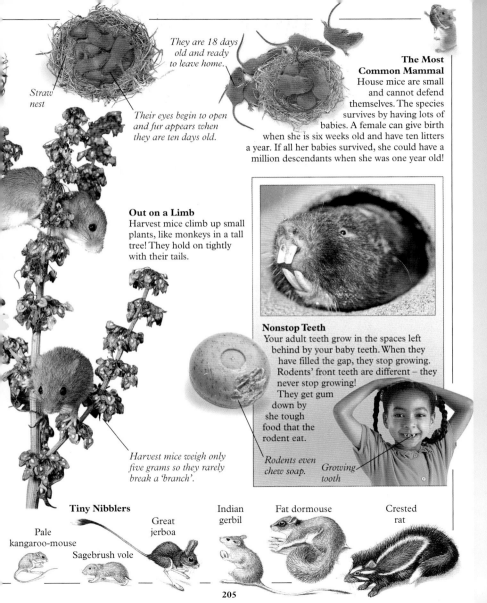

*Straw nest*

*They are 18 days old and ready to leave home.*

*Their eyes begin to open and fur appears when they are ten days old.*

## The Most Common Mammal

House mice are small and cannot defend themselves. The species survives by having lots of babies. A female can give birth when she is six weeks old and have ten litters a year. If all her babies survived, she could have a million descendants when she was one year old!

## Out on a Limb

Harvest mice climb up small plants, like monkeys in a tall tree! They hold on tightly with their tails.

## Nonstop Teeth

Your adult teeth grow in the spaces left behind by your baby teeth. When they have filled the gap, they stop growing. Rodents' front teeth are different – they never stop growing! They get gum down by she tough food that the rodent eat.

*Rodents even chew soap.*

*Growing tooth*

*Harvest mice weigh only five grams so they rarely break a 'branch'.*

## Tiny Nibblers

Pale kangaroo-mouse

Sagebrush vole

Great jerboa

Indian gerbil

Fat dormouse

Crested rat

# LARGE RODENTS

Most rodents are small and look like mice, but some are much bigger. There are two sorts of large rodents – those that look like squirrels and those, such as porcupines, that look like pigs. Rodents' teeth get worn down by gnawing, and all rodents have front teeth that keep growing throughout their lives.

Chipmunks

**Size of a Sheep!**
The capybara is the largest rodent in the world. It is a relative of the guinea pig.

**The Lion Lost**
A porcupine will run backwards and stick its quills into an attacker's face!

*A porcupine can hear fruit drop to the ground several metres away.*

*Hollow, stripy quill*

*The nest, or drey, is the size of a football.*

*Porcupines chew old bones to keep their teeth sharp.*

*Angry African porcupines stamp their back feet to rattle their quills. This warns other animals to go away*

**Giant Nibblers**

*The sharp quills only stick up when the porcupine is attacked.*

European red squirrel

Chinchilla

Rock cavy

Spring hare

Woodchuck

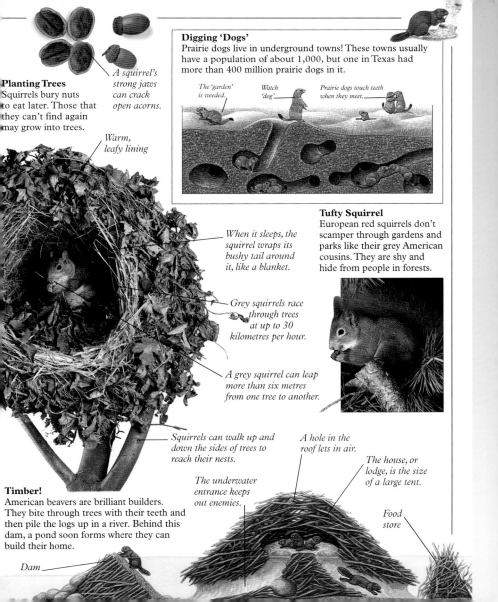

**Planting Trees**
Squirrels bury nuts to eat later. Those that they can't find again may grow into trees.

*A squirrel's strong jaws can crack open acorns.*

**Digging 'Dogs'**
Prairie dogs live in underground towns! These towns usually have a population of about 1,000, but one in Texas had more than 400 million prairie dogs in it.

*The 'garden' is weeded.*

*Watch 'dog'.*

*Prairie dogs touch teeth when they meet.*

*Warm, leafy lining*

*When it sleeps, the squirrel wraps its bushy tail around it, like a blanket.*

**Tufty Squirrel**
European red squirrels don't scamper through gardens and parks like their grey American cousins. They are shy and hide from people in forests.

*Grey squirrels race through trees at up to 30 kilometres per hour.*

*A grey squirrel can leap more than six metres from one tree to another.*

*Squirrels can walk up and down the sides of trees to reach their nests.*

*A hole in the roof lets in air.*

*The house, or lodge, is the size of a large tent.*

*The underwater entrance keeps out enemies.*

*Food store*

**Timber!**
American beavers are brilliant builders. They bite through trees with their teeth and then pile the logs up in a river. Behind this dam, a pond soon forms where they can build their home.

*Dam*

# THE HORSE FAMILY

Almost all the horses in the world are tame. The only wild species left is the Przewalski's horse. It survives in zoos. The commonest wild member of the horse family today is not a horse, but a zebra.

*Przewalski's horse*

Swift, stripy zebras are herbivores – they chew grass with their flat back teeth. Horses, zebras and asses walk on the tips of their toes, which are hidden inside hard 'shoes', called hooves.

**Desert 'Donkeys'**
Wild asses are shy and rare. They live in the dry North African deserts.

*A zebra's mane stands up straight.*

*The ears twist round to listen for danger.*

**Plains zebras** are up to 1.2 metres tall at the shoulder. They live in Africa.

*A zebra can see in colour during the day and as well as an owl at night!*

**Best Friends**
Zebras and wildebeest like to live together. The zebras keep watch, while wildebeest sniff the air for lions.

*Wildebeest eat the short grass left by the zebras.*

*The hoof is just a large toenail!*

*Foals can walk when they are a few minutes old.*

**Quick, Run!**
Asses, zebras and horses can run at speeds of up to 50 kilometres per hour.

*All four hooves leave the ground when it gallops.*

*Long legs are best for taking big steps and running fast.*

*Plains zebras are plump.*

**Spot the Zebra!**
Nobody knows why zebras are striped. Perhaps their crazy pattern puzzles lions, making it hard for them to pick their prey.

*A zebra scratches its back by rolling on the ground.*

**Trespassers will be Kicked**
Mountain zebras don't live in herds. Each male, or stallion, 'owns' a patch of land, called a territory. He will chase off any male zebra that enters his home.

*Big thigh muscles power plains zebras across the African grasslands.*

*The swishing tail swats annoying, buzzing flies.*

*Females, foals and stallions live together in the same herd.*

**Make Your Mark**
Your fingerprints are different to everybody else's. So are a zebra's stripes – each one wears a different patterned coat! Some even have thin white stripes on a black background.

*There is only one toe inside this hard hoof.*

**Born Free**
Some of the 75 million tame horses have escaped and learned to live in the wild. The ancestors of these American 'wild' horses, called mustangs, belonged to cowboys.

# HIPPOS, PIGS AND PECCARIES

Hippo is short for hippopotamus, which means 'river horse'. They are called river horses because they live in rivers and lakes and eat grass. Pigs and peccaries do not live in rivers but they enjoy wallowing in mud as much as their huge relatives. Although these water-loving mammals are not carnivores, they are all able to protect themselves. Wild pigs can stab and kill tigers with their tusks, peccaries fight jaguars, and a heavy hippo will tussle with a crocodile or smash into a boat!

**Very Important Pig**
Farmyard pigs have all been bred from wild boar.

**Built-In Suntan Lotion**
Hippo skin oozes tiny blobs of pink liquid. This oil stops their skin from drying out and also protects them from sunburn.

**Open Wide**
You yawn when you are tired or bored, but male hippos yawn when they are angry! Smaller males are frightened off by the big teeth and swim away without starting a fight.

*The eyes and nostrils are high up on a hippo's head. This means it can stick just the top of its head out of the water and still see and breathe.*

*Smooth, almost hairless, skin.*

*The half-metre-long tusks are sometimes used to stab crocodiles.*

**Hippos** are 1.5 metres tall. They live in Africa.

*This big male hippo weighs as much as 120 eight-year-old children!*

### Lumbering Lawn Mowers
Every night, hippos leave the water and spend five or six hours grazing. They troop back into the water, down well-worn paths, long before the scorching Sun rises.

### Plucky Peccary
If a mountain lion attacks a group of peccaries, one brave animal squeals loudly and runs towards the lion. This peccary dies, but the mothers and babies escape.

### Piggy Parade

Bush pig

Collared peccary

### Underwater Ballet
Hippos can hold their breath for more than five minutes. This is plenty of time to dive down and tiptoe gracefully across the bottom of the lake.

*To keep cool and moist, hippos spend 16 hours a day up to their necks in water.*

*The hippo shuts its ears and nostrils when it is under water.*

*Thick skin protects the hippo from snapping crocodiles.*

*There are four toes on each foot.*

Hippo

*Hippos do eat water lilies, but prefer grass.*

Pigmy hippo

# THE CAMEL FAMILY

You find camels and their smaller South American relatives, vicuñas and guanacos, on sandy deserts, rocky plains and bare mountains. They survive in some of the harshest places on Earth. Vicuñas can breathe thin mountain air and camels can cope with freezing nights and scorching desert days. People have made good use of these animals' amazing survival skills – most are domesticated and work for a living. There are few wild members of the camel family left.

*The fat inside a camel's humps shields its big body from the scorching Sun.*

**Domestic Dromedary**
Desert peoples could not survive without their one-humped camels. They are ridden, milked and eaten. Camel skin is made into shoes, hair is woven into clothes and dry droppings are used as fuel!

*Food is brought back up from the rumen to be rechewed.*

*The rumen is the large part of the stomach where chewed food goes first to be partly digested.*

**Swallow That!**
After going 10 months without water, a thirsty camel can gulp down nine big buckets of water in just 15 minutes.

*Third stomach*

*Second stomach*

**Twice as Tasty**
To get all the goodness out of grass, some mammals, such as camels, deer and cattle, have more than one stomach and chew their food twice!

The ears and nostrils can be pressed flat to keep out sand.

*Two rows of eyelashes keep out sand and stop the eyes from freezing on cold desert nights.*

*A camel doesn't waste water. Liquid from its runny nose drips down the split lip into its mouth!*

**Bactrian camels** are 2.2 metres tall. They live in the Gobi desert in Asia.

*Camels spit at things that annoy them.*

*Tough lips can grip thorny desert plants.*

*Camels hardly ever sweat. This saves water.*

**How Many Humps?**

Dromedary

Bactrian camel

### King of the Castle
While the females graze, the male vicuña stands on a rock. If it spots a mountain lion it whistles and the fleecy females flee.

*Camels roll from side to side when they walk because they lift both legs on one side at the same time.*

*The two toes spread out to stop the camel sinking into soft sand.*

Guanaco

Vicuña

### Hard-Working Mammals
Llamas and alpacas have been bred by people from wild guanacos. Llamas are milked and used to carry heavy loads. Alpacas are kept for their fine wool.

Alpaca

Llama

# CATTLE AND ANTELOPES

Cattle, antelopes and their relatives goats and sheep, are all bovids. This means that they have horns firmly fixed to the tops of their heads. Horns have a bony core and an outer layer made of the same stuff as your fingernails.

Gerenuk antelopes browse on leaves

Gerenuk (male)

but bison prefer to graze on grass. Like all bovids, they take the goodness out of their poor-quality food by coughing up partly digested food and chewing it a second time. This is called chewing the cud.

**Round Up**
Musk oxen form a ring around their babies to protect them from hungry wolves – who can't pass the circle of horns.

*All cattle have four stomachs!*

*These horns are about half as tall as you!*

*This rare Arabian oryx antelope chews the cud as it walks across the desert.*

Arabian oryx

*It sniffs the air for rain and then walks to where the grass is growing.*

**On the March**
At the onset of the dry season, huge herds of wildebeest walk over 1,600 kilometres to wetter, greener pastures. When the wet season begins, they wander back. These long, yearly journeys are called migrations.

*Like all cattle, bison have split hooves.*

214

**Built-In Radiator**
The Tibetan yak lives near the top of the world in the Himalayan mountains. It does not get cold though because it has its own central heating system – the moss being digested in its stomach is hot and keeps it warm.

**Heads with Horns**

*This thick, winter coat falls off in big clumps during the spring.*

*A dark coat soaks up the Sun's heat. This helps to keep the bison warm in cold weather.*

*Male bison fight for females by putting their heads together and pushing. The winner is the one who pushes the other backwards.*

African buffalo (male)

*Horns are different to antlers. They never form branches or stop growing and they are not replaced each year.*

Blackbuck (male)

*Male bison weigh more than a small car!*

**American bison** are two metres tall. They live in Canada and the USA.

Wild goat (male)

*Herds of bison spend most of the day eating grass and most of the night chewing!*

Bighorn sheep (male)

# ELEPHANTS

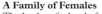
*Matriarch*

Elephants have enormous ears, long noses, tusks – and weigh more than six cars. They are the biggest land mammals. Herds of elephants shape the land they live in by treading paths that are wide enough to stop bush fires, by digging wells in dry riverbeds, by fertilizing the ground with dung and by trampling grass for zebras to eat. They also open up forests by pushing over trees!

**A Family of Females**
The leader of a herd of elephants is an old female, called a matriarch. She is followed by all her female relatives and their babies.

*Wrinkles trap water and help to keep it cool.*

**Ivory Towers**
Many elephants are shot for their valuable ivory tusks. People have burnt huge piles of old tusks to show that they want this cruelty to stop.

*Elephants never stop growing.*

**It's all Relative**
The elephant's closest relative, the hyrax, looks like a guinea pig! Millions of years ago they were huge. All that elephants and hyraxes have in common now are tusks, and nails instead of hooves.

*Tusks are teeth. They grow about 17 centimetres a year and can be as long as a car!*

**Who's Who?**
There are two sorts of elephant.

*Ankle*

*Humped back*  *Smaller ears*

*Longer tusks*

*Bigger, rounder ears*

*Taller*

*Elephants eat grass, bark and leaves for up to 20 hours a day.*

*This toenail is bigger than your whole hand!*

Asian

African

*Males leave their families when they are about fourteen.*

*Young females act as nannies.*

*An African elephant's ears are almost as big as sheets for a single bed!*

## Stay Cool
Elephants have lots of ways of cooling their big bodies. They can wallow in mud or throw water and dust over their skin. Sometimes they flap their ears like giant fans!

*The elephant spreads out its ears to make itself look bigger and more dangerous.*

*Elephants keep in touch by making deep, rumbling noises in their tummies!*

*The bendy trunk is formed from the nose and the upper lip. It is used for breathing, smelling, touching and picking things up.*

*Elephants can live to celebrate their eightieth birthdays!*

*This is one of the first four teeth.*

*The sixth, and last, set of teeth are bigger than bricks!*

## What's Inside?
Elephants may look like they have flat feet but they really walk on their tiptoes!

*Toe*

*The heel rests on a fatty cushion.*

## Always Teething!
Apart from tusks, elephants have only four teeth. These molars are replaced every few years. Bigger teeth appear at the back of the mouth and push out the old, worn teeth – like a conveyor belt of teeth!

217

# THE HUMAN BODY

Your body is one of the most amazing machines in the world. It is made up of thousands of parts all working together. Each group of parts is called a system. The body is so complicated that it is easier to imagine the different systems separately. But your digestive system, nervous system, skeleton, blood or circulatory system, and muscles all work together. You need all of them to stay alive.

When you are born, all you can do is sleep, eat and cry. It takes time to discover how the parts of your body move and to get them to work together. As you grow, you learn to do more difficult things, like crawling, walking, and riding a bicycle.

There are over 100 muscles in your face.

Human skull

Digestive system

Crawling
(about 10 months)

Walking
(about 15 months)

Hopping
(about
4 years)

Skipping
(about
5 years)

Riding a
two-wheeled bicycle
(about 5 years)

Nervous
system

Skeleton

Circulatory
system

Muscles

# HEARING

**'Canaphone'**
A piece of string threaded through two empty cans works rather like a telephone. If you speak into one can, the vibrations travel along the string to the other can – allowing your voice to be heard.

Hearing is one of your five senses. Your ears are important and delicate: they pick up sounds and send messages to your brain. Sounds travel through the air in waves. Your outer ears, the shell-shaped flaps on the side of your head, catch sound waves and funnel them inside. These waves hit the eardrum and make it vibrate. The middle ear and the inner ear change the vibrations into electrical signals, which are sorted out and recognized by your brain.

Mother

Kneel

*The outer ear collects the sounds and funnels them along the ear canal.*

**Crash!**
The loudness of sound is measured in decibels. Quiet whispering is less than 25 decibels, the clash of cymbals about 90 and a jet plane taking off can measure more than 130 decibels. Noises over 120 decibels can cause pain and may damage your ears.

Hunger

**Talking in Signs**
If deaf people have never heard speech, they may not have learned to talk. To help them to communicate, many learn a special language called signing. They also learn to spell using their hands, and to lip-read by watching the shape of people's mouths as they speak.

Hope

*Three tiny, connected bones in the middle ear – the hammer, anvil and stirrup – pass sound vibrations from the eardrum to the cochlea.*

*The semi-circular canals help you balance.*

*Nerves*

## Hello . . . Hello!
If you shout in a large, empty space, the sound waves from your voice bounce off the nearest surface, back to your ears. This is called an echo. The further a sound has to travel before it is reflected, the longer you must wait for the echo.

*Nerve cells in the cochlea send messages about sounds to the brain.*

*The inner ear is made up of the cochlea and the semi-circular canals. It is filled with liquid.*

*The eardrum is a thin sheet of skin that vibrates when sound waves hit it – just like the skin on a drum.*

## Visible and Invisible Ears
Not all animals hear in the same way as you. Some do not have any ears on the outside of their body.

*Elephants have huge ear flaps and good hearing.*

*Birds and lizards have good hearing but no ear flaps on the sides of their heads.*

*A rabbit can turn its ears to hear sounds all around it.*

# SEEING

**Tear-Full**
Tears help to keep your eyes moist and clean. When too many are made, they cannot all drain away down your nose, so tears come out of your eyes.

Sight is perhaps the most important of your five senses. Your eyes work together with your brain to help you to see. The cornea, at the front of your eye, bends light. This light is then focused by the lens, to form an image of what you are looking at on the retina at the back of your eye. But the image is upside down! Nerve cells in the retina send messages to your brain, which sorts the messages out so that you see things the right way up.

**Tricky Eyes**
Sometimes your eyes play tricks on you, called optical illusions. Try these:

Which of these two girls is the taller?

Which red circle is bigger, the left one or the right one?

Which line is longer?

**Double Vision?**
Because they are set apart, each of your eyes sees a slightly different picture. Your brain puts the two pictures together. This is called stereoscopic or binocular vision, and it means you can judge depth and distances. Try this: close one eye, point to something and keep your finger still. Now look through the other eye. Are you still pointing to the same place?

**Eye Spy**
You can have your eyes tested by an optometrist to make sure they are working properly. Glasses or contact lenses will help if you cannot see clearly. Your eyes are very important so have them checked regularly!

Eyebrow hairs stop drops of sweat getting into your eyes.

The eyelids are lowered like a protective cover if danger approaches the eye. They also wash your eyes every time you blink.

The retina is at the back of the eye. Cells on the retina, called rods and cones, help you to make sense of light and colours.

The white part of the eye is called the sclera. At the front it becomes transparent and is called the cornea. The cornea bends the light.

The conjunctiva is transparent, like a window. It protects the front of your eye.

The optic nerve takes messages from your eye to your brain.

Light enters the eye through the pupil.

Iris

The lens helps your eye to focus.

Eyelashes protect your eyes and stop dirt and grit getting in.

Six muscles control each eye and let you move your eyes in almost any direction. But both eyes work together.

Muscles around the eye allow you to blink every two to ten seconds. So even when you are awake you have your eyes shut for at least half an hour each day!

**Black Hole**
The black part of your eye is a hole, called the pupil. A coloured muscle, the iris, makes this hole get smaller in bright light, to let in less light, and bigger in dim light.

# BRAIN

Inside your head, protected by a bony skull, is your brain. It looks crinkled like a walnut and is the control centre for the whole of your body. Your heart pumps oxygen-filled blood into it through a mass of tubes, called arteries. After only four minutes without oxygen, brain cells will die and they cannot be replaced. Your brain is divided into two halves, called hemispheres. Each half controls different activities.

**Top Gear**
To stop you injuring your brain, you should wear a helmet whenever you take part in a sport that might make you knock your hea

*Musical talent is based in the right side of your brain.*

*Fantasy, imagination and dreams are all controlled by the right side of the brain.*

*Talents like drawing and painting are also right-side-of-the-brain activities.*

**Brain Control**
Your brain is the most important part of your body. It is your control centre but it is only just bigger than your two fists!

Signals coming in and going out to other parts of your body, such as your eyes, mouth, ears and skin, are all controlled by different areas of your brain.

Sight
Memory
Touch
Hearing
Hearing
Movement
Speech
Personality

### Kim's Game

When we are learning we depend on our memory to help us. Test your memory with this game. Set out a number of objects and look at them for a few moments. Ask a friend to remove an object then try to tell what is missing.

### Different Brains

Animals have brains of various shapes and sizes, suited to the things they do.

Fish

Bird

Cat

Human

*Mathematical and logical problems are sorted out by the left side of your brain.*

*Your right arm is controlled by the left side of your brain.*

*The left side of your brain remembers names, dates and facts.*

*The left side of your brain controls language skills. It enables you to speak, read and write.*

*The brain stem controls many of your automatic actions, such as your heartbeat and breathing.*

### Brain Relay

When you want to touch something, a signal is passed from your brain to other parts of your body like a baton in a relay race. It goes first to the spinal nerves then to the motor nerves, which tell muscles to move.

Brain     Spinal nerves     Motor nerves

**Left, Right, Left**
The ideas in these two large pictures are thought to be true for right-handed people. In left-handed people they may be reversed.

# NERVES

Nerves are like telephone cables carrying information between the brain and all parts of the body. One set of nerves – the sensory nerves – carries signals to your brain from your senses, telling your brain what is happening around you. When your brain has decided what to do it sends signals along another set of nerves – the motor nerves – to make your muscles work.

*Nerve network*

**Speedy Reflex**
If someone claps their hands by your face your brain thinks something is flying towards your eyes and they blink. This blink is a reflex action to protect them.

*With your eyes covered, can you tell is a teddy bear?*

**What's on the 'Feely Table'?**
The sense of touch is very important. It is one of your five senses. Receptor cells under your skin send messages, through sensory nerves, to your brain about what your fingers are feeling.

*A bottle feels hard and smooth.*

**Reading by Touch**
Blind people cannot see to read so they learn a special alphabet of raised dots, called braille. They feel these dots with their fingertips.

**Get the Message?**
Messages about how objects feel are sent through the sensory nerves and the spinal nerves to the brain to be understood.

Sensory nerves　　　　Spinal nerves　　　　Brain

*If you touch some honey, your fingers will find that it is sticky.*

*Ice is cold and slippery. When it starts to melt it feels wet.*

226

## Skin Sense

Find out which part of your skin is most sensitive with this test. Close your eyes and ask a friend to touch different parts of your body with the points of two pencils. Try this test on your fingertips and on your knee to see which parts feel two points and which feel only one.

*Blindfold*

*Your fingers can tell if something is soft. It feels good to use towels made of soft material.*

*Hot things are good to feel when you are cold – but if something is too hot your nerves will send messages to make your hand move quickly away.*

*The wood feels hard and rough.*

*Even when you are blindfolded, you can feel that this smooth, round object is a ball.*

*The bristles on this brush are sharp and prickly.*

*Feathers are very light and soft. They can sometimes tickle, especially if you stroke your face gently with them.*

*Your eyes tell your brain that something may be heavy. Your muscles are then prepared to lift a heavy weight. If you cannot see the weight you may be surprised when you try to lift it!*

# Skin

If you could unwrap your skin, you might be surprised at how much you have – enough to cover a large towel. It goes over all your bumps and curves and into every crease of your body. Your skin grows with you, so that when you are an adult it will cover an area of about 1.7 square metres. It is waterproof and protective and can heal itself if it gets damaged.

*New skin grows all the time to replace old skin that rubs off. Most house dust is really old, dead skin!*

*The thinnest skin is on your eyelids.*

**Personal Prints**
Fingerprints are patterns of lines and swirls on your fingers. Try printing yours using paint or ink! Everyone has different fingerprints so they are used to identify people. There are three basic patterns.

*Hairs grow on every part of your skin except for your lips, the palms of your hands and the soles of your feet.*

Arch          Loop          Whorl

*A fingernail takes about six months to grow from base to tip. It grows about half a millimetre a week.*

*Nails are made of dead cells which contain a protein called keratin.*

*The cuticle is the fold of skin overlapping the nail-bed from where the nail grows.*

*The half-moon at the base of your nail looks white because this part is not firmly attached to the skin below.*

228

### Shades

All skin contains a colouring substance called melanin. Dark skin contains more melanin than fair skin. As a protection from burning by the Sun, the skin produces more melanin, which tans the skin a darker colour.

*The roots of your hair are alive and grow about two millimetres a week. When the hairs reach the surface of your skin they die – so having your hair cut does not hurt!*

### Growing Old

Your skin is elastic. If you pinch the back of your hand and then release it, the skin goes back to its original place. As people get older their skin becomes less elastic and often gets wrinkled. Some people's hair turns grey because it stops making melanin.

### Dead or Alive?

Your skin has two layers. The dead, outer layer, called the epidermis, protects the living dermis underneath.

### Hair Styles

How straight or curly a hair is depends upon the shape of the pocket, or follicle, it grows from. The colour of your hair depends upon the amount of black or red melanin there is inside these pockets.

*Hair*

*A pore is the opening of a sweat gland.*

*Epidermis*

*Nerve ending*

*Dermis*

*Oil glands stop skin drying out*

*Sweat glands open to let moisture out of your skin to help keep you cool.*

*Hair follicle*

*Blood vessels bring food and oxygen to the skin.*

# BLOOD

Arteriole    Artery
Aorta
(largest artery)

Blood is pumped all around your body
by your heart. It travels in long tubes
called blood vessels. Before it begins this
journey, it is pushed to your lungs to
collect oxygen. Then it returns to your
heart to be pumped around your body.
Blood also carries nutrients
from your food to the cells.

**There . . .**
Blood vessels that
take blood away
from your heart
are called arteries.

**Power Pump**
Your heart is made of strong
muscle. In just one minute,
it can pump a drop of blood
all the way down to your toes
and back to your heart again.

*The heart is divided into four spaces
called chambers, two at the top and
two at the bottom. There is a wall
of muscle down the middle.*

*Blood enters the top right chamber
through the vena cava. It passes down
to the bottom right chamber. Then
it is pushed out to your lungs.*

*Blood, filled with oxygen
from the lungs, comes into
the top left chamber. It
passes down to the bottom
left chamber. Then it is
pumped around your body.*

*After going around your
body, the blood returns
to the right side of your
heart, to start the
journey again.*

Aorta

*Flaps, called
valves, stop blood
from flowing the
wrong way. It is the
'lub-dub' sound of
these doors closing
that you hear when
your heart beats.*

Venule Vein

Vena cava
(largest vein)

## ... and Back

Those that take blood
back to your heart are
called veins.

### Feeling the Pressure

You can feel the beat of your
heart as it pumps blood, at high
pressure, through your arteries.
This beat is called the pulse. Put
the fingers of one hand on the inside
of your other wrist, in line with your thumb.
You can feel your pulse beating there. You
can only hear a
heartbeat by using
a stethoscope or by
putting your ear
to a friend's chest.

### Heart Work

When you skip, or take any
form of exercise, your muscles
need extra oxygen and food
from your blood. To provide this,
your heart has to pump faster.

Side view of a
red blood cell

*You have about four litres
of blood in your body. An adult
has more and a baby has less.*

*A drop of blood goes round your
body more than a thousand times
a day. Every five minutes all your
blood passes through your kidneys
to be cleaned.*

### Super Cells

In one tiny drop of blood
there are red cells, white
cells and platelets, all floating
in a liquid called plasma.
The blood in your arteries is
carrying oxygen which makes
it a brighter red colour than
the blood in your veins.

*Red cells carry oxygen
around the body. They are
made in the bone marrow.*

*White blood
cells defend the
body against germs.*

*If you cut yourself, platelets
rush to the broken blood
vessel and stick themselves
together to plug the hole.*

# BREATHING

You must breathe all the time to stay alive. If you try to hold your breath for more than about a minute your body will force you to start breathing again. The air that you breathe is made up of many different gases mixed together, but your body only needs one of them, oxygen, to keep you alive. If you ran out of oxygen, even for a very short time, you would die. The air you breathe goes into two soft, moist sponges, called lungs. You have one on each side of your chest.

**Lung Capacity**
Breathe in deeply. Blow into a balloon until you run out of breath. Tie a knot in the balloon. Now you can see just how much air your lungs are able to hold.

**Bad Breath!**
The air that you breathe can contain gases that are bad for you. This woman is wearing a mask to protect herself from car fumes.

*Right lung*

*Bronchus*

*Heart*

*Blood vessels surround the alveoli.*

*Alveoli are stretchy, so they can blow up like balloons. Gases can pass right through the alveoli's stretched skin.*

*Oxygen seeps from the alveoli into the blood. A waste gas, called carbon dioxide, seeps from the blood back into the alveoli to be breathed out.*

*Some air is always left in your lungs because they would collapse if they were completely empty.*

232

*You breathe air in through a tube called the windpipe, or trachea.*

## Hot Air

The air that you breathe out is warm and has water in it. You can see this if you breathe onto a mirror. The water in your breath cools down and forms a mist as it hits the cold mirror. If you touch the mirror you can feel the moisture. You can also see the water misting-up when you breathe out on a cold day.

*Air enters the lungs through two large tubes called the bronchi. Each bronchus divides into smaller and smaller tubes ending in tiny sacs called alveoli.*

*Your ribs form a cage. They protect your lungs.*

### Breathe In
A powerful muscle, called the diaphragm, helps you breathe air into both your lungs. When this muscle is pulled tight, it moves downwards, leaving more space for the lungs. As the lungs spread out to fill this larger space, they suck in air.

### Breathe Out
When your diaphragm relaxes, it moves back up again and squashes your lungs. There is no longer enough space in your lungs for all the air, so it is squeezed up your windpipe and out of your nose or mouth.

*Mucus*

*Dirt*

*Tiny 'hairs' trap dirt.*

*Little 'brushes' help to push dirt out of your body.*

*Special cells*

*Wall of the bronchus*

### Sneezing
A sudden rush of built-up air blows dust or germs from your nose.

### Coughing
Dust or germs in the tubes of your lungs are forced out quickly.

### Laughing
The diaphragm jerks, forcing air up through your voice box and windpipe.

# TASTE AND SMELL

Your senses of taste and smell are very closely linked. They depend on each other. Tiny dimples on your tongue, and hairs at the top of the inside of your nose, detect chemicals that cause tastes and smells. Special sensory cells then send messages through to your brain to be recognized. Your sense of smell is twenty thousand times stronger than your sense of taste! Often what you think you are tasting you are really just smelling.

**Nice and Not so Nice**
You are able to distinguish several thousand different smells. The clean smell of the countryside can be lovely, but the smell of milk that has gone off is horrible. Bad smells can warn you not to drink or eat things that are not fresh.

*When you want to smell something, you have to suck air right up to the top of your nose to reach your smell sense cells.*

*The smell of tasty food automatically makes you produce saliva.*

*The roof of your mouth, the back of your throat and your tongue are covered in small dimples called taste buds.*

*As the food is pushed around your mouth by your tongue, your taste buds pick up its taste.*

*Taste buds can only detect the flavours of food that has been dissolved in saliva.*

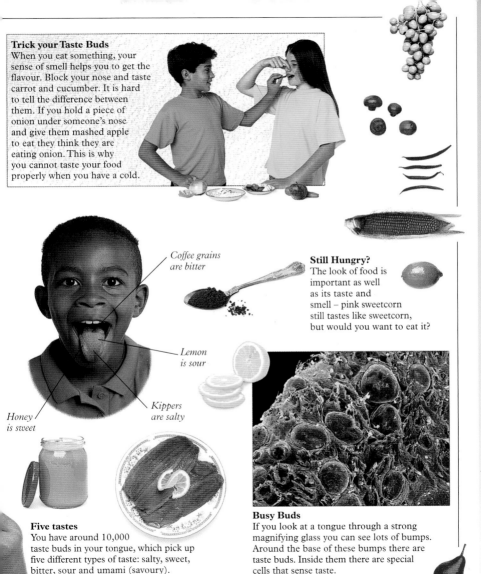

**Trick your Taste Buds**
When you eat something, your sense of smell helps you to get the flavour. Block your nose and taste carrot and cucumber. It is hard to tell the difference between them. If you hold a piece of onion under someone's nose and give them mashed apple to eat they think they are eating onion. This is why you cannot taste your food properly when you have a cold.

*Coffee grains are bitter*

*Lemon is sour*

*Kippers are salty*

*Honey is sweet*

**Still Hungry?**
The look of food is important as well as its taste and smell – pink sweetcorn still tastes like sweetcorn, but would you want to eat it?

**Five tastes**
You have around 10,000 taste buds in your tongue, which pick up five different types of taste: salty, sweet, bitter, sour and umami (savoury).

**Busy Buds**
If you look at a tongue through a strong magnifying glass you can see lots of bumps. Around the base of these bumps there are taste buds. Inside them there are special cells that sense taste.

# TEETH

You use your teeth to break up food into pieces that are small enough to swallow. Some are shaped for biting and others for chewing. You have two sets of teeth. The first set are called milk teeth and there are 20 of them. At the age of about six, you start to lose your milk teeth. One by one the second set, the 32 adult teeth, grow in their place. Teeth are strong and keep working for many years.

**Gappy Grin**
Children are left with gaps where their milk teeth have fallen out and they are waiting for their adult teeth to grow.

*Healthy gums are just as important as healthy teeth – they help to hold your teeth in place.*

**Cases for Braces**
Sometimes teeth grow crookedly or become overcrowded in the mouth. Often this can be put right by wearing teeth braces.

**Still Rooted**
This skull shows how teeth are rooted into the two powerful jawbones.

— *Jawbone*

**Complete Set**
A full set of adult teeth has eight incisors, four canines, eight premolars and twelve molars. Four of the molars are called wisdom teeth.

 **Incisors**   **Canine**    **Premolar**    **Molars**

### Inside Story
Your teeth are alive. The part that sticks out from your gum is the crown. The part under the gum is the root.

*Enamel is the hardest substance your body makes. A thin layer of it covers all your teeth.*

*Nerve*

*Gum*

*Under the enamel, there is a layer of hard, bone-like material called dentine.*

*Jawbone*

*The soft, middle part of the tooth is called the pulp. It contains nerves and blood vessels.*

### Brushing Up
Saliva and bits of food form a mixture called plaque. If plaque builds up on your teeth it can cause them to decay and even fall out. Brushing your teeth and gums after meals and before going to bed helps to remove the sugary foods that lead to tooth decay.

*Your knobbly back teeth are called molars. They crush and grind food when you chew.*

*Sometimes people have extra teeth.*

*The sharp, chisel-shaped teeth at the front of your mouth are incisors. They can cut and bite tough food.*

*At about the age of eighteen, wisdom teeth may grow at the back of your mouth – but they don't make you wise!*

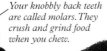

*There are molars on the bottom too.*

*Premolars have two edges, or cusps. They tear and grind up your food.*

*Canine teeth are sharp and pointed. They are used for tearing food.*

# EATING

Food is the fuel that provides energy for your body. The energy is measured in units called kilojoules. Before your body can use the food you eat, it has to be broken down into tiny bits that are small enough to pass into your blood. This digestion takes about 24 hours, as the food flows through a long tube winding all the way from your mouth to your bottom.

**In and Out**
The inside wall of the small intestine has a very bumpy surface.

*1. Food starts being digested in your mouth. Your spit, or saliva, has a digestive juice which starts to break down the food.*

*Your liver is a 'chemical factory'. It also stores vitamins.*

*Windpipe*

*2. The food travels down a foodpipe, called the gullet.*

*3. Your stomach is a thick bag. Food is churned up inside it and mixed with strong stomach juices to make a kind of soup.*

*4. After leaving your stomach, your food flows down your small intestine. Goodness from the food seeps through the thin walls into your blood.*

*Large intestine*

*Small intestine*

**Fats**

**Vitamins**

**Minerals**

**Proteins**

**Get into Groups!**
Foods can be put into groups. Fats and carbohydrates provide you with energy. Vitamins and minerals keep you healthy. Proteins build cells and so help your body to grow and repair itself.

*5. Your large intestine holds the food that your body cannot digest. Later it is passed out of your body through your rectum.*

*6. Your bladder stores urine. When it fills up you feel the need to go to the toilet to empty it.*

238

### A Lump in the Throat

You can swallow even if you are standing on your head! This is because your food does not slide down through you – it is squeezed along by muscles in your digestive tube. This is called peristalsis and it happens all the time, without you having to think about it.

The muscles of a snake can squeeze an egg through its body in the same way.

*Walking uses about 1000 kilojoules an hour*

*Sleeping uses about 275 kilojoules an hour*

*Drawing uses about 350 kilojoules an hour*

*Netball and other vigorous sports use about 2300 kilojoules an hour*

### Fuel Burning

If a car travels very fast it uses up more fuel than if it goes slowly. The same is true of your body. When you exercise you use up more kilojoules than when you are asleep.

*You have two kidneys. Each one is about the size of your clenched fist.*

*Narrow tubes, called ureters, take urine from the kidneys to the bladder.*

**Carbohydrates**

*Any water your body does not need is turned into urine by your kidneys.*

### How Long?

If you could stretch your whole digestive system out in a straight line it would be about as long as ten metre rules!

# MUSCLES

Try to sit as still as you can. Is anything moving? Even when you think you are completely still, many parts of your body are moving. Your heart is beating and your intestines and lungs are working. All these movements are made by muscles. You have more than 600 muscles spread throughout your body. Every bend, stretch, twist and turn you make depends on them. You use about 200 muscles each time you take a step, and many more when you jump.

*Your brain sends messages to your muscles and makes them move.*

*The largest muscle in your body is the gluteus maximus muscle in your thigh and bottom.*

*If you stand on tiptoe, you can see your calf muscles in the back of your leg.*

*Before you begin to make any strenuous movements you should always warm up your muscles by doing gentle loosening-up and stretching exercises.*

**Muscle Food**

To keep your muscles working properly you need a diet that includes protein. Foods that are full of protein include eggs, cheese and dried beans.

Biceps contracts

Triceps relaxes

Biceps relaxes

Up

Down

Triceps contracts

**Arm Bend**

Muscles are attached to bones and make them move. But they can only pull, they cannot push – which is why they always work in pairs. In your arm, the biceps and triceps muscles work together to move it up and down. When the biceps pulls, or contracts, it gets shorter and fatter and bends the arm. As the biceps pulls, the triceps muscle relaxes.

**Holding Hands**
The muscles in your hands allow you to make delicate, accurate or powerful movements. Your flexible fingers have many small muscles which are useful for precise jobs. Your fingers and thumb work together to let you grasp things tightly. Your hands are strong enough to support you if you hang from a bar.

**Cheeky!**
Your tongue is a group of strong muscles which help you to eat and speak – and also to lick your lips . . .

or your chin . . .

or your nose . . .

or your cheek!

*The longest muscle in your body is the sartorius muscle in the upper leg.*

*Some of your arm muscles are joined on to bones in your back. This strong anchor enables you to pick up heavier things.*

*It takes about 15 muscles to smile!*

*You learnt how to control your bladder muscles as you grew older.*

*The muscles in your intestines are pushing food along all the time.*

*Tendons are the tough cords that join the muscle firmly to the bone. You can feel one of them, called the Achilles tendon, in the back of your ankle.*

241

# SKELETON

Without a frame to support your body you would collapse, lose your shape and be unable to move. Your body's frame is called a skeleton. It gives your body strength and it protects the soft parts inside. Your skeleton is made up of more than 200 bones. They are light enough to allow you to move about easily and they have joints so that you can bend your body to do many things.

*You have twelve pairs of ribs. They are all joined to a row of bones in your back called your spine.*

*From the side, your spine looks curved, like the letter S. It helps you to stand up straight.*

*Ulna*

*Femur*

**Yes and No Bones**
The bones of your spine are called vertebrae. The top two vertebrae, the atlas and axis, fit together to allow your head to nod and to move from side to side.

Atlas

Axis

*Your nose is not made of bone but of rubbery material called cartilage. If you look at a skeleton you will not see a nose bone, only a nose hole.*

*Radius*

*Fibula*

*Tibia*

*Your ankle is a joint. It is made up of bones in the foot and the ends of the leg bones, the tibia and fibula.*

## A Tall Order
Your bones keep growing until you are in your early 20's. You cannot change your height – it is decided in your genes and passed on from your parents. But you are about one centimetre shorter in the evening than you are in the morning! This is because the pads of cartilage in your spine get squashed as you walk about all day.

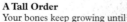

## Soft Centre

Some animals, such as this crab, do not have a skeleton inside them. Instead, they have a hard outer covering, called an exoskeleton.

## Inside Information

Your bones are all hidden inside your body. So if doctors want to look at them, they have to take special photographs, called X rays. The X-ray camera can see straight through your skin and show what the bones look like. On this X ray of a hand, you can see that the bone connected to the little finger is broken.

*Your hip joint is where the end of the thigh bone, or femur, fits into a socket in your pelvis. This joint helps you to bend your body almost in half.*

*Bones give muscles a place to hang on to, but without these muscles, the bones would not be able to move. Muscle power is transferred to the bones along strong bands called tendons.*

*Your basin-shaped pelvis supports the upper half of your body and also protects soft parts, such as your bladder.*

*Your spine can only curve gently. If it bent any further it would damage your spinal cord – the nerve cable that carries messages to and from your brain.*

*Skull*

*Your arm can only bend at the elbow.*

*The muscles that control the thumb and fingers begin here. They are attached to two arm bones called the radius and ulna.*

# BONES

Your bones are hard and strong. They are not solid though, so they are not as heavy as you would think. In fact, they only make up 14 per cent of your total body weight – they are lighter than your muscles. Bones are not dead and dry – they are living, and can repair themselves if they break. Your body is made up of lots of bones all working together and linked by joints. If you had no knee joints, you would have to walk with stiff legs.

## What's Inside a Bone?

The outer part of all your bones is hard and tough but the inside of many of them is spongy. These lightweight, soft centres are criss-crossed by small struts which make your bones strong, but not too heavy. This idea of strength without weight is copied in buildings such as the Eiffel Tower.

*Criss-cross struts*

*The spongy inner bone looks like a honeycomb.*

*Blood vessels take oxygen and food to bone cells.*

*Some bones are filled with jelly-like marrow. Red blood cells are made in the bone marrow.*

*Your two feet contain one quarter of the bones in your whole body!*

*Your neck is much shorter than a giraffe's, but it has the same number of vertebrae!*

*The tiny tail bones at the end of your spine, called the coccyx, protect your spinal cord.*

### Baby Bones

Newborn babies have soft bones. Their bones are mostly made of cartilage, a tough, rubbery material that gradually becomes hard. In this drawing of a child's hand you can see the areas of cartilage where, later, bones will grow.

Cartilage

*The bones in your hand are all linked together by muscles, tendons and ligaments.*

*There are 27 small bones in your hand.*

*Bones fit together like a jigsaw puzzle.*

### Bone Work

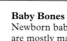

You have three kinds of bone – long bones like those in your legs, short bones such as those in your hand and spine, and flat bones like your shoulder and skull. Bones are linked by different kinds of joints, which allow them to move in different ways.

*Your thumb is special. It has a saddle joint in it which allows you to move your thumb in two directions.*

*You have flat gliding joints in your foot.*

*Your kneecap, or patella, protects your knee.*

*The shoulder has a ball-and-socket joint. The round end of one bone fits into a cup-shaped hole in the other. Your shoulder can move in a complete circle.*

*Your knee joint, like your elbow, is a hinge joint. The end of one bone fits into a sort of hollow in the other. This kind of joint will only bend in one direction.*

# WHERE DO I COME FROM?

You began your life as an egg, which was only about the size of this full stop. This tiny fertilized egg grew for about nine months inside your mother before you were born. While a baby is growing, it relies on the mother for everything and although a baby cannot do very much when it is first born, already it is a complete and very special person.

## The Beginning

Everyone is made of billions of living units, called cells. A baby starts when an egg cell from a woman and a sperm cell from a man join together to make one new cell. For the egg and sperm to meet, the man and woman must have sexual intercourse. This is sometimes called making love because the man and woman treat each other lovingly. The man's penis gets firm and he puts it into the woman's vagina. The penis releases a mixture called semen, which has sperm in it, to join the egg.

Egg tube

Egg

Ovary

Uterus

Vagina

Bladder

Penis

Testes make sperm

*The fertilized egg grows and divides into two.*

*It divides into four, eight, sixteen, and so on . . .*

*Sperm are like tiny tadpoles with long tails. They swim to the tube where the egg is waiting. One sperm may then fertilize the egg.*

*While it is dividing it is travelling to the womb, or uterus.*

*After about eight weeks the group of cells starts to look more like a baby.*

*The fingers, toes and face are formed.*

*After nine days the egg attaches itself to the wall of the uterus.*

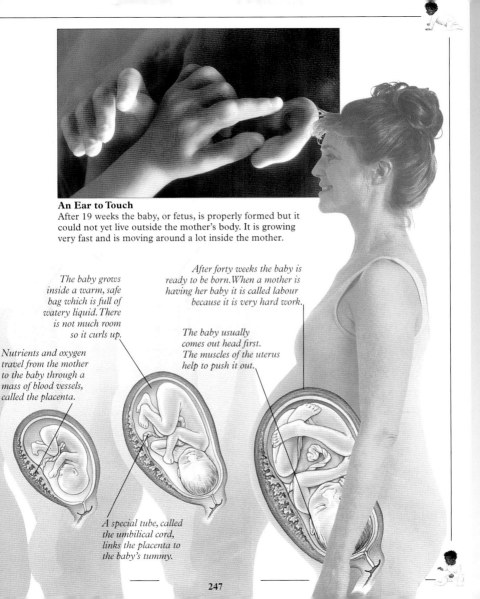

**An Ear to Touch**

After 19 weeks the baby, or fetus, is properly formed but it could not yet live outside the mother's body. It is growing very fast and is moving around a lot inside the mother.

*The baby grows inside a warm, safe bag which is full of watery liquid. There is not much room so it curls up.*

*After forty weeks the baby is ready to be born. When a mother is having her baby it is called labour because it is very hard work.*

*Nutrients and oxygen travel from the mother to the baby through a mass of blood vessels, called the placenta.*

*The baby usually comes out head first. The muscles of the uterus help to push it out.*

*A special tube, called the umbilical cord, links the placenta to the baby's tummy.*

# CHAPTER 3

# OUR WORLD

Early people hunted for food only when they were hungry. Later, they learned to farm, growing crops and keeping animals so they had a more regular supply of food. Today, most of the food in shops and supermarkets still comes from farms – meat and dairy products, grains and rice, fruit and vegetables. However, machines now do most of the work, and special chemicals kill pests and help crops to grow.

As their lives became more settled, our ancestors formed into communities, and had more time to enjoy themselves. The simple entertainments of singing, dancing and drawing branched out over time into plays, and, much later, films and television.

Today, whether they live on high mountains, dry deserts, or swampy marshlands, all men and women have to feed, clothe and house themselves. But from country to country, people do these things in an enormous variety of ways.

**People in the Past
Arts and Entertainment
Food and Farming
People and Places**

# PEOPLE IN THE PAST

The lives of men and women who lived a long time ago were very different from ours. The first people made their homes in caves and had to kill their food or find it growing wild. For a long time, no one could read or write, so information and stories had to be learned by heart so they could be passed on.

Changes in the way people lived came gradually, when travellers – traders, or soldiers who went to war in foreign lands – took new ways of doing things, new foods, or new materials from one place to another. Sometimes, changes were particularly important, like the invention of the wheel or the printing press. These changes tended to spread quickly, and alter everyday life completely.

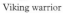
Viking warrior

18th-century gold doubloons

Ancient Peruvian pot

Pottery beaker
c2200 BCE

19th-century
Russian
cossack
pistol

17th-century samurai sword

Illuminated manuscript

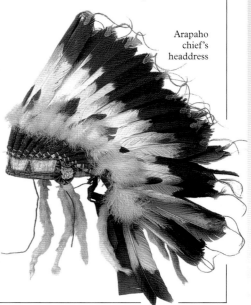

Arapaho
chief's
headdress

Egyptian wall painting c1400 BCE

Ancient
Egyptian
reed pens

Beaded
Blackfoot
moccasins

# HUNTERS AND GATHERERS

Horse

The earliest people lived by hunting and gathering to find their food – meat, fish, vegetables and fruit. They moved with the seasons, sheltering in caves or tents. The animals they hunted gave them food to eat, fat to fuel lamps, skins to make tents and clothes, and bones to make weapons, tent supports, jewellery and playthings.

Some European hunter-gatherers, who lived 16,000 years ago, painted animal pictures in caves. We don't know exactly why they did this but cave painting may have been part of their religion or a kind of magic.

**Making Flint Tools**

Flint was a stone that was easy to work and could be given a sharp edge. The hunter-gatherers used it to make tools and weapons. A pebble or bone hammer was used to strike long flakes of flint from the main stone. The flakes were shaped and then the edges were chipped to make them razor sharp.

*The mammoth was like a modern-day elephant, but covered in fur. It was hunted for its meat, skin and tusks.*

An axe with a flint blade

A spear with a bone tip

## Animal Magic
Beautiful pictures of the animals hunted by these people were painted on the walls and ceilings of caves in southwest France and in parts of northern Spain.

Bison

Reindeer

*The hunters hurled heavy stones at their prey.*

*The spears used for hunting were often made from a flint or bone arrowhead tied onto a wooden shaft.*

*The hunters wore clothes made from animal skins.*

## Unusual Decoration
Teeth and bones from animals were made into pieces of jewellery, such as this necklace.

## First Fashion
Animal skins were used to make clothes. First the skins were pegged out and then scraped to clean them and make them soft. Next the skins were cut to shape. The pieces were sewn together using needles made from animal bone and long, thin strips of hide.

Skin scrapers

A thong made from animal hide

A knife used to cut animal hide

# THE EARLY FARMERS

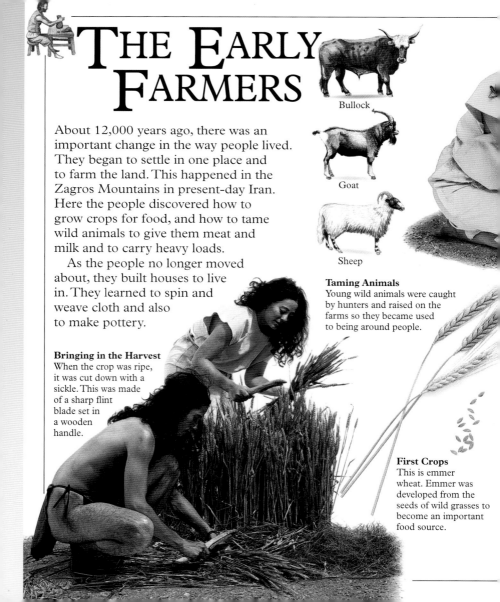

Bullock

Goat

Sheep

About 12,000 years ago, there was an important change in the way people lived. They began to settle in one place and to farm the land. This happened in the Zagros Mountains in present-day Iran. Here the people discovered how to grow crops for food, and how to tame wild animals to give them meat and milk and to carry heavy loads.

As the people no longer moved about, they built houses to live in. They learned to spin and weave cloth and also to make pottery.

**Taming Animals**
Young wild animals were caught by hunters and raised on the farms so they became used to being around people.

**Bringing in the Harvest**
When the crop was ripe, it was cut down with a sickle. This was made of a sharp flint blade set in a wooden handle.

**First Crops**
This is emmer wheat. Emmer was developed from the seeds of wild grasses to become an important food source.

*Before it is ground, this ear of corn will be beaten to separate the grains from the husk.*

**Coiling Clay**
This girl is making a pot by coiling long, thin rolls of clay on top of a flat clay base. She is making the pot in the same way the first potters did, 9,000 years ago.

*The flour would be mixed with water and made into round, flat loaves.*

*The grain was ground between two heavy stones and made into flour.*

**From Farm to Town**
Farms attracted people. As they grew larger, villages and towns were formed. The first known town, Çatal Hüyük, was built in Turkey about 9,000 years ago.

*The walls of the houses were made of mud. Because of this, the houses were not very strong and could only have a few windows.*

*The roofs were made of branches, reeds and straw covered in mud.*

*The houses touched each other and there were no streets.*

*People got into their houses by climbing a ladder and going through a hole in the roof.*

# THE SUMERIANS

About 7,000 years ago, farmers began to move into an area of land between the Tigris and Euphrates rivers. This fertile land was called Mesopotamia, in what is now Iraq. In the south of Mesopotamia was the land of Sumer. The Sumerians were very inventive. They developed the first form of writing and recording numbers, and invented the wheel and the plough.

The Sumerians grew bumper crops of cereals, which they traded for things they needed: wood, building stone or metals. Wheeled carts and their skills in writing and using numbers helped them develop long-distance trade.

*A merchant makes a record of the goods he has sold.*

**How Writing Began**
The Sumerians drew pictures on soft clay with a pointed reed. The pictures were drawn downwards in lines, from the right-hand side.

Fish

Bird

Barley

Ox

Later, they started to write across the tablet, from left to right. The reed tip became wedge shaped, as did the marks it made.

The signs were then joined together to build up words and sentences.

In time, the picture signs changed so much that the original objects were hard to recognize. This writing is called cuneiform, which means 'wedge shaped'.

**It's a Deal**
Instead of writing their names, the Sumerian traders used a seal to sign their contracts.

**Flooded Fields**
Mesopotamia was watered by the Tigris and Euphrates, which flooded in the spring. The farmers dug out basins and canals so the river water could be stored and used to water fields away from the river. Because of this, land was very fertile and harvests were good.

*Wood was imported from Syria and the Lebanon.*

*Wheeled carts were able to carry heavy objects over long distances.*

*Pots were used to store grain and oil.*

*Crosspiece*

*Spokes*

**Tilling the Soil**
The first ploughs were made of wood. Later, the blade was made of bronze. Despite the flooding from the rivers, Sumer was baked hard in hot weather. The plough made it possible to break up the hard-to-work soil.

**Revolutionary Invention**
The first wheels were made of planks of solid wood held together with crosspieces.

They were clumsy and heavy. In time, lighter wheels were made. These had many spokes.

# THE EGYPTIANS

The Egyptians believed that when they died they went on to another, everlasting, life. To live happily in the

afterlife, they needed their earthly bodies and great care was taken to ensure that they arrived in style. The dead bodies were preserved in a special way called mummification.

To mummify a body took a long time, as much as 70 days. First, parts of the body were taken out and put in tightly sealed jars. Next, the body was dried out by covering it with natron, a white powder like salt. It was left for 40 days, rubbed with sweet-smelling oils and then covered in molten resin. Finally, the body was wrapped in linen to make a neat parcel.

**Well Kept**
This is how the mummy of King Seti I looks underneath all his bandages. He was buried at Thebes over three thousand years ago. Despite his age, you can still see his face very clearly.

*A picture of the dead person is painted on the mummy case or coffin.*

*On this coffin, the arms are shown crossed over the chest.*

*The coffin is made to follow the shape of the body inside.*

*These little drawings are called hieroglyphs. Each picture means a word or sign in the ancient Egyptian language.*

**Royal Tombs**
Egyptian kings, called pharaohs, were buried in tombs known as pyramids.

## Creatures Great and Small

The Egyptians believed in many different gods and goddesses, some of which took the form of animals. They mummified these creatures, as well as people. When treated, they made some odd shapes.

Mummified crocodile

Mummified cow

Mummified cat

*Red straps painted on the coffin show that the mummy was a priestess.*

*The lid of the coffin is decorated with symbols of the gods. These are the wings of the sky goddess, Nut.*

*This coffin is made of wood. Early ones were made of clay or woven out of reeds like a basket.*

### All Wrapped Up

All mummies were wrapped up tightly in lots of material. As much as 375 square metres of linen might be needed to wrap up a single mummy.

*The hieroglyphs may have been spells to help the priestess on her journey to the next life.*

*Brightly coloured figures and symbols are painted on the inside of the coffin.*

*This mummy case may have been one of a nest of coffins, each fitting inside the next like a set of Russian dolls.*

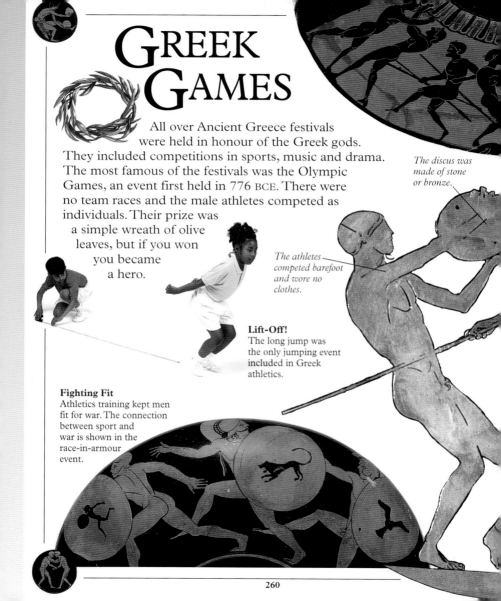

# GREEK GAMES

All over Ancient Greece festivals were held in honour of the Greek gods. They included competitions in sports, music and drama. The most famous of the festivals was the Olympic Games, an event first held in 776 BCE. There were no team races and the male athletes competed as individuals. Their prize was a simple wreath of olive leaves, but if you won you became a hero.

*The discus was made of stone or bronze.*

*The athletes competed barefoot and wore no clothes.*

**Lift-Off!**
The long jump was the only jumping event included in Greek athletics.

**Fighting Fit**
Athletics training kept men fit for war. The connection between sport and war is shown in the race-in-armour event.

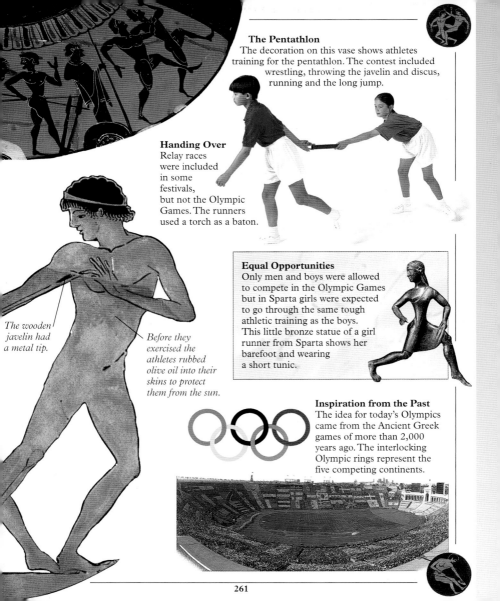

### The Pentathlon
The decoration on this vase shows athletes training for the pentathlon. The contest included wrestling, throwing the javelin and discus, running and the long jump.

### Handing Over
Relay races were included in some festivals, but not the Olympic Games. The runners used a torch as a baton.

*The wooden javelin had a metal tip.*

*Before they exercised the athletes rubbed olive oil into their skins to protect them from the sun.*

### Equal Opportunities
Only men and boys were allowed to compete in the Olympic Games but in Sparta girls were expected to go through the same tough athletic training as the boys. This little bronze statue of a girl runner from Sparta shows her barefoot and wearing a short tunic.

### Inspiration from the Past
The idea for today's Olympics came from the Ancient Greek games of more than 2,000 years ago. The interlocking Olympic rings represent the five competing continents.

# ROMAN LIFE

The Romans planned their towns to include magnificent public buildings such as temples, the town hall, baths and places of entertainment. There were also grand houses for wealthy families. But side by side with these were the tumbledown dwellings where most people lived – overcrowded flats built over shops and workshops. They had no toilets or kitchens and the poor cooked out of doors or bought hot food from stalls. Since the Romans lived, traded and ate in the streets, their towns were noisy places. Traffic was bad, too, with carts and wagons bringing country goods through the busy streets.

**In the Kitchen**
This scene shows what a typical Roman kitchen was like. You would have found it in the town house or villa of a rich family.

**Country Living**
Fine houses, called villas, were built on estates in the countryside.

*Building being built of bricks*

*Wharf*

*Fishing nets drying*

*A wooden bridge over the river*

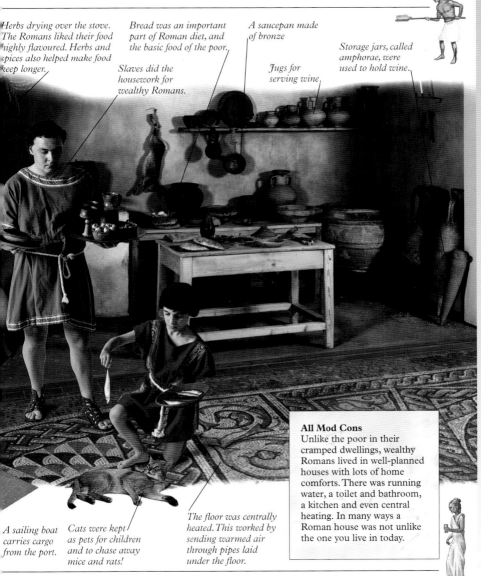

Herbs drying over the stove. The Romans liked their food highly flavoured. Herbs and spices also helped make food keep longer.

Bread was an important part of Roman diet, and the basic food of the poor.

A saucepan made of bronze

Storage jars, called amphorae, were used to hold wine.

Slaves did the housework for wealthy Romans.

Jugs for serving wine

A sailing boat carries cargo from the port.

Cats were kept as pets for children and to chase away mice and rats!

The floor was centrally heated. This worked by sending warmed air through pipes laid under the floor.

**All Mod Cons**
Unlike the poor in their cramped dwellings, wealthy Romans lived in well-planned houses with lots of home comforts. There was running water, a toilet and bathroom, a kitchen and even central heating. In many ways a Roman house was not unlike the one you live in today.

# RAIDERS FROM THE SEA

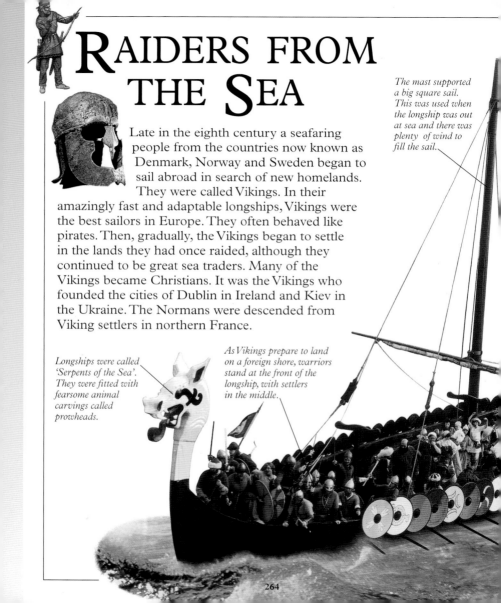

Late in the eighth century a seafaring people from the countries now known as Denmark, Norway and Sweden began to sail abroad in search of new homelands. They were called Vikings. In their amazingly fast and adaptable longships, Vikings were the best sailors in Europe. They often behaved like pirates. Then, gradually, the Vikings began to settle in the lands they had once raided, although they continued to be great sea traders. Many of the Vikings became Christians. It was the Vikings who founded the cities of Dublin in Ireland and Kiev in the Ukraine. The Normans were descended from Viking settlers in northern France.

*The mast supported a big square sail. This was used when the longship was out at sea and there was plenty of wind to fill the sail.*

*Longships were called 'Serpents of the Sea'. They were fitted with fearsome animal carvings called prowheads.*

*As Vikings prepare to land on a foreign shore, warriors stand at the front of the longship, with settlers in the middle.*

## Strange Stones

The Vikings set up stones, called runestones. They were carved with many beautiful patterns and with letters developed by the Vikings called runes.

*Runes*

## Where the Vikings Went

The Vikings roamed great distances. Merchants travelled to Russia, Persia and around the Mediterranean Sea. They traded such northern things as furs and walrus tusks for southern things such as silk and silver. Explorers sailed to Europe, Iceland, Greenland and to Newfoundland in North America. They called this Vinland.

*Longships were made of overlapping planks of wood. They were very light and could be carried overland for short distances to get from one river to another.*

## Fascinating Tales

Story telling was very popular. These stories, or sagas, were long poems telling of brave deeds, journeys to strange lands and victories in battle. When people couldn't read or write, they remembered stories by learning them off by heart.

In the map legend:
Land and river routes
Sea routes
Possible sea routes
Homeland
Viking settlements

# THE CRUSADES

The city of Jerusalem and the Holy Land of Palestine (now Israel and Jordan) are special to people of three faiths – Jews, Muslims and Christians. Nine hundred years ago several wars were fought in the Middle East for control of Jerusalem. Muslims seized the city and refused to allow in Christians. As a result, European Christians – called crusaders from the Spanish word *cruzada*, meaning marked with a cross – set out to take Jerusalem.

After four years of struggle, the crusaders captured Jerusalem in 1099 and held it for nearly one hundred years. Then it was recaptured by a great Muslim leader called Saladin. More crusades followed, but none was successful. However, the returning crusaders brought many new objects and ideas back to Europe.

*This crusader knight is wearing armour called chain mail.*

*Over his armour, the knight is wearing a loose white coat with a cross on it – the sign of a crusader.*

*The leg-pieces are made of chain mail.*

**Stronghold**
The crusaders built strong castles in the Arab style to defend the land they had captured. This is Krak des Chevaliers in Syria.

## Body Beautiful

The crusaders took back to Europe new customs that they learned in the Middle East. Cosmetics such as rouge to redden the cheeks and henna to colour hair became common for women. Glass mirrors replaced polished metal discs. Perfumes to scent clothes and the body were used. Being clean became popular!

Roman numerals
I   II  III  IV  V  VI  VII  VIII  IX
Arabic numerals
0 1 2 3 4 5 6 7 8 9

### One, Two, Three . . .
The Muslims developed a series of numbers, called Arabic numerals, which were much easier to use than those of the old Roman system. They are used today throughout the world.

### Bookworms
Arab learning was more advanced than that of the crusaders. They had lots of books and libraries at a time when there were very few in Europe. The crusaders took many books back with them.

*This puppet of a Muslim Arab is fighting a Christian knight. For centuries, puppets have been used to act out folk tales, religious stories and famous scenes from history.*

### Healing Arts
Muslim doctors were very good surgeons and were skilled in using plants and herbs to make medicines. They used opium and myrrh to ease pain when people were having operations.

*A Muslim foot soldier usually carried a round shield for protection. It may have been made of wood or of layers of hardened leather sewn together.*

### Musical Instruments
The Muslims invented a musical instrument called the al'ud, which was called the lute in Europe. The modern guitar was developed from this instrument.

### Great Inventors
The Muslims made fine scientific instruments like this astrolabe. It used the positions of the stars and planets to show travellers which way to go in the empty deserts.

*Boots made of leather or felt were the most common footwear for a Muslim soldier.*

# MARCO POLO

In 1271 a merchant called Marco Polo and his family set off from Venice on an extraordinary journey to China. They travelled along the Silk Road, an important trading route between Europe and the Far East. Merchants had been using the route for more than 1,700 years before the Polos, but they were the first to travel its whole length. In an age when there were no planes, trains, coaches or cars, they crossed thousands of kilometres of mountains, deserts and plains on foot, horseback and even on camels. Their journey to China took them over three years. The Silk Road could be very dangerous and the traders were sometimes attacked by bandits. Because of this threat, they travelled together in groups.

**Making a Swap**
The Venetian merchants exchanged jewels, silver and gold for goods from the East that were highly valued in Europe. These included spices, silks, porcelain or 'China' and fine carpets.

**Wealthy Traders**
Venice was the most important port in Europe. Its merchants travelled by sea and land to bring back goods from the East to sell to other towns in Europe.

*Camels were used by merchants when crossing the desert regions of central Asia. Unlike horses, they were able to travel long distances without needing water.*

*Besides the barren deserts, the merchants travelling on the Silk Road had to climb over fearsome mountain ranges and cross flooded rivers.*

Pepper

Cloves

Cinnamon

Mace   Nutmeg

Silk tunic

*In the desert, travellers had to take all their own food and water with them.*

*A camel train was part of a caravan, a large group of people who travelled together.*

Persian carpet

Porcelain jar

*The camel driver is covered from head to foot in heavy clothing to protect him from the harsh winds of the desert.*

### In the Court of Kublai Khan
When the Polos arrived in China they found it under the control of the Mongol emperor Kublai Khan. Marco Polo stayed at the Mongol court for 17 years and became a trusted advisor to Kublai Khan.

# THE RENAISSANCE

In the 15th century, Europe was bursting with new ideas about art, learning and religion. Many of the people who could read and write began to ask questions and to do experiments for themselves rather than follow what their rulers and priests told them to think. They rediscovered many of the ideas that the Greeks and Romans had about life and the world. As a result this period became known as the 'Renaissance', a French word meaning rebirth. The Renaissance started in the cities of northern and central Italy but gradually spread all over Europe.

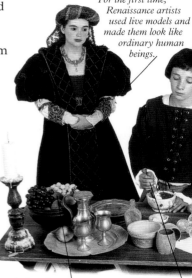

*Before the Renaissance, most paintings showed mythical scenes or Bible characters, and everything in them looked perfect.*

*For the first time, Renaissance artists used live models and made them look like ordinary human beings.*

*A letter of type used in the printing press*

### The Printed Word
Before the printing press was invented by Johannes Gutenberg, books had to be copied by hand. Only the rich could afford them.

*During the Renaissance, everyday objects appeared in paintings for the first time.*

*The apprentice is grinding colours to make paints for his master. He will mix the powder with oil to produce oil paints.*

### The Gutenberg Bible
These pages come from one of the three books that made up the Gutenberg Bible. It was printed in the 1450s and was much admired for its quality.

*In the 15th century, artists began to paint on canvas using oil paints. Before then they had mainly used water-based paints.*

*Artists were no longer unknown craftsmen, and their names became famous throughout Europe during the Renaissance.*

### The Quest for Knowledge

During the Renaissance, scholars and scientists began doing experiments and inventing things to find out more about the world they lived in.

With the invention of the telescope, faraway planets could be seen in detail for the first time.

The artist Leonardo da Vinci was interested in the workings of the human body. This is one of his drawings.

This model was made from a design by Leonardo, showing an early form of tank.

Leonardo's creative imagination led him to produce designs for a flying machine.

# FOOD FROM THE NEW WORLD

From 1492 onwards, European explorers sailed across the Atlantic to what they called the New World of North, Central and South America. There they discovered a treasure trove of gold and silver. But they found other treasures, too. These were foods that grew only in the New World, such as sweetcorn (sometimes called maize) and potatoes, and plants that could be made into medicines. In fact, you may be surprised to find out how many of the foods you eat come from the New Word. Every time you eat a tomato or some mashed potato or have chocolate for a treat, just think, you owe them to the people of the Americas.

Sunflower

Cocoa

**A World of Golden Treasure**

The Indian peoples of America had vast quantities of gold which they used to make into jewellery. The Europeans plundered most of this treasure.

*Maize was eaten boiled, roasted or ground into flour. The explorer Christopher Columbus took it back to Europe when he returned from his voyages.*

*This is cornmeal, made out of ground maize. It was used to make bread-like foods.*

Peanut

**Native American Plants**
These include cocoa (for chocolate), sunflowers (to give us oil to cook with) and peanuts.

## Healing Plants

When the explorers reached the Americas, they found skilled healers among the people living there. These healers used thousands of plants to make medicines. Their remedies were used to cure many illnesses, including stomach pains, headaches, coughs and fevers. Many of these plants are still used today to make medicines.

*Cinchona leaf*

Quinine is used to prevent an illness called malaria. It is made from the bark of the cinchona tree.

*Cinchona bark*

*Quinine tablets*

*'Pyne fruit' or pineapple, was one of the new fruits found by the explorers. Pineapples were also used to make wine.*

*Black beans*

*Lots of different beans came from Mexico. These are red beans.*

*These small, hot peppers are chillies. They were used to flavour the bowls of maize porridge that the Mexicans ate for breakfast.*

*Sweet potatoes*

*Tomatoes started off as weeds growing in the maize fields. In time, different kinds were grown to eat. The first ones to reach Europe were probably yellow.*

*Potatoes were first grown in the Andes Mountains. They were loaded aboard the treasure ships as food for the sailors.*

*Avocados look like pears with rough, tough skins. They were first grown in Central America.*

# THE LIFE OF THE SAMURAI

For about seven hundred years the Samurai were the honoured knights of Japan. Fierce fighters, they had a tough training, becoming experts in fencing, wrestling, archery and acrobatics, and they had a special code of behaviour. The word 'samurai' means 'one who serves' and any Samurai worthy of the name was absolutely loyal to his lord, ready to obey any command without question.

But although the Samurai were professional fighters, away from battle they were not violent men. The Samurai believed in Zen Buddhism, a religion that taught respect for all living things. The Samurai were also taught to love art and learning, taking pride in their skill at painting, writing poetry and even flower-arranging.

*The large horned helmet was mean to terrify enemies as much as to protect its wearer.*

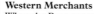

**Western Merchants**
When the Portuguese arrived in Japan in 1543, they brought guns with them. The guns changed the nature of warfare in the country completely.

## Women and Ladies

Just as the Samurai obeyed his lord, so the women of his own family had to obey him. Graceful, musical and artistic, these Samurai ladies were expected to make homes for their lords and masters.

By contrast, the peasant women who laboured in the fields had to work as hard as beasts of burden.

*A Samurai's most important weapons were his two razor-sharp swords, one long, the other short. At birth every Samurai boy was presented with a sword, which he kept for life.*

*A Samurai's armour consisted of six main pieces: the helmet, the face mask, the breast plate, the sleeves, the shin guards and the loin guard.*

## Knowing Their Place

Life in Samurai Japan was strictly organized. From birth, everybody had a fixed place in society. Samurai families belonged to the upper classes.

The god-like Emperor was the official ruler, but the Shogun, his chief general, was really the most powerful person in Japan.

Shogun

Daimyo

The Daimyo were the nobles of Japan, and they were supported by Samurai warriors. They preferred to have nothing to do with money or the buying and selling of goods.

Samurai

Merchants and traders were not given much respect, in spite of their wealth.

Merchants

Lowest of the low were the peasants. They worked on the farms of the Daimyo and were treated like slaves.

Peasant

# NEWCOMERS TO A NEW LAND

The Europeans who began arriving in North America in the beginning of the 17th century were traders and settlers rather than soldier-conquerors. At first the contact between them and the people already living there, whom they called Indians, was friendly. The Native Americans showed the newcomers how to hunt, fish and farm in a land of plenty. In return for their help and animal furs, the Native Americans were given objects such as knives, needles, fish hooks and cloth. But before long, the settlers were taking more and more land for themselves, and trying to change the ways of the Indians.

*Warm furs from the forest animals of North America were taken back to Europe and sold for high prices.*

*European weapons, tools and machines completely changed hunting and warfare for the Indians.*

*European cloth was prized for its bright colours and silkiness.*

Creek
(Southeast)

Iroquois
(Northeast)

Tlingit
(Pacific Northwest)

Hidatsa
(Plains)

Hopi
(Southwest)

Sauk
(Great Lakes)

Paiute
(Great Basin)

*The settlers gave the
Indians silk thread
and glass beads.
The Indians used
feathers and animal
teeth to decorate
themselves.*

## Warriors and Hunters

The work that men and women
did varied from tribe to tribe, but
usually the men were the hunters
and warriors, while the women were
the farmers and home-keepers.
Most Indians wore their hair long
and they enjoyed decorating their
bodies and clothes.

## Tepees, Longhouses and Pueblos

There was great variety in the lives
of the Native American peoples.
How they lived – their clothes,
their food, their religious beliefs –
depended on the land and the
weather. Some of the differences
between the tribes are shown
by their homes.

*For comfort
and protection
against ants, snakes
and other dangers, the
Indians wore slipper-
like leather shoes called
moccasins.*

*veetcorn, squash and
mpkins were among
e exotic American foods
that the European
settlers tasted for
the first time.*

*Tlingit cedar-
plank house*

*Plains Indian
animal-skin tepee*

*Sauk mat-covered
dome lodge*

*Paiute brush
and reed
encampment*

*Iroquois
wooden
longhouse*

*Hopi stone
and sun-baked
mudbrick pueblo*

*Creek
storehouse*

# THE ASHANTI KINGDOM

*Ghana*

The Ashanti kingdom flourished for 200 years after its emergence in the 17th century, in what is now Ghana in West Africa. The Ashanti were a highly organized people: the king had his own civil service, which carried out his commands throughout the country. The Ashanti were also fine warriors and much of their wealth was based on selling slaves from the prisoners they captured in battle. They had vast quantities of gold which was used to make jewellery and as decoration for musical instruments and weapons. Ashanti goldsmiths were highly skilled in their craft. They used a special method to cast the metal, called the lost-wax technique.

*The item to be cast in gold was modelled in melted beeswax.*

*The wax was made into thin sheets. These were cut into strips, which were used to make the model.*

*Clay was moulded around the model and a hole made in the clay. As the mould was baked, the wax melted and poured out through the hole. Molten gold was then poured into the space.*

*When the metal had cooled and hardened, the mould was smashed open. The gold object was taken out and cleaned up.*

**Beautifully Made**
These royal sandals have flowers of gold sewn onto them.

*Ashanti goldsmiths worked gold into all kinds of objects. The handle of this sword was covered in a fine sheet of gold.*

278

## Hub of the Kingdom
Kumasi, the capital, was a teeming, bustling city. Many sumptuous parades and celebrations were held there.

Kente cloth

## Fine Cloth
The Ashanti were experts at making beautiful cloth. One, known as kente, was made from cotton woven into narrow strips that were then sewn together. Adrinka was another sort of cloth. Large pieces of material were printed using stamps dipped in dyes. Patterns were built up in blocks or panels.

## Printing Blocks
The stamps used to print cloth were made out of the shell-like fruits of calabash trees.

*Elephant symbols were used in Ashanti jewellery to show the power of the wearer.*

## Dripping with Gold
The Ashanti wore rings on their fingers as well as gold bracelets on their wrists and at their knees.

# CATHERINE THE GREAT

Catherine II, Empress of Russia during the 18th century, was called 'Great' because she worked hard as ruler of her vast empire. She asked the advice of many of the major thinkers in Europe and because she was interested in education she started the Russian school system.

Catherine also loved clothes and spectacular entertainments, and so did her nobles. Under her rule they became even more powerful than they had been before. They were the owners of land and of people. These people were known as serfs and, like slaves, they had to do whatever their masters wanted. Serfs could be bought and sold by their masters.

**Miserable Existence**
Nine out of ten Russians were serfs and life for them was grim. Often, they lived in poor log huts with only one room for an entire family.

*Catherine's palaces and the homes of the nobles were filled with furniture, ornaments, carpets and other luxuries in the latest fashions.*

## The Hermitage
Catherine built a Winter Palace in St. Petersburg. She called it the Hermitage, because it allowed her to shut herself and her court away like hermits. Today it is a famous museum.

*During court entertainments the wearing of masks became popular.*

*The court entertainments were dazzling to look at, with gorgeous costumes.*

*The playing of music was encouraged at court. Catherine invited foreign musicians to Russia to perform their work.*

*The nobles dressed in clothes that came from fashionable France. They were the finest clothes money could buy.*

## Revolt of the Serfs
In 1771 a Cossack soldier called Emilian Pugachev set himself up as a rival emperor to Catherine. The Cossacks were a warlike people who lived in southern Russia. Thousands of serfs who wanted to get rid of the nobles joined in their revolt.

The number of rebels under Pugachev grew and in 1773 they swarmed across Russia, destroying the city of Kazan. Catherine ordered her army to attack the rebels and in July 1774 the serfs were defeated. Pugachev was captured, brought to Moscow and executed. The revolt was over.

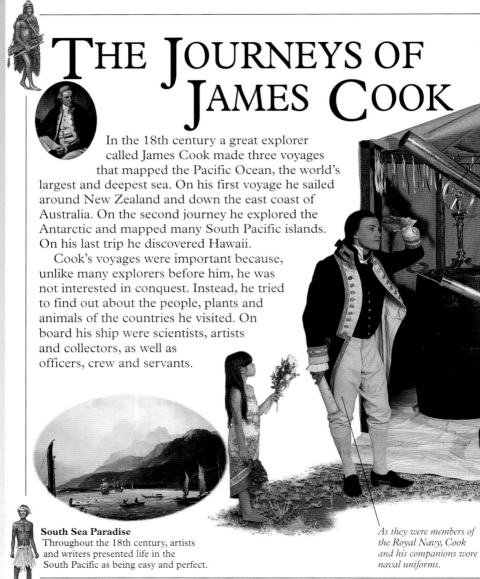

# THE JOURNEYS OF JAMES COOK

In the 18th century a great explorer called James Cook made three voyages that mapped the Pacific Ocean, the world's largest and deepest sea. On his first voyage he sailed around New Zealand and down the east coast of Australia. On the second journey he explored the Antarctic and mapped many South Pacific islands. On his last trip he discovered Hawaii.

Cook's voyages were important because, unlike many explorers before him, he was not interested in conquest. Instead, he tried to find out about the people, plants and animals of the countries he visited. On board his ship were scientists, artists and collectors, as well as officers, crew and servants.

**South Sea Paradise**
Throughout the 18th century, artists and writers presented life in the South Pacific as being easy and perfect.

*As they were members of the Royal Navy, Cook and his companions wore naval uniforms.*

*The first voyage to the South Seas was made to watch the movement of the planet Venus. The scientists looked through a telescope like this.*

*This very accurate astronomical clock was used for timing the observations of the stars and planets.*

### Art for All

Drawings and paintings made by the artists on Cook's voyages were published. People in Europe could see illustrations of new plants and animals discovered on the explorations.

Erythrina

Hibiscus

Wild cat

*This is a quadrant. It was another means of helping sailors find their way.*

Butterfly fish

Blue-crowned lory

*Artists were taken on the voyages to draw the plants and animals they saw, just as a photographer might take pictures today.*

# REVOLUTION

In the 18th century an important revolution started in France. It happened because the king, Louis XVI, and his nobles held all the power and wealth in the country. He could rule the people as he pleased. The way he chose to do so was unfair. For example, the nobles, who were already rich, paid no taxes while the poor peasants did.

In 1789 the king had nearly run out of money. He wanted to increase taxes. At the same time, food was very scarce because of bad harvests. The ordinary people had had enough and decided that they didn't want to be ruled by the king. Louis was executed and a new government was set up.

*The revolutionaries were against organized religion and many clergymen fled the country.*

*Nobles were thought to be enemies of the revolution. Some were arrested and went to the guillotine.*

*The revolution was supported by people who thought they had been badly treated by their rulers. They included lawyers, traders, small farmers, workers and ordinary soldiers.*

*The nobles made fun of the simple clothes of the revolutionaries. They called them sans-culottes, people without the fine knee-length breeches the nobles wore.*

*Women played an impo[rtant] part in revolutionary e[v]... They led many of the marches.*

### The Guillotine
Anyone who was not loyal to the revolution faced arrest and possible death by guillotine. The guillotine cut off the heads of the victims. It was made of a heavy, sharp blade that fell between two posts. Death by guillotine was very quick. It caused less suffering than other methods of execution.

*Victims of the guillotine rode to the place of execution in open carts, called tumbrels.*

*The revolutionaries wore a red bonnet that looked like a nightcap. It was decorated with a blue and white ribbon.*

### American Revolution
In the 17th century people left Europe to live in America. They were ruled from Britain and were called colonists. Eventually they wanted to rule themselves and fought the British for their independence. The French revolutionaries were encouraged by the American success.

*This painting shows colonists fighting the British in Massachusetts in 1775.*

# RICHES OF INDUSTRY

*Modern photography was invented by the British scientist William Fox Talbot during the 1830s. It soon became popular for people to have their photograph taken.*

One of the biggest changes in the history of the world, the Industrial Revolution, started in Britain in the late 18th century. As the 'Workshop of the World' Britain was the first home of new machines, new types of materials and new ways of making power. This was the age of coal and iron, of gas and electricity, of railways and factories.

Within 50 years this series of mighty inventions had dramatically changed the way in which people lived. Railways and steamships made it possible to travel quickly from place to place. Instead of living in the country, many more people lived in towns and cities. There they worked in factories where machines made things in vast numbers, quickly and cheaply.

**Grim Conditions**
The big industrial cities were very smoky and many people were crammed together in badly built houses.

*The railways and cheaper paper provided many more readers with news of events from all over the world.*

*With the arrival of trains, which had to run according to timetables, people began to live their lives by the clock.*

**Iron Foundry**
Abraham Darby replaced charcoal (made from wood) with coke (made from coal) for making a new kind of tough iron.

*The invention of electroplating made it possible to coat iron objects with silver. They looked like solid silver but were far cheaper to make.*

Ironbridge

**Made of Metal**
Engineers soon made use of iron and steel. In 1789 Abraham Darby III built the first iron bridge across the river Severn. The place is now called Ironbridge. The Eiffel Tower was built in France in 1889 and was nearly 300 metres high.

*Vast numbers of machine-made cups and plates were turned out for everyday use.*

Eiffel Tower

*The invention of artificial dyes in the 1850s meant that cloth did not fade when it was washed.*

**The Great Exhibition**
In 1851 the Great Exhibition was opened in London, inside a huge glass building called the Crystal Palace. The Exhibition displayed all the latest industrial developments.

**Factory Life**
The first factories were built to contain the heavy machinery needed to produce cotton cloth. Whole families – even young children – kept the machines going night and day.

# PIONEERS

During the 19th century European settlers travelled across America in search of land to farm. They were called pioneers. Some of them travelled in wagon trains so long that they stretched as far as the eye could see. The wagons were packed tight with provisions – food, tools, ploughs, household goods and even chamber pots. There was room only for small children, the sick and some women to ride in the wagons. Everyone else walked alongside.

Tormented by the heat and dust, or by gales, rain and snow, the pioneers trudged across prairies and climbed over mountains. They lived and slept outdoors and often went short of food and water. The pioneers also faced attacks from Native Americans who resented the Europeans taking their land from them.

*The wagons were pulled by teams of horses, mules or oxen.*

**The Lure of Gold**
Prospectors were people who hunted for gold. They would fill a shallow pan with gravel from a riverbed and wash the stones out of the pan with water. Then they looked for any gold that might have sunk to the bottom.

*When gold was discovered in Australia, America, South Africa and Canada in the 19th century, Europeans flocked to these countries to make their fortune.*

*The wheels at the front were made smaller than those at the back, so that the wagon could be steered more easily.*

**Self Assembly**
When the pioneers came to set up home, they had to build their own houses. Some made them out of logs but others used chunks of dry earth cut from the ground.

**The Great Trek**
In 1835 Dutch settlers in South Africa moved in wagons to new land to escape being ruled by the British. This journey was called the 'Great Trek'. For safety against the black Africans whose land they had entered, the settlers would carefully form their wagons into a circle at night.

*The top was made of canvas held up by a frame of hoops. It helped keep out rain and dust.*

*The hoops were made of strong and flexible hickory wood.*

*The pioneers had to bring all their cooking equipment with them.*

*The wheels were made of wood and the rim was covered in iron. Wheels often broke and held up the wagon train.*

# THE AMERICAN CIVIL WAR

In 1861 a civil war started in America between states in the South who owned slaves and states in the North who thought this wrong. The South tried to break away from the Union to form a separate nation but the North went to war to prevent this. After four years of bitter fighting the North won and the South was forced to return to the Union. But the price paid by both sides was terrible. Some 620,000 soldiers died, over half of them victims of disease, not of battle. When they fell ill or were wounded, their treatment was as likely to kill them as cure them. The field hospitals were filthy and the surgeons often poorly trained.

*If they were lucky, soldiers were given drugs to make them unconscious during surgery. But often they had nothing to ease the pain.*

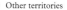

■ Northern states

▨ Confederate states

▢ Border states that fought on the Northern side

▨ Areas with the most slaves

▢ Other territories

**The Confederates**
The soldiers of the South, or Confederacy, were given uniforms of grey coats and caps and blue trousers. When uniforms were in short supply the men wore whatever they could find.

## The Unionists

The soldiers of the North, or Union, wore dark-blue coats or jackets and sky-blue trousers. They had more and better weapons than the troops from the South because most of the factories making weapons were in the North.

*The surgeons who treated the soldiers often worked with dirty hands and clothes spattered with blood.*

## The Slave States

The wealth of the Southern states of America came from plantations producing cotton, sugar and tobacco.

The work on the plantations was carried out by slaves – black Africans who had been captured and shipped from Africa over to America. Their masters could do what they liked with them and they were often ill-treated. Slavery was finally ended in America in 1865.

*Slaves could be bought and sold at market like animals. Often families were split up.*

*Women volunteered to help the wounded. In the North, teams of trained nurses were set up.*

*Most medicines were not very effective, and a few were actually dangerous.*

## Special Kit

With its pliers and saw, this box looks like a tool kit. In fact, it was a surgeon's case used during the American Civil War.

# IN THE SCHOOLROOM

*The blackboard was double-sided. It was on wheels so it could be moved easily.*

Until 1870, children in England did not have to go to school. Children from rich families went to school but poor families could not afford to pay for education. Poor children had to go to work to help their parents. After 1870 the government made school places available to young children for a very small payment. By 1902 education was free and every child aged between five and thirteen had to attend school.

*The globe of the world was used to teach geography to the children.*

At school, children were taught reading, writing, arithmetic and religion. The children sat at their desks, chanting spellings and tables over and over again and copying words onto slates. At other times they did some geography and history, drawing, singing and physical exercise. Discipline was very strict and children were beaten if they made mistakes in their work.

*A wooden hoop used for playing.*

**Playtime**

When they were not in school, children amused themselves with outdoor games like the ones played today – marbles, skipping, hopscotch and football. Hoops were popular too – they were rolled along the ground, thrown in the air or whirled around the body.

*China inkwells in a tray were filled and given out to the older children by a monitor. The children wrote with pen and ink in a special copybook.*

*The ink to fill the inkwells was kept in a special container that looked like a small watering can.*

The window was built high up so that the children could not look out and be distracted from their work.

Teachers often carried a cane with them. If the children were bad they would be smacked.

This is an abacus, or counting frame. Children learned to add up and take away by moving the beads along the wires.

Each child in the class had only one reading book. It contained stories and poems and had to last the whole year.

Young children did their writing on slates, using slate pencils. The slates were cheap and could be used over and over again.

The desks were very simple. The shelf underneath held the children's books.

Pencils were made of a single piece of lead, without a wood casing.

The desks had special holes made in them to hold the inkwells.

## Stitch by Stitch

Samplers were very popular in schools. They consisted of a piece of embroidery designed to show a girl's skill in using different stitches. Girls began to make them at an early age. They were a way of teaching them their letters and their sewing at the same time.

# ARTS AND ENTERTAINMENT

Today we are very lucky because we have lots of interesting and entertaining things to see and do. At one time, though, people had to put all their time and energy into finding food, keeping warm, and protecting themselves from attack. It was not until they solved these problems that they began to look for ways of having fun. The earliest forms of entertainment were drawing pictures and telling stories. Later, men and women made simple music and sometimes danced to it.

Now, machines do most of our work for us, and we have time to create and enjoy exciting plays, films, music and ballets, and amazing photographs, paintings and sculptures.

Recorder      Violin      Trumpet

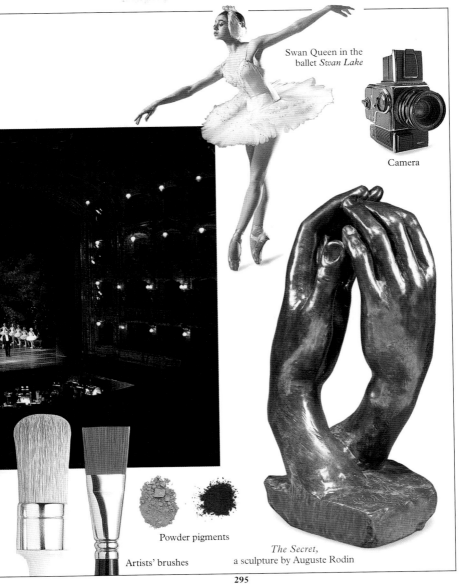

Swan Queen in the ballet *Swan Lake*

Camera

*The Secret,* a sculpture by Auguste Rodin

Powder pigments

Artists' brushes

# THEATRES

People have enjoyed going to the theatre to watch plays for centuries – the first theatres were built by the Greeks about 2,500 years ago. Stone seats were carved into the hillside.

The actors did not need microphones, as sound carried right up to the back row. Until the 17th century, most plays were staged in the open air. But by the 1650s, bare stages had been replaced by elaborate sets that had to be kept inside, so indoor theatres became common. Lights transformed theatres too. Realistic acting began with the invention of limelight – for the first time, players' expressions could be seen.

**Wagons Roll**
In the Middle Ages actors took their shows, called miracle plays, from town to town. These plays were about the battle between Good and Evil.

*The upper gallery was about eight metres above the ground.*

*Stage door*

*The Globe theatre was first built in 1599.*

*More than 2,000 people could crowd in to watch a good play. Only a few could afford to sit in these galleries.*

**Ancient Art**
Noh is an old, traditional type of Japanese theatre. Religious stories and ancient myths are performed on a stage that has very little scenery. The plays, some of which are more than 500 years old, can go on for as long as six hours!

## The Globe Theatre

William Shakespeare, the most famous of all playwrights, acted on the Globe's wooden stage. The theatre was rebuilt and opened again in June 1997.

*Stage*

*The Globe was octagonal.*

*Way in*

## Setting the Scene

Theatres come in all sorts of shapes and sizes. Early ones were open to the air. Most modern stages have roofs so that plays can be staged when it is raining.

*Musicians played on this balcony.*

*When the flag was raised, people knew that a play was going to be performed.*

*There was no scenery on the stage.*

*This model of the Globe theatre has been cut in half to let you see inside.*

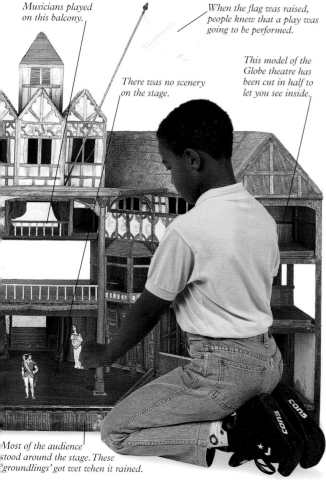

*Most of the audience stood around the stage. These 'groundlings' got wet when it rained.*

Greek theatre
200 BCE

Roman theatre
100 CE

Elizabethan theatre
16th century

'Modern' theatre
19th century

# PLAYS AND PLAYERS

Playwrights write stories, or plays, that are performed on stage by players, called actors and actresses. Molière and Shakespeare both lived more than 300 years ago but their plays, such as *L'Avare* and *Macbeth*, are still popular. Laurence Olivier, one of the last century's most famous actors, starred in *Henry V* by Shakespeare and also in more modern plays, such as *The Entertainer* by John Osborne. Like all good players he could make an audience believe that what they are seeing is real, not just an act.

**Not a Word**
Marcel Marceau is a famous French mime artist – he acts out stories without speaking.

*The actor playing Romeo shows that he likes Juliet by giving her a rose.*

*The players wear costumes like those worn by rich Italians in the past.*

**Happy Ending**
Plays that make people laugh are called comedies. Molière wrote many wonderful plays in the 17th century that are still funny today.

**Sad Ending**
Tragedies are plays with sad endings. *Cat on a Hot Tin Roof* was written by Tennessee Williams and is a famous modern tragedy.

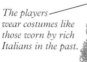

## Setting the Scene

*Romeo and Juliet* is one of Shakespeare's saddest plays. The couple can never be together because their families hate one another.

*These are the first words Romeo ever says to Juliet.*

ROMEO *(to Juliet, touching her hand)*
If I profane with my unworthiest hand
This holy shrine, the gentle sin is this:
My lips, two blushing pilgrims,
    ready stand
To smooth that rough touch with a
    tender kiss.                    95

JULIET
Good pilgrim, you do wrong your hand
    too much,
Which mannerly devotion shows in this;
For saints have hands that pilgrims'
    hands do touch,

*Juliet replies – she is not upset at him holding her hand.*

*This line is not spoken – it tells the actors what to do.*

*There are 145 lines in this scene, or part of the play. This is line 95.*

## Make-up Magic

To make an audience believe what they are seeing, players often change the way they look by using make-up.

Young

*Talcum powder and special white mascara makes brown hair and eyebrows look grey.*

Going grey

*Pale powder takes away the rosy cheeks.*

*Lines are drawn on the face with a special dark pencil.*

Old

*The actress pretends to be shy, yet pleased to receive the rose.*

## Staged in the East

Spectacular, traditional Chinese plays are known as Peking opera in the West. Every action and colour has a special meaning – blue and yellow costumes show that a person is bad tempered and proud.

# MUSIC

Musical sounds can be made with your voice or by playing an instrument. The first instruments were played more than 35,000 years ago – people blew into shells and hollow mammoth bones! Today's instruments are more complicated. The sounds they make can be high or low: this is known as the pitch of the note. The way these sounds are arranged is called the tune. Rhythm is the pattern of long and short notes. A skilful musician can make the same tune sound slow and sleepy or loud and jazzy.

**Beat the Clock?**
A metronome can tick at different speeds. Musicians listen to it to make sure they are playing at the right speed. This is called keeping the beat.

**Stylish Groups**

Jazz band

Pop group

String quartet

Electric drum

**Wired for Sound**
Electronic instruments are actually almost silent! When you twang the steel strings on an electric guitar, they vibrate. This movement is changed into tiny electrical signals by pick-ups beneath the strings. These signals are then increased by an amplifier and finally turned into sounds by a loudspeaker.

Electric guitar

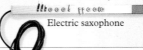
Electric saxophone

*A pick-up*

**Note it Down**
Music is written down in a special language. Instead of words, there are notes. These are the notes for 'Here Comes the Bride'.

*Deeper notes are wrtiien on lower lines or in lower spaces.*

*This number tells you there are four beats in each bar.*

*The way a note looks indicates how long it lasts. Notes like this are the shortest in this time.*

*Notes are named after letters. This one in the second space up is A.*

Bagpipes

You blow here.

*Scotland is famous for bagpipes. They are played by blowing air into a bag and then squeezing the air up through the pipes.*

## A World of Music

Different countries and regions have very different instruments and styles of music. This traditional music is played by local people, or folk, so it is often called folk music.

Banjo

*People who live in the eastern mountains of the United States are famous for their banjo playing. Banjos were first brought to the United States by enslaved Africans.*

*Panpipes are made from pipes of different lengths and are popular in South America. You play them by blowing over the top of the pipes. Longer pipes make lower sounds.*

Panpipes

*Australian aboriginals are the only people to play the didgeridoo. It is made from a hollow bamboo branch. It is very difficult to play well.*

Didgeridoo

# ORCHESTRAS

Many musicians play music in groups called orchestras. Most orchestras have four sections: string, percussion, woodwind and brass. The different sounds and notes, from as many as 120 instruments in a symphony orchestra, combine to form marvellous music. Orchestras usually play classical music, often written by great composers of the past, such as Mozart and Beethoven.

*Cymbal*

*Principal violinist*

*Clarinet*

*Percussion players play many different instruments, such as drums, triangles and gongs.*

*Violin*

**Sounds Different**

Most of the instruments in a gamelan orchestra are percussion instruments – there are no violins at all. This music comes from Indonesia.

*The leader of an orchestra is always a violin player who sits near the conductor.*

*Woodwind instruments, including recorders, are played by blowing down a tube that has holes in it.*

**Two beats to a bar**

**Three beats to a bar**

**Four beats to a bar**

*The conductor stands in front of the musicians so that they can see the baton.*

*The French horn, like a trumpet or a trombone, is a long curving tube that is made of brass.*

*Bow*

## Keeping the Beat

If all the instruments in an orchestra played at different speeds they would sound dreadful. The musicians keep in time by watching a conductor who waves a baton to the beat of the music.

*Conductor*

*Short stick, called a baton*

*This cello, like the violin, is part of the string section. It is played by drawing a bow across the strings.*

## Which Section?

The clarinet player is sitting on a yellow seat. By using the key shown below, you can see that a clarinet is a woodwind instrument.

*Strings*

■ String   ■ Percussion   □ Woodwind   ■ Brass

## Child Genius

Wolfgang Amadeus Mozart wrote, or composed, over 600 pieces of music. He completed his first symphony when he was eight years old!

303

# DANCE

Dancing is a way of moving your body in time to music. Early peoples danced to please their gods. Today most people dance purely for fun. It was not until the 12th century that dancing in pairs became popular. The arrival of the waltz in the 1800s was shocking – it was the first time that couples had held one another closely as they danced. A revolution has taken place this century too – set steps have been replaced by solo dancers who make up all their own moves.

*This is an imaginary 'bow'.*

*The dancer pulls back an 'arrow'.*

*There are more than 25 different finger positions – each one has a different meaning.*

**Proud to Dance**
The spectacular flamenco dance comes from the gypsy peoples of Spain. The dancers hold their heads up high as they stamp their feet and turn round. The women wear long, colourful dresses but the men wear black.

**Head Over Heels**
Jive dancing, has few rules. The dancers twist, spin, jump, leap around – whatever the music makes them feel like doing!

*Taking a bow*

*The dance begins*

*Taps are fitted to the heel and toe of each shoe.*

**Tap, Tap, Tap**
Fred Astaire was one of the most famous dancers of this century. He tap-danced his way through many shows and films. Small pieces of metal, called taps, were fixed to the soles of his shoes. When his feet touched the ground, you could hear the quick clatter of clicking metal.

*Classical Indian dancers use the whole of their body. Their neck, wrists and even their eyes move to the rhythm of the music.*

*As she pretends to put a grip in her hair, the dancer looks into the 'mirror'.*

*Her hand is held out flat to form a 'mirror'.*

**Moves Matter**
Classical Indian dance has been performed for more than one thousand years. Sometimes the dancers just create shapes and patterns with their body. In other dances they use hand movements and mime to tell stories of Hindu gods.

*She stamps her bare foot in time to the drumbeat of an instrument called a tabla.*

*The pleats in the special dance dress let the dancer move freely.*

**One, Two, Three**
The waltz is danced in triple time – each bar of music has three beats. As the dancers swirl round and round they draw their feet together once every three steps.

# BALLET

Louis XIV

Ballet is a graceful type of dance that uses particular positions and steps. It began in Italy but was developed by the French into the style you see today. Louis XIV of France started the first ballet school in 1661. But the dancers in his 'ballets' at the French court sang and recited poems! The first true ballet, without words, was not performed until 1789. The basic steps and jumps taught by Louis' school are still used today – which is why many of them have French names. *Glisser* means to glide and *pas de chat* means cat step!

**At the Barre**
Ballet dancers must warm up their muscles before they dance. They do this by stretching while holding onto a pole, called a barre.

*This short, stiff skirt is called a tutu. It allows the dancer's legs to be seen.*

**Hopping Frogs**
*The Tales of Beatrix Potter* is an amazing ballet. The dancers wear wonderful costumes and animal masks.

*Women did not dance in ballets until 1681. Then, they had to wear long, flowing dresses.*

*'Turning feet out' takes years of practice.*

First position
(en première)

Second position
(en seconde)

Third position
(en troisième)

Fourth position
(en quatrième)

Fifth position
(en cinquième)

**The Five Positions**
In the 17th century, a ballet teacher, called Beauchamps, developed five feet and arm positions that enabled dancers to keep their balance and still look elegant. Most ballet steps begin or end with one of these positions.

Long hair is always tied back in a bun.

Male dancers need to be strong. They have to lift ballerinas high up in the air.

## This is Ballet Too!

During this century some very adventurous ballets have been performed. These modern ballets use many of the classic steps, but often have no story. The imaginatively dressed dancers simply express a mood.

Ballerinas sew on their own ribbons.

The ballerina keeps her foot pointed.

The leg is held very still and straight.

A female ballet dancer is called a ballerina.

Ballerinas put cotton wool inside their shoes to stop their toes hurting.

Ballet dancers wear tights.

Dancing on tiptoes makes the ballerina's legs look longer and more graceful.

## Ballet Shoes

To dance on tiptoe, or *en pointe*, ballerinas wear special satin slippers with stiffened toes. Girls have to be at least twelve years old before their feet are strong enough to dance like this.

Male dancers' shoes do not have stiffened toes.

# OPERA

Inside Paris opera house

Operas mix music with theatre in a most spectacular way. The performers on stage act out a story, but instead of speaking the words they sing them. A performance usually begins with an overture. This is a piece of catchy music, that features snatches of the tunes that will be heard during the rest of the opera. As well as singing the story, the stars on the stage also perform solo songs, called arias. These are often the most beautiful songs.

## Smashing Note
When you rub your finger around the rim of a glass it makes a high sound. If a person with a strong voice sings this note loudly, and for a long time, the sound waves can shatter the glass!

## Stylish Surroundings
Operas are usually staged in special buildings that are designed to help the whole audience hear the sound clearly. The Sydney opera house in Australia is one of the most modern. It was finished in 1973.

*The jagged roof looks like waves or the sails on a yacht.*

*Just one of the two main halls holds 1,500 people.*

Sydney opera house

Paris opera house

### Crowded Stage

Operas sometimes have spectacular stage sets and, as well as the soloists, a large group of singers, called the chorus.

### A Choice of Voices

The soprano is the highest female voice. It is a brilliant and exciting sound.

The contralto, or alto, has a slightly lower voice than the soprano. It has a warmer tone.

The tenors sing many of the important male songs in an opera.

The bass sings the lowest notes, and his voice is deep and strong.

### Dressed to Impress

Opera singers wear incredible costumes to play their parts. In *The Cunning Little Vixen* their make-up is amazing too.

### On Song

Luciano Pavarotti was one of the world's greatest tenors. He had a powerful and beautiful voice.

*Operas are mostly sung in Italian, French or German.*

*Powerful lungs enable the singers to sing without a microphone!*

### Foxy Tale

Operas tell stories. *The Cunning Little Vixen,* by Leos Janacek, is about a crafty female fox who escapes from a forester and has many exciting adventures.

# PAINTING

This cave painting is believed to be 30,000 years old.

Many thousands of years ago, people painted pictures of bulls, horses and antelopes on the walls of their caves. We will never be sure why they did this – perhaps it was to make magic and bring people luck in their hunting. Since then, artists have painted pictures to record events, to honour heroes and heroines, to make people wonder about the world, to tell stories, or simply for pleasure. All artists have their own painting style and you may not like them all – it's simply up to you.

*This says 'Jan van Eyck was here, 1434'. It may be to prove the artist was a witness to the marriage.*

*If you look closely in the mirror you can see the reflections of two other people. Perhaps one is the artist himself.*

*Things that are farther away look smaller, so the artist has made the shoes at the front bigger than those at the back. This gives the picture depth.*

**Hills and Valleys**
Paintings of the countryside are called landscapes. This Chinese scene looks very different from a Western landscape. It is painted on silk, using a fine and detailed style.

King Ramses II

by an unknown Egyptian artist
(detail)

Lucrezia Panciatichi

by Il Bronzino
(detail)

Self-portrait

by Vincent Van Gogh
(detail)

Woman Weeping

by Pablo Picasso
(detail)

*The Arnolfini Marriage*, painted by Jan van Eyck in 1434

## Looking for Clues

This painting records a couple's marriage. But if you look closely you will see it is much more than just a wedding picture.

*One candle is left to burn, even though it is daylight, to show that the couple will always love one another.*

*Like the merchant, his wife is wearing expensive clothes. It was the fashion to hold your skirts in this way.*

## Action Painting

In this painting the modern American artist, Jackson Pollock, was not trying to show objects or people, but feelings. He worked by dripping and splattering paint on the canvas.

*The light shines on the couple's hands, and the artist has shown every tiny line.*

Son of Man

by René Magritte
(detail)

Marilyn Monroe

by Andy Warhol
(detail)

## Painting Portraits

For thousands of years artists have enjoyed painting pictures of people. Not all of them painted the person true to life – there are many different styles of painting.

# SCULPTURE

Sculptures are three-dimensional, not flat like paintings. Bricks, plastic, even rubber tyres, have all been used by sculptors but the traditional materials are wood, stone and clay. Some sculptors build up their image by adding small pieces of material, such as clay. Others start with a big block of wood or stone and cut away, or subtract, material. When Michelangelo carved, he believed he was setting free a stone person, or statue, that was trapped inside the stone!

**Mystery from the Past**
Strange statues were carved on Easter Island more than one thousand years ago. Nobody knows for sure what they were for, or how they were built.

*Many of Moore's sculptures are based on natural, shapes, such as smooth pebbles.*

**In Touch With Nature**
Some of the sculptures created by Henry Moore (1898–1986) look like everyday things, but many are just interesting shapes.

*This rounded sculpture is meant to be touched.*

*If you walk around this sculpture you see different, exciting shapes.*

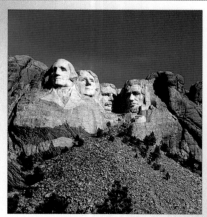

**Mountain Men**
Mount Rushmore has the heads of four American Presidents cut into it. It took 14 years to blast and drill Presidents Washington, Jefferson, Roosevelt and Lincoln out of the rock.

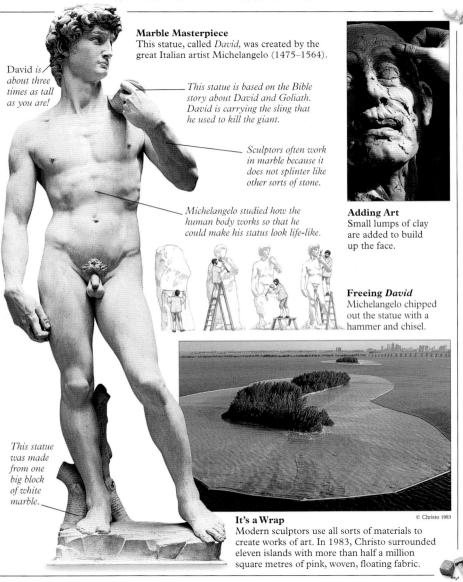

**Marble Masterpiece**
This statue, called *David*, was created by the great Italian artist Michelangelo (1475–1564).

*David is about three times as tall as you are!*

*This statue is based on the Bible story about David and Goliath. David is carrying the sling that he used to kill the giant.*

*Sculptors often work in marble because it does not splinter like other sorts of stone.*

*Michelangelo studied how the human body works so that he could make his status look life-like.*

*This statue was made from one big block of white marble.*

**Adding Art**
Small lumps of clay are added to build up the face.

**Freeing *David***
Michelangelo chipped out the statue with a hammer and chisel.

© Christo 1983

**It's a Wrap**
Modern sculptors use all sorts of materials to create works of art. In 1983, Christo surrounded eleven islands with more than half a million square metres of pink, woven, floating fabric.

# PHOTOGRAPHY

Every day millions of photographs are taken around the world. These photos are not just snaps of birthdays and holidays, but pictures of goals being scored, models in studios and important news events. No matter how complicated the camera, all photographs are made in much the same way as when the process was invented more than 150 years ago. A camera is basically a box with a hole in it. Light that enters through this hole is either captured on film inside the camera or as a digital image you can see on a screen.

**Say Cheese!**
In early photographs, it took a long time for the picture to form. People had to stay still for up to 20 minutes to stop the picture from blurring.

*Flash*

*This tough camera will not break if it is dropped!*

*This spare camera has a long 'telephoto' lens. It makes things that are a long way off, look closer.*

*Before digital cameras, photographers had to carry lots of rolls of film.*

Click – A sinking bus is snapped

**Right Time, Right Place**
Newspaper photographers have to be ready for action all the time. They may not get a second chance to snap an amazing event or famous person.

*Flash*

**Camera Collection**

35mm professional camera

Instant camera

High-quality studio camera

Underwater camera

This flash is mush bigger than the flash on your camera!

Light bounces back off this board, onto the person being photographed.

White paper reflects light back onto the model.

### Lights, Camera, Keep Still!
Wind, rain and poor light can ruin your shots when you take pictures outside. This is why photographers work in studios. Many of the pictures in this book were taken in a studio.

Small spotlights light up the white background.

The photographer takes pictures when the model is in the right position.

The person having their photo taken is called the model. You can see the final pictures of this dancer on pages 304–305.

Camera

An assistant hands film to the photographer.

This box is called a power pack. It provides the energy to run the flashlights.

A cable connects the camera to the power pack. This makes sure the flash goes off when the camera clicks.

The camera sits on a three-legged frame, called a tripod. This prevents the camera from moving.

Spare films

315

# FILMS

From the first flickery film, people have loved the world of movie make-believe. The early films were made in black and white and did not have any sound. They were called silent movies. In the cinema, a pianist played along with the film and the audience had to read words on the screen. It was not until 1927 that the first 'talkie', called *The Jazz Singer*, came out. Colour films, such as *The Wizard of Oz*, were made in 1939, but only became common in the 1950s.

**A Star is Born**
The dry weather in California is ideal for filming. Hollywood, once a sleepy suburb of Los Angeles, was the centre of the American film industry by 1920.

**Silent Star**
Charlie Chaplin (1889–1977) was one of the first movie stars. He starred in more than 80 films. His most famous character was a little tramp who had a funny walk.

**Cue Clapperboard**
When a clapperboard is clicked shut it is seen on the film and heard on the soundtrack. The pictures and words can then be matched.

**Moving Pictures**
A film is made of many still pictures called frames. The frames pass before your eyes so quickly that the pictures look as if they are moving.

*Small holes keep the film steady in the camera.*

*Frame*

**Eastern Promise**
More than 800 films a year are made in India – double the number made in Hollywood. Streets in Mumbai and Delhi are lined with bright posters that advertise these dramatic films.

*The lighting crew sets up the lights so that the actor looks as if he is outside and not inside a bright studio.*

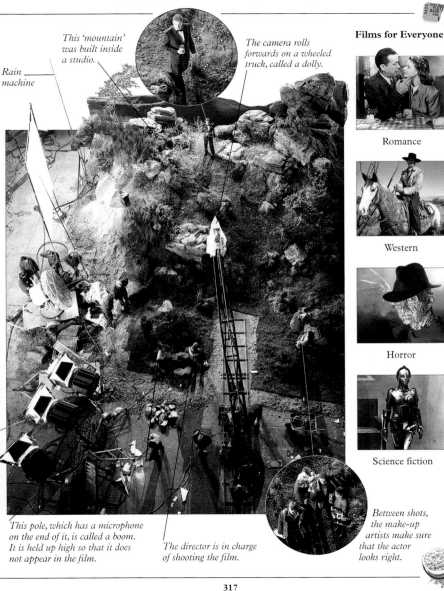

This 'mountain' was built inside a studio.

Rain machine

The camera rolls forwards on a wheeled truck, called a dolly.

**Films for Everyone**

Romance

Western

Horror

Science fiction

This pole, which has a microphone on the end of it, is called a boom. It is held up high so that it does not appear in the film.

The director is in charge of shooting the film.

Between shots, the make-up artists make sure that the actor looks right.

# SPECIAL EFFECTS

Have you ever wondered how alien worlds are filmed or how actors and actresses survive death-defying leaps? These amazing events are not real, they are created by special effects. With clever camera work and special equipment, such as wind machines, film directors can make us believe that what we are seeing is real. These tricks of the trade are used when shooting the action in the normal way would be too expensive, too dangerous, or just impossible!

**Size Isn't Everything**
This tiny, detailed model of a Y-wing spaceship appeared in *Return of the Jedi*. On screen it looked big enough to carry people!

*A wind machine can make a gentle breeze or a howling gale.*

**Cue Weather**
Film makers can't wait for the right weather. In this scene from *The Mosquito Coast* giant fans whipped up the waves that battered the boat.

*The lights shining through the glass look like real camp fires.*

*The special effects expert pulls the trigger to fire the red pellet.*

**Blood Gun**

People often have to pretend to be shot in films. Real guns can't be used as this would be too dangerous, so special blood guns are used. A small pellet is filled with red liquid. When this hits bare skin, it bursts and looks like a nasty bullet wound.

*Air is forced down this hose to push out the blood bullet.*

*The highly trained stunt man leaps from the building.*

*The audience must think that the actor is falling so the stunt man wears the same clothes.*

**Land of Make Believe**

This tree-top village appeared in the film, *Return of the Jedi*. It was not built in trees but painted onto glass! Small parts of the painting are scraped away and live action is shown through these holes. In the finished film, actors, dressed as alien Ewoks, look as if they are in the village!

*This special trick painting and filming is called matte painting.*

*The stunt man waves his legs and arms about, to look as though he is terrified.*

*The camera stops running when the stunt man prepares to land.*

**Falling for You**

Jumping from a high building is dangerous and difficult! In films, it is only done by experts, called stunt people. They take the place of the actor or actress who is supposed to be falling to the ground in the story.

*The stunt man twists in the air so that his shoulders will hit the bag first.*

**Fire!**

Film makers don't just throw bombs to make flames and smoke. Explosions are carefully set up and controlled.

*Fuse*

Smoke cylinders

Explosives

*This can makes orange smoke.*

*Actor*

*The stunt man hits the soft air bag at more than 80 kilometres per hour!*

# FOOD AND FARMING

Most of us buy our food in shops or from market stalls, but it has probably been produced somewhere far away. This could be a large farm in the country, or a small plantation halfway around the world.

We eat some things – fruit, raw vegetables and nuts, for example – just as they are picked. Other types of food have lots of things done to them before we put them on the table. Cocoa beans, for example, which grow in huge pods on cacao trees, are made into delicious chocolate. Grains of wheat are threshed to separate them from their husks, then milled into flour. Flour is used to make the bread, biscuits, and pastry that most people eat every day.

Chocolate cake

Baby pigs are called piglets.

Baby sheep are called lambs.

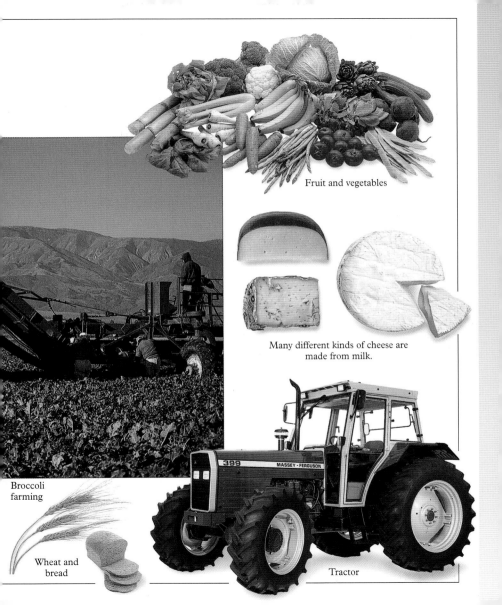

Fruit and vegetables

Many different kinds of cheese are made from milk.

Broccoli farming

Wheat and bread

Tractor

# WHEAT

What have breakfast cereals, breads, cakes, pastries, pasta and couscous all got in common? The answer is that they are made out of wheat, the most important crop in the world. Wheat is the main food eaten every day by 35 per cent of the world's people, and is so important it is called a staple food. Like barley, oats, rye, maize, rice, sorghum and millet, wheat is a cereal. Cereals are grasses and we eat their seeds.

## Crop Rotation

If the same crop is grown on the same land year after year, the soil may lose its fertility and pests and diseases build up. The farmer can prevent this by changing the crops grown each year. In the first year, rapeseed may be grown, then wheat, field beans, wheat, and barley.

rapeseed

barley

wheat

field beans

wheat

## Machine Power

This is a combine harvester. It cuts the crop and separates the grain from the straw.

*This is the unloading spout. It is used to empty threshed grain from the harvester.*

*In the harvester, the grain is shaken off the stalks. The stalks fall to the ground at the back.*

*These are straw walkers. They carry the crop through the machine.*

## Edible Ears

Other cereal crops include oats, barley and rye. Like wheat, these plants have an 'ear' of grain on each stem. Each grain is protected by a husk and inside the husk is the seed. The grain can be eaten whole or ground into flour.

Rye

Oats

Barley

## Wheat Products

Wheat can be used for many different foods. You would never guess these items are all made from the same ingredient.

Wheat germ

Cracked wheat

Breakfast cereal

Pasta

## Monsters on the Move

These wheatfields in the prairies of Manitoba, Canada, are so vast that several combine harvesters can work the fields at the same time.

*The cab is air-conditioned to keep the driver cool and also to filter out all the dust produced during harvesting.*

*The reel sweeps the crop into the cutter bar. The cutter bar cuts the crop.*

*An ear of wheat is made up of 40 to 60 grains. When wheat is ripe and ready for harvesting, it turns golden yellow.*

## Home Sweet Home

The wheatfield is a world of its own. It is home to mammals, insects, birds and wild flowers.

# MAIZE

In many tropical and subtropical countries maize (sweet corn) is the main food that people eat. It is eaten as a vegetable or ground into flour or cornmeal. Maize is also made into oil for cooking and for salad dressings. Maize needs lots of sunshine to grow – it will grow in hot climates but also in cooler, mild ones as long as there is plenty of sun. However, the varieties of maize grown in these different climates are not the same.

*The flower at the top of the plant is called the tassel.*

*This is the stalk. Some kinds of maize have stalks as high as six metres.*

*Maize is, in fact, a huge grass.*

*The maize ear, or cob, is protected by a husk of tightly wrapped leaves.*

*These long, soft threads are called the silk.*

*The cob is covered in neat, straight rows of kernels. The kernels are the plant's seeds and the part you eat.*

*Short side roots spread over the surface of the soil. They anchor the tall plant like the guy ropes of a tent and stop it falling over.*

*Deep roots go down into the soil and take out the food and water the plant needs to grow.*

## Pest Problems

In warm and tropical areas, one of the pests most feared by farmers is the locust. They travel in huge swarms of over 50 billion insects, stripping plants of their leaves and stems as they feed. Locusts can destroy crops and cause famine and starvation.

## Sun Ripened

Maize is the staple food of the warmer parts of North, Central and South America, and also of Africa. It can be grown in huge fields with the help of machinery, or tended by hand.

**Maize Foods**

Sweetcorn

Breakfast cereal

## Mountain of Maize

After the maize has been harvested, it is sorted. Some will be kept as seed for the next crop, some kept for food and some used as animal feed.

Tortilla chips

## Amazing Maize

Maize comes in all sorts of colours and it may even be striped, streaked, speckled or spotted.

Taco

## Tough Grains

In dry parts of Africa and Asia, people mainly eat sorghum and millet. These cereals are tough and will grow with little water. This woman is pounding sorghum grain. It is mixed with water or milk until it becomes soft and sticky, like semolina. Sorghum is eaten with spicy stews, which give it flavour. It is also ground into flour. Millet is cooked like porridge, baked into a flat bread or used in soups and stews.

Maize oil

# RICE

Like maize and wheat, rice is a staple food. It is the main food of at least 1.6 billion people. Ninety per cent of the world's rice is grown in Asia. However, the Asian countries eat most of what they grow. The USA also produces huge amounts of rice, but sells much of what it grows to the rest of the world.

*Rice is a swamp plant. It grows with its roots in water. It has hollow stems which take oxygen to the roots.*

*In Asia, the work of sowing, planting out the seedlings and harvesting the rice is usually done by hand.*

## How the Rice Plant is Used

*The grain is the part of the plant we eat. Damaged grains are used to make beer, and flour for cakes and noodles.*

*Husks are used as animal feed or to make fertilizer.*

Grain

*The stems are woven into baskets, mats and hats.*

**Preparing the Fields**
The paddy fields are flooded, ploughed, raked and flattened. In Asia, buffaloes are used to do the heavy work.

**Planting Out**
The pre-sprouted seedlings are moved to the paddy fields. They are planted far apart so they have plenty of space to grow.

*While water helps the rice to grow, it kills off weeds that can't grow in such watery conditions.*

*Rice is a type of grass.*

*Most rice is grown in flooded fields called paddies.*

*The fields are flooded for much of the growing season.*

*The rice is planted in straight lines.*

**Machine Power**

In the USA, growing rice is highly mechanized. Tractors prepare the fields, the seed may be sown from aeroplanes and combine harvesters gather the ripe plants.

**Safekeeping**

Special buildings are used to store the rice until it is needed. They are called granaries. A granary keeps the grain dry and safe from hungry animals.

**All Rice**

Puffed rice cakes

Rice noodles

Sticky rice cakes

Rice paper

**Harvesting**

The rice is ready for harvesting in three to six months. The fields are drained and the plants cut down, tied in bundles and left to dry.

**Winnowing**

The rice is beaten to remove the grains. The grains are crushed and then sieved and tossed to remove any fine pieces of husk.

327

# VEGETABLE OILS

Vegetable oils are made from the seeds and fruits of many plants growing all over the world, from tiny sesame seeds to big, juicy coconuts. The oils are used for cooking, as salad dressings and to make cooking fats and margarine. Soya beans are the most important source of oil worldwide, especially in the USA. In western Europe, the oil most widely produced is rapeseed oil.

## Harvesting
Olives are picked in the autumn when they are ripe. They are shaken from the trees and gathered up, usually by hand. Next, the olives are sorted out to remove the leaves and twigs, and taken to be pressed.

*Olive trees are often quite small but can live for hundreds of years. They develop very wrinkled, knotty trunks.*

## How Olive Oil is Made
The olives are ground to a thick paste which is spread onto special mats. The mats are then layered up on the pressing machine which will gently squeeze them to produce olive oil.

*Olive trees are planted in rows. Fields of olive trees are called groves.*

### Edible Olives

There are many varieties of olives – black and green, large and small. Most are used for making oil, but some are eaten whole, too. Raw olives are very bitter, but once they have been treated, fermented and pickled, they taste delicious!

*The trees are shaken to make the olives fall. Sometimes, machines are used to do this job.*

*Each long, flexible branch has lots of flowers and about 30 clusters of fruit.*

*Nets are laid down so that the fallen fruit can be gathered easily.*

### Surprising Sources

Oil can be produced from lots of very different fruits and seeds.

Groundnuts (Peanuts)

Cottonseeds

Sesame seeds

Rapeseed

Soya beans

### Sunflower Oil

Every sunflower is made up of hundreds of tiny flowers, surrounded by a fringe of petals. It is the seeds of the flowers that are rich in oil. Sunflowers are ready for harvesting when the flowers are dead and the heads have dried out. Sunflower oil is good for cooking oil, salad oil and for making margarine.

# CATTLE AND DAIRY FARMING

Cattle are very popular domesticated animals because they provide us with a lot of food. They are kept for their meat, which is called beef, and also for their milk. Milk is full of calcium and protein, which make it a very complete and nourishing food. Because of this, milk-giving animals are kept all over the world – but they are not always cows. Goats, sheep, camels, reindeer and llamas give us milk, too!

*A cow gives milk for ten months of the year, then she has a rest for two months. Most cows are milked twice a day.*

*To produce milk, a dairy cow must have a calf once a year.*

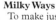

### Milky Ways
To make just one kilogram of butter, you need around 22 litres of milk! The liquid that is left over is called buttermilk.

*A calf born to a dairy cow stays with its mother for just 48 hours.*

### Hard Cheese!
Foods made from milk, such as butter, cheese, yoghurt and cream, are known as dairy products. Making cheese is the best way to turn milk into a food that can be stored for some time. Thousands of different cheeses are made all over the world. Soft, creamy cheeses must be eaten promptly, but hard, crumbly cheeses will last for months and even years!

*Reticulum*

*Omasum*

*Rumen*

*Abomasum*

*Animals that chew cud are called ruminants.*

## Second Helping

Cows eat grass without chewing it properly. It goes to the rumen and reticulum to be broken down into cud. The cow sicks this up and chews it again. When it is swallowed, the cud goes through the stomachs in turn, being finally digested in the abomasum.

*This is the udder, where the milk is produced. It is in four parts. Each part has a teat.*

## In the Milking Parlour

When cows are milked, special suckers are attached to the teats. They squeeze the milk gently from the cow just like a calf does. Most cows give about 11.5 litres of milk per day.

## Bred for Beef

Big, heavy breeds of cattle are kept for beef because they have more meat on them. The world's largest herds of beef cattle are found in North and South America. Here there are lots of wide, open spaces where the cattle can graze until they are fat and ready for eating.

**Dairy Cattle**

Holstein Friesian

Jersey

**Beef Cattle**

Hereford

Charolais

**Dairy and Beef**

Simmental

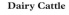

# SHEEP

Sheep are raised for their meat, for the foods that can be made from their milk, and for their wool. There are more than 200 breeds of sheep and different sorts are able to live in very different places – in lands that are hot with little water, in areas that are cold and wet, in the lowlands and on the hills. The kind of place where it lives affects the quality of the sheep's meat and wool.

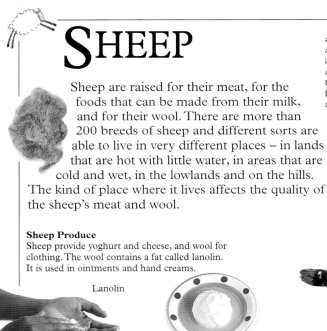

## Sheep Produce
Sheep provide yoghurt and cheese, and wool for clothing. The wool contains a fat called lanolin. It is used in ointments and hand creams.

Lanolin

Yoghurt

Cheese

Milk

*It takes the wool from one average-sized fleece to make this jumper.*

*Hand-operated shears or electric clippers are used by the shearer.*

*Sheep are shorn in the spring and early summer when they no longer need their long coats to keep them warm.*

*The fleece is made into wool for knitting and for making carpets and fabrics. Sometimes, it is even used to fill mattresses.*

### Bathtime

Once or twice a year, the farmer drives the sheep through a chemical dip. This keeps them free of pests and diseases.

### Domestic Sheep

Suffolk

Wensleydale

### Mummy!

Some lambs are orphaned or not wanted by their mum. These may be bottle-fed by the farmer or shepherd or adopted by another ewe.

### Working Dogs

Dogs are used to gather the sheep in flocks and move them from place to place. Sheepdogs naturally like to herd animals but they need to be trained to follow instructions. The shepherd controls the dog using special calls and whistles. Sheep are timid, so the dog will run low in the grass to avoid frightening them.

Karakul

Scottish blackface

### In a Spin

To produce wool for knitting or weaving, many strands are twisted together to make one long thread. Spinning was first done by hand using a spindle. Later, the spindle was attached to a wheel and wool could be spun more quickly. Now, most spinning is done by machine.

### Wild Sheep

Bighorn

*The shearer shears the sheep so that the fleece comes off in one piece.*

# PIGS

Domestic pigs are mainly kept for their meat, especially in China, which has the most pigs in the world. Pigs raised for their meat are usually kept in pens and are fed on cereals, potatoes, fish meal and skimmed milk. Pigs kept for breeding often live outdoors in fields. The farmer feeds them but they also search for their own food. They like worms, snails, roots and plants.

Duroc

**Mud, Glorious Mud**
Despite their reputation, pigs are not dirty animals. They cannot sweat so in hot weather they roll about in mud to help cool themselves down.

*A female pig is called a sow.*

*The piglets go to the same teat every time they want to feed. When they are six weeks old, they move on from milk to solid food.*

**Intensive Farming**
When pigs leave their mothers, they are normally housed in piggeries. This is so they can be looked after properly and kept warm. The pigs are fed a special diet, and because they have less space to run around, they put on weight quickly.

*A sow makes a 'nest' before she has her litter. In a pen, she paws straw into a heap. In a field, she lines a hole with leaves and straw.*

Landrace

British saddleback

Piétrain    Vietnamese pot-bellied pig

*Domestic pigs don't have a hairy coat to protect them, just a few short bristles. Because of this, pink pigs can get sunburned. Black pigs are protected by their dark skins.*

### Pig Products

The meat from pigs, which is called pork, is used to make a variety of foods, including sausages, all kinds of hams and spiced meats.

*The last piglet born is often smaller and weaker than the rest. It is called the 'runt' and it might not survive.*

### Detective Work

Pigs have a good sense of smell and use their snouts to dig up food. In France, pigs are used to search for truffles, which are difficult to find because they can grow as much as 30 centimetres under the ground.

Truffles are like mushrooms and are a great delicacy.

*A sow usually has about ten to twelve piglets in a litter. She can have more than two litters every year.*

# CITRUS FRUITS

*The ugli fruit is a cross between a tangerine, a orange and a grapefrui...*

The third largest fruit crop in the world, after grapes and bananas, is citrus fruits. This is the family of fruits that oranges, lemons and satsumas all belong to. Citrus fruits are grown mainly in tropical and subtropical parts of America, in countries around the northern and eastern Mediterranean, and in Australia.

*A tree can produce a thousand oranges each year.*

*This is a white grapefruit. The flesh inside is a pale yellow.*

*Lemons, like other citrus fruits, are rich in minerals and vitamins, especially vitamin C.*

*Tangerines are like small, sweet oranges. They have several small pips.*

*Limes have thin skins and very sharp juice.*

## Fighting Frost

Citrus trees need just the right climate to produce good fruit – sun to make them sweet and then cold to make them sharp. But the trees' greatest enemy is frost, which will kill the fruit. So modern plantations often have wind machines and special orchard-heaters in case it is frosty.

*Orchard-heaters protect the trees from frost.*

*This is a pink grapefruit. Inside it has a sweet, pink flesh.*

## The Perfect Package

Citrus fruits are perfectly packaged foods. In the middle is the juicy flesh, a wonderful source of food and drink that is rich in vitamin C. Next comes a spongy layer, called the pith, which cushions the flesh. On the outside is a protective skin.

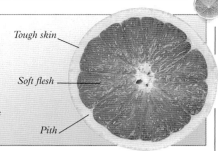

Tough skin

Soft flesh

Pith

*Navel oranges are very juicy. Usually they have no seeds.*

*Clementines, like satsumas and tangerines, have a loose skin that is easy to peel.*

*Satsumas are like tangerines, except they don't have pips.*

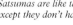

*You can eat kumquats whole, including the rind.*

## Mix and Match

By mixing pollen from the blossom of different citrus trees, new varieties can be developed. The limequat, for example, is a cross between a lime and a kumquat.

## Juicy Fruit

These oranges are being sorted and packed, and will be sold for eating. Many oranges are pulped to be made into juice. This pulp is frozen for transporting round the world.

*Fresh orange juice contains the most goodness, so squeeze it yourself if you can.*

# GRAPES

*Grapes need rain to swell them and sun to ripen them.*

There are two different types of grapes, black and white. But black grapes are really dark red and white grapes are light green. Grapes are delicious to eat fresh, and keep their sweetness when dried, too. But most of the grapes grown in the world are used for making wine. Grape plants are called vines and they are planted in rows in vineyards. Vines need a lot of care, and it takes much hard work and skill to produce a bottle of fine wine.

**Pruning**
As vines grow, they are often cut back so they have a few strong branches rather than lots of weaker ones. This work is called pruning and must be done by hand.

*The broad vine leaves shade the grapes from the direct glare of the sun and the battering rain.*

**Bitter Wine**
Red and white wine can also be made into vinegar. It is produced when special vinegar yeasts ferment the wine, and turn it sour. Vinegars can be made from other liquids, like cider or malt, and are used as a flavouring. They can also be mixed with foods to pickle and preserve them.

**From Grapes to Wine**
First the grapes are crushed and pressed to mix the yeast with the sugar in the grapes. This is called fermentation. Then the juice is filtered and poured into vats. These are left in a cool place for the flavour of the wine to develop.

Grapes

Press

*There is a natural yeast on the grape skin that is needed to turn the grape juice into wine.*

*Black grapes can be made into red or white wine. To make red wine, the skins of black grapes are left in the wine mixture.*

## Dried Goods

Grapes for drying must be very sweet because it is their natural sugar that preserves them. They can be dried on racks, in the sun or in ovens. Only seedless grapes are used for drying. Sultanas are dried white grapes. Raisins and currants are dried black grapes and are usually smaller.

Currants

Raisins

Sultanas

*Grapes grow in tight bunches.*

## Grape Harvesters

Most wine grapes today are picked by machine, except in small or sloping vineyards. Special grapes for making rare wines are carefully picked by hand.

## Digging Deep

The type of soil in a vineyard is very important and affects the flavour of the wine. Yet some of the best wines are produced from poor soils. This is because the vine can find regular supplies of food and water by pushing its roots deep into the earth.

Vats

Wine

# UNDERGROUND VEGETABLES

Some plants are not grown for their leafy tops but for the parts of them that grow beneath the soil. Carrots, turnips, radishes and parsnips are the fat roots of plants and are known as root vegetables. Potatoes are the swollen part of the underground stem of the plant. They are called tubers. Onions, too, grow in the dark earth, but it is the bulb of these plants that we eat.

*The flowers produce seeds that can be used to grow new plants, but it is more usual to use seed potatoes.*

**Farming with Nature**
Many farmers use chemical fertilizers and pesticides to help them grow crops efficiently, but some farmers use only natural products. They use fertilizers such as manure, and encourage pest controllers like ladybirds, which eat all sorts of flies and larvae. This helps to stop a build-up of chemicals in the environment and is called organic farming.

*Potato plants grow well in cool climates, but are killed by frost.*

Radish        Carrot                    Beetroot

*These are the tubers. Each plant has between 15 and 20 tubers.*

**Types of Tuber**
Tubers come in all
shapes and sizes.

Sweet potato

Cassava

Yam

Cocoyam

**Harvest Time**
In the autumn,
the potatoes are
fully-grown and
special harvesters,
pulled by tractors,
are used to lift
them carefully
from the soil.

**Tasty Bulbs**
Bulbs, like
onions, are not
roots. Instead,
they are made
up of clumps

Garlic

of tightly curled leaves.
Leeks, garlic, shallots
and spring onions are all
members of the same
plant family and they
are all valuable for
the flavour that they
can give to many
other foods.

Shallot

*When the leaves
wither in the autumn,
the farmer knows the
potatoes are ready
to harvest.*

Stem

*Some potatoes may be harvested and put to
one side. These will then be used to grow
new plants, and are called seed potatoes.*

*From these tiny scars, called
eyes, new shoots will grow.*

Onion

Roots

# HOTHOUSE VEGETABLES

In countries with cool climates, there is not usually enough heat to grow the most delicate or exotic vegetables. But in special hothouses, with glass or clear plastic walls, a farmer can grow almost any crop. This is because the temperature inside a hothouse can be controlled. Hothouses are useful in warmer countries, too. They mean the farmer does not have to follow the seasons of the year and summer vegetables, that do not store, can be grown fresh all year round.

**Computer Controlled**
Tomatoes are quite fragile plants so this hothouse, where the temperature and feeding are controlled by a computer, is a good place to grow them. Tomatoes grown in hothouses are usually top quality and are picked by hand.

**Nature's 'Hothouse'**
Some of the world's hottest spots are dry deserts. But if a water supply can be set up, the desert heat can be put to good use. Fertile gardens can be created, like this fruit orchard in Jordan.

**Short Showers**
Most of the work in large hothouses today is done by machines. These young sweet pepper (capsicum) plants are watered by overhead pipes. Hothouse crops must also be sprayed to protect them from the pests and moulds that like the damp, warm conditions.

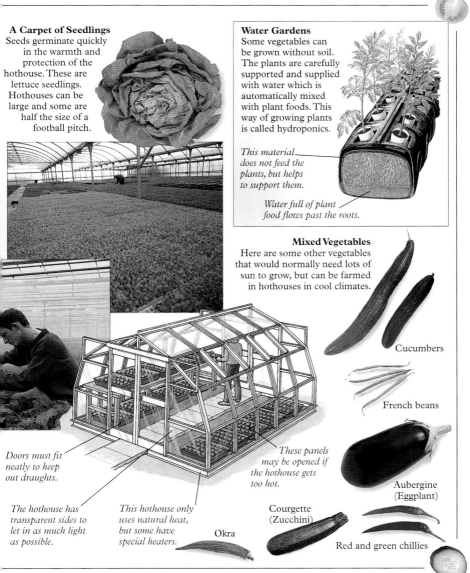

**A Carpet of Seedlings**
Seeds germinate quickly in the warmth and protection of the hothouse. These are lettuce seedlings. Hothouses can be large and some are half the size of a football pitch.

**Water Gardens**
Some vegetables can be grown without soil. The plants are carefully supported and supplied with water which is automatically mixed with plant foods. This way of growing plants is called hydroponics.

*This material does not feed the plants, but helps to support them.*

*Water full of plant food flows past the roots.*

**Mixed Vegetables**
Here are some other vegetables that would normally need lots of sun to grow, but can be farmed in hothouses in cool climates.

Cucumbers

French beans

Aubergine (Eggplant)

*Doors must fit neatly to keep out draughts.*

*These panels may be opened if the hothouse gets too hot.*

*The hothouse has transparent sides to let in as much light as possible.*

*This hothouse only uses natural heat, but some have special heaters.*

Okra

Courgette (Zucchini)

Red and green chillies

# COFFEE, TEA AND COCOA

Coffee, tea and cocoa are drunk in most countries of the world. Cocoa is also used to make chocolate. Coffee and cocoa grow in the tropics. They are grown on huge plantations but a lot is produced on small farms as well. Tea is grown in the tropics and subtropics, on plantations. Altogether, millions of people are employed to produce these crops. Coffee, tea and cocoa are important to the countries that grow them because they are cash crops. This means they are grown to be traded with other countries rather than for home use.

### Picky Pickers
Tea comes from evergreen trees that are pruned into bushes. This makes it easy to pick the leaves. The best quality teas are produced by plucking only the bud and the first two leaves on each shoot. A skilled plucker can pick enough leaves in one day to make 3,500 cups of tea.

Green tea      Black tea

### Special Treatment
The leaves are made into black or green tea. For green tea, the leaves are dried, heated and crushed. For black tea, the leaves are dried, crushed, fermented and dried again.

A coffee tree produces about 2,000 fruits each year. It takes twice this amount to make one kilogram of roasted coffee.

The fruits are called cherries because of their colour and size.

There are two green coffee beans inside each cherry. They only go brown after they are roasted.

The coffee is harvested twice a year.

The trees are pruned to stop them growing more than three metres high.

When the fruits first appear, they are green. Gradually, they turn bright red. They are then ready to be picked.

The ripe fruit is picked by hand or shaken from the tree onto a cloth spread out underneath it. On some plantations, machines are used to pick the fruit.

**Heavy Load**
Cocoa pods are large and heavy. They grow on the trunk of the cacao tree or from its thick branches.

The pod has a thick skin.

Each pod may contain 20 to 50 cocoa beans.

The pod grows up to 38 centimetres long, about the size of a rugby ball.

# SUGARS

Most people like sugar. Nearly 100 million tonnes of it are produced each year. Over half of it comes from sugar cane. This is grown on a large scale on plantations in the tropical areas of Brazil, Cuba, India, China, Australia, Mexico, the Philippines, Thailand and the USA. The rest of our sugar comes from sugar beet, which is a vegetable. Sugar beet grows in the cooler climates of Europe, the USA, Canada, China and Japan.

**Workers Watch Out!**
The sugar plantations can be home to the deadly bushmaster snake. Enormous bird-eating spiders also nestle among the thick foliage.

**Sugar Cane**
Sugar cane is a tropical plant. It grows best in places that get plenty of sunshine and lots of rain.

*The canes are cut close to the ground because this is where the most sugar collects.*

*After the cane has been harvested, healthy stumps will regrow into new plants.*

*Sugar cane is a very tall grass, like rice and cereals.*

*The sugar is stored inside the stalk, in a firm pulp.*

*The stalks of a mature plant are about five centimetres thick.*

**Sugar Beet**
Sugar beet is a root vegetable. It looks like a giant parsnip. It grows best in places that have warm summers and cool or cold winters.

*The leafy tops of the plants are cut off before the sugar beet is lifted. The tops can be used for animal feed.*

*The sugar is stored in the thick root.*

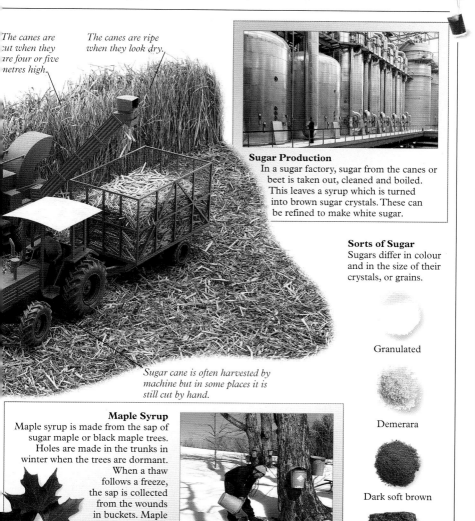

*The canes are cut when they are four or five metres high.*

*The canes are ripe when they look dry.*

## Sugar Production

In a sugar factory, sugar from the canes or beet is taken out, cleaned and boiled. This leaves a syrup which is turned into brown sugar crystals. These can be refined to make white sugar.

## Sorts of Sugar

Sugars differ in colour and in the size of their crystals, or grains.

Granulated

Demerara

Dark soft brown

Muscovado

*Sugar cane is often harvested by machine but in some places it is still cut by hand.*

## Maple Syrup

Maple syrup is made from the sap of sugar maple or black maple trees. Holes are made in the trunks in winter when the trees are dormant. When a thaw follows a freeze, the sap is collected from the wounds in buckets. Maple syrup is only produced in North America.

# PEOPLE AND PLACES

In lots of ways, people are the same everywhere: they build homes, they wear clothes, they eat meals, and they have fun. However, men and women in different countries have developed their own languages and customs, which vary widely from place to place.

Did you know, for example, that in Spain, there is a festival in which people throw tomatoes at each other? Did you know that the Chinese language has 50,000 written characters? Did you know that in Denmark, there is a theme park built out of Lego bricks?

Learning about other ways of life is not only interesting, it also helps you to understand and get along with people in other countries who may be very different from you.

Inuit boy from northern Canada

African jewellery

The Eiffel Tower in Paris, France

Indonesian boy on a water buffalo

Talking drum
from Nigeria

Antipasto
from Italy

Vegetable market in Guatemala

Buckingham Palace in London, England

Woven bag
from Peru

Indian snake
charmer

# THE ARCTIC & ANTARCTICA

The Inuit people live in the icy lands of the Arctic North. For many generations, they have found practical ways of coping with their cold surroundings. But no one has settled for very long on the southern extremes of the planet. Antarctica is the coldest and windiest place in the world. This huge continent is lashed by freezing blizzards and gales, with temperatures as low as -89°C.

### Icy City
Murmansk is a Russian city 200 kilometres north of the Arctic Circle. No other city is farther north than this. The sun does not rise between November and the middle of January.

### Homes in the North
In the past, the Inuit were self-sufficient and lived a life on the move, hunting and fishing to survive. They built temporary homes, called igloos, from solid snow. Today, most Inuit live in wooden houses and earn a living by working for other people, often in fish-canning factories or for mining companies.

### Speedy Ski-Doos
Today, the Inuit people get about on motor sledges, called Ski-doos. This is much faster than using dogs to pull a sledge, which is the traditional method of travel.

*Warm clothes are vital in the Arctic.*

### Long-Lost Relations
For many years, Inuit families on either side of the Bering Strait were not allowed to meet, for political reasons. Nowadays, the North American Inuit and their relations in northern Asia can visit one another once again.

*The Bering Strait is a narrow stretch of sea that separates northern Asia from North America.*

*The Arctic*

*Antarctica*

### Antarctic Science
Scientists from all around the world are the only people who live and work in Antarctica. Some study the effect of the enormous sheet of Antarctic ice on the world's weather patterns. Others observe the behaviour of living things in the freezing conditions.

*This scientist is measuring the density of Antarctic snow.*

*This emperor penguin lives in the Antarctic. No penguins live in the Arctic.*

### Exploring the Unknown
Antarctica was the last continent to be explored. The first successful expedition in search of the South Pole took place in 1911, led by a Norwegian called Roald Amundsen. The British expedition led by Captain Scott ended in disaster, when the team froze to death on the trek home.

*A windscreen protects the riders from the biting wind.*

### What a Mess
Alaska is an important producer of oil. In 1989, an American oil tanker ran aground just off Alaska, causing one of the world's worst environmental disasters. Over 2,000 kilometres of the Alaskan shoreline were covered with oil.

*Runners on the front of the Ski-doo spread the weight of the vehicle evenly, to prevent it sinking into the soft snow.*

ski-doo

# CANADA

*Totem poles often guarded doorways to village homes.*

Canada is an enormous country. A journey from the east to the west coast on the world's longest national highway will take you through almost 8,000 kilometres of beautiful landscape. Canada's population of 34 million is small for the country's huge size. Most Canadians live in cities in the warmer southern part of the country, close to the border with the United States.

*Some carvings show off the family possessions.*

**Quebec City**
Quebec City is the capital of the province of Quebec. It is Canada's oldest city and the only walled city in North America. Many of its distinctive buildings are in the original French style.

*The animals are symbols of the family's ancestors.*

**Timber!**
Half of Canada's four million square kilometres of forest are used for timber. Logging is a very important Canadian industry. On the west coast, large areas of forest are disappearing. Logging companies are being asked to slow down the destruction and to replant more trees.

*Modern machinery fells giant conifer trees.*

**Totem Pole**
The Native Americans of British Columbia, on the west coast of Canada, carved giant totem poles out of trees. Some totem poles celebrated special events or the lives of leaders.

### Inuit Victory

The Inuit people have lived in the Arctic north of Canada for thousands of years. They have persuaded the Canadian government to give them back control of four regions of native land that cover around 40 per cent of Canada. The biggest region, Nunavut, is home to more than 33,000 people.

### Is There Anybody Out There?

The first long-distance phone call was made in Canada in 1876. A century later, Canada was the first country to set up a satellite network. Satellites provide a vital link to many remote communities.

### Two Languages

Canada has two official languages, English and French. The first Europeans to settle in Canada were the French, followed by the British. Today, the majority of Canadians speak English, but French is the official language in Quebec, Canada's largest province.

### Winter Sports

Winters are very harsh all over Canada. Ice hockey and skating are national sports – some families flood their back gardens in winter, so that the water freezes to make a temporary ice rink.

*A tug pulls the timber down the river. Water transport is used when there are no major roads through the forest.*

*The timber is taken to a riverside sawmill, where it is cut into planks or pulped for papermaking.*

# THE UNITED STATES

The United States of America is an exciting mixture of different cultures and traditions. Over the last 500 years, more than 70 million people from all over the world have made America their home, many entering the country through New York City. The families of the new arrivals now help to make up the American population of about 313 million. The United States is a superpower, and is probably the most powerful nation in the world.

**Leading Light**
The Statue of Liberty has been a welcoming sight to many immigrants arriving in the America over the last hundred years. The statue is a symbol of freedom, and was built to celebrate the 100th anniversary of American independence. It was given to the Americans by the French in 1884.

**Lots of Languages**
Most Americans can trace their family trees back to other parts of the world. Four out of five Americans speak English, but other European and Asian languages are also widely spoken.

*Three-quarters of the American population live in cities. This is San Francisco, in the West Coast state of California.*

United States

*Jeans are made of tough material called denim.*

## Jean Genie

Jeans are an American invention. The first pair was made in 1874 by Levi Strauss. Levi jeans are still sold all around the world. Today, the jeans industry makes millions of dollars for the American economy.

## Drive Time

America is a huge country, and many Americans are used to driving long distances to visit friends or family. Driving is a popular American pastime. Large cars are not as fashionable as they used to be. This is because smaller cars use up less petrol and are better for the environment.

*Many American children grow up in suburbs. It is easy to drive from the suburb to the nearest shopping mall or city.*

*More corn is grown in America than in any other country. Much farming is done by machines, so only three per cent of the labour force work on farms today.*

## Modern Motorbikes

Today, many Native Americans try to keep up traditional ways and beliefs alongside their modern lifestyles. But many young Native Americans ride motorbikes rather than horses these days!

# CENTRAL AMERICA & THE CARIBBEAN

Central America is made up of a narrow strip of eight countries that link the continents of North and South America. Just like the long chain of islands that makes up the Caribbean, Central America is surrounded by clear blue oceans. Today, the beautiful Caribbean Sea and the sunny, sandy beaches attract many tourists. In the past, the sea brought visitors who were less welcome, like the first settlers from Europe five hundred years ago.

## Weaving for a Living

Over half the people of Guatemala are Amerindian. Their ancestors go back a thousand years to the days of the ancient Maya. Guatemala now sells Mayan crafts to the rest of the world.

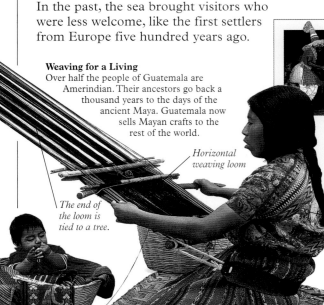

*Horizontal weaving loom*

*The end of the loom is tied to a tree.*

## Carnival Time

The Caribbean is famous for its carnivals. For two days and nights at the start of the Christian festival of Lent, people dance through the streets wearing fantastic costumes.

*It is often possible to tell which village a weaver lives in from the patterns in her cloth.*

*A strap around the weaver's back holds the loom steady.*

Belize
 Costa Rica
 Cuba
Dominica
 Dominican Republic
El Salvador
 Grenada
Guatemala

## Pollution City
The four million cars in Mexico City cause awful traffic jams. Pollution from traffic and industry can reach dangerous levels, and mountains around the city stop the bad air escaping.

## The Day of the Dead
Every year in Mexico, a festival is held to remember people who have died. It is called The Day of the Dead and takes place at the end of October. Families have picnics by the graves of their relatives. When night falls, they keep watch over the graveyard by candlelight.

*A sugary souvenir of the festival.*

## A Modern Mix
Many Caribbean people are descendants of African slaves, who were forced to work on sugar plantations. Slavery was stopped in the 19th century, and many Asians then came to work in the Caribbean. Their descendants still live there today.

## Terrific Temples
More than 1,000 years ago, the ancient Maya peoples built impressive temples, especially in Mexico. Mayan society was very sophisticated long before the Spaniards invaded in the 16th century.

## Difficult Life
An army helicopter causes these children in El Salvador to take cover. Central America has seen many revolutions and long wars. This area has natural hazards too, such as volcanoes, earthquakes and hurricanes.

 Haiti

 Honduras

 Jamaica

 Mexico

 Nicaragua

 Panama

 St Kitts-Nevis

 St Lucia

 St Vincent and the Grenadines

 Trinidad and Tobago

## Caribbean People
More than fifty different ethnic groups live on the islands of the Caribbean. Here are just a few.

Asian

Arawak

Afro-Caribbean

European

# SOUTH AMERICA

Most South Americans are Roman Catholics. A huge statue of Christ towers over the Brazilian port of Rio de Janeiro. This is a reminder of three centuries of Spanish and Portuguese rule, when the first peoples of South America were almost wiped out. Today, most South Americans still speak Spanish and Portuguese. South America is a growing industrialized area, but many people are still very poor.

## Galloping Gauchos

Large areas of northern and central Argentina are covered with a grassy plain, called the pampas. Huge herds of cattle are kept on the pampas, and are looked after by cowboys known as gauchos. Most gauchos are descendants of European settlers in South America.

*These gauchos from northwest Argentina are wearing traditional Spanish hats and neck kerchiefs.*

*Stiff, flared leather flaps protect the gaucho's legs from high-growing thistles when he is riding his horse in the pampas.*

*Heavy leather riding crop*

## Rich and Poor

São Paulo, in Brazil, is South America's biggest industrial city. The city centre is very modern and wealthy. Many people from the surrounding areas travel to São Paulo in search of work. Their children often end up living in terrible poverty on the streets.

Colombia  Ecuador  Guyana  Paraguay  Peru Surinam Uruguay Venezuela

*Gauchos are very proud of their horses. They work on ranches called 'estancias'.*

*A thick poncho is used as a blanket at night. It can also be used as a shield in a fight.*

## Machu Picchu and La Paz

South Americans have always been clever at building cities high up in the mountains. The ruins of Machu Picchu are hidden 2,280 metres up in the Andes, in Peru. The city was built over 500 years ago, without the help of modern machinery.

La Paz is the capital city of Bolivia. It is the world's highest capital city, 3,636 metres above sea level. The city's steep streets are surrounded by snow-capped mountains. The thin mountain air often makes visitors breathless.

## The Yanomami

In 1991, an area of the Brazilian rainforest about the size of Portugal was set aside for the Yanomami tribe. This did not stop miners from invading the land, bringing diseases that have wiped out large numbers of the Yanomami population.

## South Americans

South America is a huge continent, with a wide mix of different people.

Highland Amerindian

Lowland Amerindian

South American of African descent

South American of European and Indian descent

# NORTHERN AFRICA

The spectacular pyramids and priceless treasures of Ancient Egypt are world famous. Art and culture are still very important to people all over northern Africa. A great range of musical and artistic traditions have been passed down through African families for generations.

**The Berber People**

Most North Africans are now Muslims. But in Morocco and Algeria, one in five people are still Berbers. Their nomadic way of life has hardly changed for centuries.

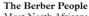

*The big bass drums are called brekete drums.*

**Making Music**

African rhythms have influenced modern jazz and blues music, and are now an important ingredient of African pop music. These drummers are from Ghana in west Africa.

**Famine**

Africa has the fastest-growing population in the world. It is hard to grow enough food to feed all these people. Even in a normal year, up to 150 million Africans suffer from a lack of food. When the rains don't come, crops fail and disaster strikes. These children in the Sahel region of northern Africa are in danger of starving.

Egypt
 Eritrea
Ethiopia
 Gambia
Ghana
Guinea
Guinea-Bissau
Ivory Coast

## City Growth

Most Africans live in the countryside, but a steady flow of young men are moving from the villages to look for work in the big cities. Lagos in Nigeria is Africa's fastest-growing modern city.

### Chocolate Centre

Well over half the world's cocoa is grown in western Africa. More cocoa is grown in the Ivory Coast than anywhere else. About a fifth of Ivory Coast farmland is used to grow cocoa crops.

*The drummers' clothes and music come from Dagbon, in northern Ghana.*

*The smaller drums are called talking drums. The tighter the strings are squeezed, the higher the note.*

### African Crafts

Wood carving, weaving and jewellery making are traditional African crafts.

Nigerian wood carving

Narrow-strip woven trousers from Ghana

Bronze bracelet from Mali

Algerian silver jewellery, with enamel decoration

Brass bracelet and earrings from Sudan

 Liberia
 Libya
 Mali
 Mauritania
 Morocco
 Niger
 Nigeria
 Senegal
 Sierra Leone
 Somalia
 South Sudan
 Sudan
 Togo
 Tunisia

361

# SOUTHERN AFRICA

A rich variety of peoples make up the African countries in this region. Huge grassland savannahs support an amazing variety of wildlife. Game parks were first set up in Kenya to protect animals from hunters. Today, these parks are big tourist attractions. Across the whole region, traditional lifestyles, like those of the Kalahari Bushmen, have slowly been replaced with new ways. There have been many personal and political changes for the peoples of southern Africa.

### A New Start

The San, or Bushmen, live in the Kalahari desert. For about 20,000 years, they hunted animals and gathered plants to survive. Very few of them still hunt, and most now find work on local farms or in nearby towns.

*Today, most Bushmen settle in one place. They have given up a life on the move.*

### On the Move

Only a few small groups of Bushmen still hunt in the Kalahari desert. Each group has a territory of up to 1,000 square kilometres. The men hunt while the women find tasty fruit, nuts and roots.

*Much of the Bushmen's land is now used for farms, cattle ranches and nature reserves.*

Botswana
 Burundi
Comoros
Congo
 Equatorial Guinea
 Gabon
 Kenya
 Lesotho
Madagascar

## Market Day
African women often earn money by selling surplus vegetables from the family farm at the market. Village markets are lively and noisy occasions, where friends meet to exchange the latest news.

 Malawi

 Mauritius

 Mozambique

 Namibia

 Rwanda

 São Tomé & Príncipe

 South Africa

 Swaziland

 Tanzania

 Uganda

 Dem. Rep. Congo

 Zambia

 Zimbabwe

## Black and White
In 1948 the white government of South Africa passed apartheid laws that were unfair to black people. The African National Congress fought the laws and their leader, Nelson Mandela, was jailed for 26 years. He was let out in 1990 and in 1994 he became the first black president of South Africa.

## Going to School
Many African children have a long journey to school. A bus takes these Zimbabwean children part of the way, and they have to walk the last few kilometres.

## Rise of the Zulus
Two hundred years ago, the Zulus were a small clan of a few hundred people, but they fought wars with similar clans to become one big Zulu nation. Today, the Zulus are an important political force in South Africa.

## White Tribe
This Afrikaner family lives on a farm in South Africa, near the border with Zimbabwe. They are descendants of the first Dutch South African settlers, who started arriving from Europe in 1652. Like their ancestors, the Afrikaners are still dominant in many aspects of South African life.

# THE MIDDLE EAST

The discovery of oil has made parts of the Middle East very rich and powerful. Huge oil refineries are a common sight in the region. But the oil will not last for ever, and other industries are being developed to keep the money coming in when the oil has run out. The Middle East has always been a very productive area. Its age-old civilizations have exported farming techniques, beautiful crafts and three major religions all around the world.

**Turkish Bazaar**
In the Middle East, many people shop in markets and bazaars. This shopkeeper is hoping to sell some of his brassware at the Great Covered Bazaar in Istanbul, Turkey.

**Desert Survivors**
This family lives on the edge of the desert in Oman. They belong to a group of travelling Arabs called the bedouin. For 4,000 years, nomadic bedouin have survived in the hottest parts of the Middle East, leading camels and goats in search of water and pasture.

*Bedouin women dress modestly in traditional masks and black overdresses.*

*Bedouin girls wear colourful clothes and silver and gold jewellery.*

**It's a Camel's Life**
Most bedouin families own a pick-up truck. These do much of the work once done by camels. Camels are prized as symbols of wealth. A camel may be sold to a camel racer for several thousand dollars.

**Living on a Kibbutz**
In Israel, big farms, called kibbutzim, were set up so many Jewish families could live and work on the same farm and share the produce.

*The Dome of the Rock*

**City of Faith**
Jerusalem is a special city for Jews, Christians and Muslims. Jews come to pray at the Western Wall, the only remaining part of the ancient Temple. Christians believe Christ came back to life after his death in Jerusalem. The Dome of the Rock marks the spot where Muslims believe Muhammad rose to heaven.

*The Western Wall is the holiest site in Judaism.*

*A decorative silver dagger is a sign of power and wealth.*

*White clothes reflect bright sunlight and help people keep cool.*

*Bedouin men and boys wear head shawls to protect their heads from the sun. In June, the Omani desert can reach 45 °C in the shade.*

**Trip of a Lifetime**
At least once in a lifetime, every Muslim must try to make a special journey, or Hajj, to Mecca in Saudi Arabia. During the Hajj, visitors crowd into the Great Mosque, and walk seven times around the shrine, called the Ka'ba.

Afghanistan

Bahrain

Iran

Iraq

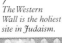
Israel

Jordan

Kuwait

Lebanon

Oman

Qatar

Saudi Arabia

Syria

Turkey

Yemen

United Arab Emirates

# SCANDINAVIA

Scandinavia is the name give to the countries of northern Europe. The far north of this region lies inside the Arctic Circle, so the winters are very harsh.

The people of northern Scandinavia enjoy winter sports in the cold climate. Cross-country skiing was invented in Norway, and is still a quick way of getting about during the snowy winter months.

**City slickers**
About a quarter of the Danish population live in Copenhagen, the capital of Denmark. Most Scandinavians choose to live in cities in the warmer south of the region.

**Sweat it Out**
Saunas are wooden rooms, steaming with heat from a stove. Invented in Finland over 1,000 years ago, they are found in many homes in Scandinavia. After a sauna, people often enjoy a cold showers or a roll in the snow.

**Escape to the Country**
Many Scandinavians enjoy a high standard of living. Some can afford to buy or rent a second home in the mountains, in the forest or by the sea. They escape to these 'holiday huts' at weekends and during the summer months.

**Land of the Midnight Sun**
Imagine waking at midnight, to find the sun shining outside! At the height of summer, the tilt of the Earth causes northern countries to get more of the Sun's light. In northern Scandinavia, it doesn't get dark at all in the middle of summer.

*It is still light at midnight, because the Sun hasn't set.*

**Lighting Up the Sky**
The northern nights, or aurora borealis, can be seen in many parts of the Arctic Circle, especially the far north of Scandinavia. The colourful, dancing lights appear in the sky when a cloud of gas released from the Sun collides with the magnetic field around Earth.

## Out in the Cold

The Saami, or Lapp people, are traditionally nomadic, travelling throughout northern Scandinavia and Russia herding their reindeer. It is getting harder to make a living in this way, so many young Saami have become fishermen and farmers.

## Legoland

Denmark is the home of Lego, one of the world's most popular children's building toys. A theme park has been built entirely from Lego bricks near Billund. It is a big tourist attraction.

## Earthly Energy

These Icelanders are swimming in waters warmed by energy deep under the Earth. This geothermal energy is also used to generate electricity and heat houses.

*At seven o'clock in the morning, the Sun is already well up in the sky.*

*At midday, the hot Sun is at its highest position in the sky.*

*It is six o'clock, and the long, light evening is just beginning.*

# THE BRITISH ISLES

The Republic of Ireland is an independent country, with its own government and traditions. England, Scotland, Wales and Northern Ireland make up the United Kingdom. Many aspects of British life, such as its historical buildings and customs, have been preserved. But the United Kingdom is also good at adapting to change. A rich variety of ethnic groups now live in the United Kingdom's multicultural society.

**Beside the Seaside**
Britain is surrounded by the sea. British seaside holidays first became popular in the 19th century. Today, many British people go on holiday abroad, where it is less likely to rain!

**The Oldest Democracy**
The Houses of Parliament in London have been the home of British democracy since 1512. The political party with the most representatives, called MPs, forms the government. MPs are voted in at national general elections.

*The Commons' Chamber is where the 650 MPs debate government decisions.*

*Big Ben is the name of the bell inside Elizabeth Tower.*

**Howzat!**
Sunday afternoons in summer would not be the same in many English villages, without the familiar sight of a cricket match on the village green. Cricket is an English invention, and is usually followed by another well-known English tradition, afternoon tea!

**Guy Fawkes Night**
A plot to blow up the Houses of Parliament almost succeeded in 1605, but the ringleader, Guy Fawkes, was caught and executed. Guy Fawkes Night is still celebrated all over England on November 5, when home-made straw dummies – called guys – are burnt on big bonfires at firework parties.

Republic of Ireland

United Kingdom

### Arty Edinburgh

For three weeks every August, a big arts festival takes place in Edinburgh, the historic capital of Scotland. The festival gives amateur and part-time entertainers the chance to perform, and also attracts some of the world's best musicians, theatre companies and artists.

### Foot-Tapping Folk

Traditional folk music is extremely popular in Ireland. The accordion is a typical folk instrument, often played to accompany singers. Irish bands have been very successful on the world pop scene. Many songs were first written in Gaelic, the original language of Ireland.

*Possible new laws are debated in the Lords' Chamber.*

### A Divided Community

Northern Ireland is part of the United Kingdom, but is divided along religious lines. The Protestant majority want to stay under British rule, while the Catholic minority want to join the Republic of Ireland. Politicians are working towards a peaceful agreement while ordinary people try to carry on with their lives.

### National Pride

The Welsh are proud of their culture, and enjoy celebrating national festivals. St David is the patron saint of Wales, so on St David's Day, children go to school wearing traditional Welsh costume.

*The leek is the national emblem of Wales.*

# FRANCE & THE LOW COUNTRIES

The Netherlands, Belgium and Luxembourg are sometimes called the Low Countries, because much of the land is flat and low-lying. France and the Low Countries are powerful farming and trading nations, thanks to their good soil and large natural harbours. The people of the region are fond of good food. French chefs are world famous for their fine cooking skills.

**European Dream**
Many European countries are working together by being members of the European Union. The parliament is at Brussels, in Belgium, and also at Strasbourg, in France.

*This stylish outfit is by Christian Lacroix, a top French fashion designer.*

**Style Capital**
Paris, the capital of France, is at the heart of the world fashion industry. Every season, famous designers display new creations at big shows.

**Chocolate Secrets**
Many Belgian chocolate makers keep their recipes secret, so no one can copy them.

Brandy

Coffee

Mint

Nougat

Mixed nuts

**City Canals**
Amsterdam is the capital of the Netherlands. It is built around a network of canals that were once used for trade and transport. By tradition, the Dutch find their way about the city on bicycles.

**At War with the Sea**
Nearly half of the Netherlands was once under sea water. Over the centuries the Dutch have reclaimed this land from the sea, draining it by using a clever system of canals and sea walls, or dykes. Much of the reclaimed land is now used for intensive crop and dairy farming.

Belgium   France   Luxembourg   Monaco   Netherlands

## Land of Wine
France produces some of the world's best wines. Each region has its own wines, with their own special flavours. In the Rhône valley in southeast France, grapes ripen in the summer sun. They are then harvested and fermented in vats.

## Small But Rich
Luxembourg is a tiny country that nestles between France, Belgium and Germany. Its small population has a high standard of living, because of the country's success as a financial centre.

## Fabulous Food
The French love their food, and take care to buy it as fresh as possible. Most French people are careful shoppers, closely inspecting food and even sampling it before they buy.

*Attractive vegetable displays are arranged to catch the shopper's eye.*

*Many French shops sell only one kind of produce, but offer a wide range of choice.*

*Crusty French bread is bought every morning, as it does not keep fresh for long.*

# SPAIN & PORTUGAL

Both Spain and Portugal have warm, sunny climates and long coastlines. The blue skies and dazzling white beaches of Spain's Mediterranean coast attract millions of tourists every summer. The sea is also an important source of food and employment. Fishing is a major industry in Portugal and on Spain's Atlantic coast.

*Young Spaniards can ride scooters from the age of 14.*

**Easy Riders**

Scooter-riding is a craze for young people in many parts of Spain, especially the regions of Valencia and Catalonia. Bikers meet in the evenings, to compare bikes and arrange races.

*This scooter can reach a top speed of 95 kilometres an hour.*

**Fiesta!**

Spain has more festivals than any other European country. Some are religious – others are just for fun. One of the messiest festivals takes place in Bunyols, in Valencia. The villagers pelt each other with tomatoes, to celebrate the time when a lorry spilled its load of overripe tomatoes all over the village square.

**Tide of Tourists**

Mediterranean countries are very popular with tourists. In 2010, around 210 million tourists flocked to the coasts of southern Europe. Every year the Spanish population doubles when tourists arrive to enjoy the hot summer weather and sandy beaches.

Andorra     Portugal     Spain

## Take Your Pick
These Portuguese farmers grow oranges, lemons and olives. Orchards of sweet, juicy oranges are a common sight in the hot countryside of southwest Portugal.

## City of Seven Hills
Lisbon, the capital of Portugal, is the smallest capital in Europe. It is built on seven steep hills. Old electric trams carry the townspeople up and down the sloping streets.

## Eating Around Spain
Here are some tasty dishes from different regions of Spain.

Gazpacho – cold tomato soup from Andalusia

## Fire Dance
Flamenco dancing was developed many hundreds of years ago by the gypsies of Andalusia. It is still popular all over Spain. Many Spanish children learn the dance from a young age, and enjoy wearing the colourful flamenco costumes.

Cocido – meat stew from Castile and Estremadura

Zarzuela de Pescado – seafood stew from Catalonia

## First Communion
Most Spanish people are Roman Catholics. From the age of seven or eight, children are taught the main beliefs of the Catholic church, ready to take their first communion at the age of ten. The ceremony is a religious and social occasion – an important event for all the family.

Paella – chicken, seafood and rice from Valencia

Doughnuts – a popular sweet all over Spain

# GREECE & ITALY

Greece and Italy lie in southern Europe, where the warm summers and beautiful Mediterranean coastline draw millions of tourists every year. Many magnificent buildings, dating back to the days of the Ancient Greeks and Romans, are also popular attractions. A lot of these sites are in urgent need of repair. Both Greece and Italy are struggling to keep their ancient monuments in good condition.

**Priests on Parade**
Greek Orthodox priests are allowed to get married, unlike Roman Catholic priests. Priests play an important part in both Greek and Italian society and are given great respect.

**Café Talk**
In some parts of Greece and Italy, far away from the busy towns and cities, life carries on at a very relaxed pace. Many families rest in the strong heat of the day. In the cooler evenings, men often gather in cafés for a drink and a chat.

*Chemicals from car exhausts are eating away at the ancient stone.*

*Parts of the Parthenon have been so badly damaged, they need to be restored or replaced.*

*So many tourists visit the Parthenon that its steps are being worn away.*

**Temple under Threat**
The Parthenon in Athens is an ancient Greek temple, built to honour Athene, the goddess of wisdom. It is now under threat from air pollution and the tramping of millions of visitors' feet.

### The Pope's City
The Pope is head of the Roman Catholic Church. He lives in a tiny country called the Vatican City, which lies within the walls of Rome, the capital of Italy. This state has its own laws, police force and even its own postal service!

### Car Italia
The Fiat car works, in Turin northern Italy, is one of the largest car factories in the world. Over 140,000 people work there to make more than one and a half million cars every year.

### Pasta Preparations
More types of pasta are made in Italy than anywhere else in the world. Flour, eggs, vegetable oil and salt are mixed to make dough, which is then rolled out and cooked. Pasta is often eaten with a tasty sauce.

*Spaghetti Bolognese*

*Big arches reduce the weight of this typical Venetian building.*

*Brick foundations are laid on wooden posts, which are driven deep into the mud.*

### Grand Passions
Opera and soccer are two of Italy's top obsessions. The soccer World Cup took place in Italy in 1990. Luciano Pavarotti, the world-famous Italian opera singer, sang at a gala concert to celebrate this important tournament.

### Sinking City
Venice was built over 300 years ago on the mudbanks of a lagoon on Italy's northeast coast. The floating city is slowly sinking. Many of its buildings have been damaged by pollution and constant contact with water, and need to be carefully restored.

# GERMANY, AUSTRIA & SWITZERLAND

Germany, Austria and Switzerland lie at the heart of Europe. Central Europeans share a love of traditional food, drink and festivals. They also share a language, as German is the most widely spoken language of the region. Germany is a powerful country. After years of separation for political reasons, East Germany rejoined West Germany in 1990 to become one big country. The wall dividing East from West Berlin was torn down amidst great celebrations.

**Fantasy Castle**
The castle of Neuschwanstein nestles among the Bavarian Alps in south Germany. It was built about a hundred years ago by a rich Bavarian king with a wild imagination.

*Tall turrets give the castle a fairy-tale appearance.*

*King Ludwig II died in 1886, before this spectacular castle was finished.*

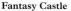

**Starting School**
German children start primary school at the age of six, although most have been to a nursery, or kindergarten, for three years before this. On their first day, children are sent to school with a large cone stuffed with everything they will want, including sweets, pens and books.

*The castle attracts tourists from all around the world.*

Austria

 Germany

 Liechtenstein

Switzerland

## Coming Down the Mountain

The return of cows from the Alps is celebrated in August. It is called the Einabtrieb. The cows are usually decorated in bright colours. But if somebody has died, the decorations are black or dark blue.

## Snowy Holiday

Every year, thousands of skiers visit resorts in Austria and Switzerland. Some people worry that mountain tourism spoils the environment. But it brings lots of money for both countries and is a big employer of local people.

## The Biggest Wheel

The Riesenrad in Vienna is one of the largest big wheels in the world. The wheel is 61 metres across, and it turns round at the slow speed of 75 centimetres a second.

## Very Viennese

One in five Austrians lives in Vienna, the capital of Austria. The city was once at the centre of the great Austro-Hungarian empire. It is still an important city, and is the home of many United Nations organizations.

*The highest point of the wheel is nearly 65 metres above the ground.*

*Each carriage takes up to 12 passengers.*

## Three Languages

Switzerland is surrounded by Germany, Austria, Liechtenstein, France and Italy. Three main languages are spoken in Switzerland – French, German and Italian. Most Swiss people speak German, but many speak at least two of these languages.

# CENTRAL AND EASTERN EUROPE

Central and eastern Europe has been invaded many times but is now a meeting place for different cultures and religions. The downfall of communism in the 1980s and 1990s has liberated the countries of the region, but has also allowed old tensions between many of the ethnic groups to flare up again. Several new countries have been created, including the Czech Republic, Croatia, Slovenia, Bosnia and Herzegovina.

### Lake Bled

The picturesque snow-covered mountains and clear lakes of north-western Slovenia draw tourists to the area. Lake Bled, with its beautiful village overlooking the waterside, is one of the most spectacular holiday resorts in Slovenia.

### Hungarian Dress

This traditional dress is covered in detailed embroidery. Colourful sewing is a typical Hungarian handicraft. Today this costume is only worn on special occasions.

### Prague's Town Hall

Prague is the capital of the Czech Republic and one of the most beautiful cities in Europe. The Old Town Hall looks huge, but is really a row of small adjoining buildings.

### Fishermen of the Adriatic

These fishermen are from the island of Korcula, off the coast of Croatia. Local people have made a living from fishing since prehistoric times. Many families have their own boat and a private jetty.

*Above the inscription 'Prague, Head of the Kingdom' is the city's coat of arms.*

Albania

Bosnia and
Herzegovina

Bulgaria

Croatia

Czech
Republic

Hungary

Kosovo

Macedonia

Montenegro

**Bratislava Castle**
Bratislava is the capital of Slovakia
and is situated on the
River Danube. The oldest
parts of the city date back
to the middle ages.

*To get to the steeple
you have to enter
the main doors,
which are Gothic
in style and carved
from wood.*

*The face of this
famous clock
not only tells
the time, but
shows the
movement of
the sun and the
moon through
the twelve signs
of the zodiac.*

*Pictures on the
calendar show
how the world
changes with the
four seasons.*

**City of Learning.**
Many of Poland's buildings were lost
in World War II but Krakow's buildings
escaped and the impressive streets are
a reminder that Krakow was once the
capital of Poland. The oldest university
in Poland is situated in Krakow – the
university of the Jagellonians.

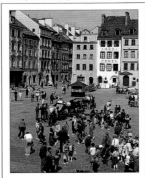

**Historic Square**
Warsaw, the capital of Poland,
is over 700 years old. Today its
old town is a popular tourist
attraction and people can
explore the area in traditional
horse-drawn carriages.

Poland

Romania

Serbia

Slovakia

Slovenia

**Favourite Foods**
Here are some
typical central and
eastern European
dishes.

Red borsch

Pork with cabbage
and dumplings

Goulash

Dalmation bake

Armenia
 Azerbaijan
Belarus
 Estonia
 Georgia
 Kazakhstan
Kyrgyzstan
 Latvia

# NORTHERN EURASIA

Northern Eurasia stretches across a vast area, from Ukraine in the west to the frozen wastes of Siberia. For centuries, northern Eurasia has been controlled by powerful rulers and governments. But in 1991, the communist Soviet Union split into 15 independent states. Mongolia had close links with the former Soviet Union, but was never part of it.

**Daring Dance**
This energetic dance celebrates the courage of cossack soldiers from the Ukraine.

**Rocking Russia**
These rock fans are enjoying a concert in Moscow, the capital of Russia. Big changes happened for the Russians in the late 1980s. Strict communist rules were relaxed and the people began to enjoy new freedoms.

**Going to Church**
Orthodox Christianity has been the traditional Russian religion for over 1,000 years. The cathedral of St Basil is one of the most spectacular Russian Orthodox churches.

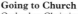

*The cathedral lies in Red Square, right in the heart of Moscow.*

*St Basil's was built for Tsar Ivan the Terrible in the 1550s, to mark his military successes.*

**Keeping the Faith**
The Communist Party disapproved of all religions. The Jews suffered badly – their synagogues and schools were closed down. Jewish traditions survived, but they are now practised mainly by older people.

Lithuania   Moldova   Mongolia   Russian Federation   Tajikistan   Turkmenistan   Ukraine   Uzbekistan

### High Fliers
The circus is a popular form of entertainment all over Russia. One of the most famous circuses in the world is based in Moscow. The New Moscow Circus boasts a high standard of acrobatics. Its grand Big Top was opened in 1971 and seats an audience of up to 3,400 people.

### Northern Eurasians
The largest ethnic group of northern Eurasia is made up of Slavs. Next biggest is the Turkic-speaking population. Smaller groups include Mongols and Inuit.

### Eastern Promise
The people of Central Asia look very different from the Russians who live farther north. They speak languages similar to Turkish and many are Muslims, like their neighbours in the Middle East. These women are selling bread at a market stall in Uzbekistan.

Ukrainian Slav

### Yesterday's Hero
Ancestors of these Mongol horsemen fought in the army of the fierce Mongol emperor, Ghengis Khan, 1,000 years ago. Today, Ghengis Khan is once again a Mongolian national hero.

Turkic-speaking Uzbek

*Colourful onion-shaped domes top the nine chapels of St Basil's.*

Mongol

### Ripe Old Age
In the Caucasian mountains, people live long lives and marry young, sometimes staying together for 100 years! Perhaps the fresh air, healthy food and hard work keep them young.

Russian Inuit

# CHINA AND TAIWAN

There are more than 500 million bikes in China, including 100 milllion electric bikes – four times as many e-bikes as there are cars. There are over a billion people in China – more than in any other country. Fifty-seven different ethnic groups make up the population, but by far the largest group is the Han, traditionally a peasant farming people.

**Communism in China**
The Communist government in China plays an active role in people's everyday lives. This official government poster encourages couples who live in cities to have only one child.

**Food and Farming**
Two-thirds of the Chinese people are farmers, growing crops on every spare patch of suitable land. Up to three crops of rice may be grown on the same paddy field each rice-growing season.

*Rice is the basic food for China's huge population.*

**Bringing up Baby**
The 'one child per family' rule was introduced in 1979 to try to control the fast population growth. It aimed to keep the population under 1.2 billion by 1995, but in 2012 there were 1.3 billion people in China.

**Words and Pictures**
The Chinese written language is based on pictures, which describe objects, actions and ideas. There are about 50,000 pictures, or characters. A simplified list of about 2,000 is commonly used today.

男人 *Man*

女人 *Woman*

*Lettering brush*

China    Taiwan

**Folk Art in Taiwan**
Taiwan has some colourful folk traditions. A sticky mixture of rice and flour is dyed and moulded to make these decorative figures. In the past, the flour and rice recipe was used to make children's snacks. Today, the figures are kept, not eaten.

*Many Chinese people would like to be allowed to have bigger families. It is hard for them not to spoil their 'only' children.*

*Most Chinese mothers are in full-time work. Their children are looked after in crèches at the workplace, until they are old enough to go to to school.*

## Hong Kong
More than seven million people live in the 1,045 square kilometres of Hong Kong, making it the world's most crowded place. Hong Kong is a busy trading centre and the world's biggest exporter of watches, clocks and toys.

**Get Well Soon**
This street trader is selling herbal medicines. Ancient, natural ways of treating illnesses are very common in China.

*Angelica root*

**Buddhist Tibet**
Most people living in Tibet are Buddhists. They believe their past leaders are alive now in the body of their present leader, the Dalai Lama. In 1959, the Dalai Lama fled his home, the Potala Palace, to escape the invading Chinese army. He now lives in exile in India.

383

# JAPAN & KOREA

Japan is famous for its electronic gadgets and machines. In the last 50 years, Japan has become one of the world's richest countries, and many Japanese people enjoy a high standard of living. Japan's neighbour, Korea, is split into two separate countries. North Korea has cut off its links with the South and is one of the world's most secretive societies. South Korea is a successful industrial country, like Japan, and trades with the rest of the world.

**Fish Food**
The traditional Japanese diet of fish is very healthy. Many Japanese people live to be very old – in 2010, nearly a quarter of the population was aged over 65.

**Children on Parade**
The Seven-Five-Three Festival in Japan is named after the ages of the children who take part. Every year on November 15, girls and boys are dressed up in traditional costume and taken to a Shinto shrine. It is a very sociable occasion.

**Dinner Time**
The evening meal is an important time for busy Japanese families to get together and relax. Parents often get home late from work, and children have lots of homework to do in the evenings.

*Rice is cooked until it is sticky, so it is easy to eat with pointed chopsticks.*

*An electric rice cooker sits close to the table.*

*Japanese tea is drunk without milk, and is called green tea.*

**Mind Your Head**
These pupils are not hiding from their teacher! They are practising what to do if there is an earthquake. Earthquakes do not happen often in Japan, but they could happen any time. In the past, they have caused terrible damage.

書店

Japan

North Korea

South Korea

**Colourful Koreans**
This woman is wearing the national costume of South Korea. It is made of brightly coloured material. South Korea sells huge amounts of material to the rest of the world. About 600 million square metres of cotton were produced in South Korea in 1990.

*The food is placed on the table before the family sits down to eat.*

*The family sits on cushions around a low table to eat their meal.*

**Selling Ships**
Most of the ships in Asia are made at the Hyundai shipyard in South Korea, the biggest shipyard in the world. It has 9,000 employees, and in 2011 it became the first shipbuilder to deliver its 1700th ship.

**Watch This Space**
The big cities of Japan can get extremely crowded. Space is often very hard to come by, but the smallest places are always put to good use. This electronics shop had hundreds of gadgets for sale in a tiny kiosk in Tokyo.

*Chopstick rest*

*Presentation is very important with Japanese cookery. Portions are always small and dainty.*

**Climb Every Mountain**
Japanese people work hard, but they also enjoy their hobbies. Japan has some stunning mountain ranges, and many Japanese people keep fit with mountain climbing. These hikers are up Mount Furano-Dake, on the island of Hokkaido in north Japan.

書店

# THE INDIAN SUBCONTINENT

The Indian subcontinent includes India, Sri Lanka, Pakistan, Bangladesh, Bhutan and Nepal. Most people in this part of the world follow the Hindu, Muslim or Buddhist religions. In India, eighty per cent of the huge population are Hindus. Every year, millions of Hindus make pilgrimages to the holy city of Varanasi in north India, to wash away their sins in the River Ganges.

## Country Life
Eight out of ten Indians live in small country villages. Cows are kept in each one, and the human population is only three times bigger than the cow population! Hindus believe that cows are holy, so they don't eat them. According to Hindu teaching, 330 million Hindu gods and goddesses live in the body of a cow.

*The bride is nine years old. After the wedding she will return to her family until she is old enough to live with her new husband.*

*The beautiful wedding sari is made of expensive silk.*

*The people in this village make combs for a living.*

## Hindu Theatre
The Dusserah festival celebrates the end of the rainy monsoon. Groups of actors perform episodes from the story of Ram, a Hindu god in human form. The main parts are played by the top class of Indian society, called the Brahman caste.

## Wedding Day
Most Hindu parents choose the person their son or daughter will marry. It is important that the partner they pick belongs to the right class, or caste, of Indian society. Children are often engaged and married when they are quite young. Their weddings are colourful and happy family occasions.

Bangladesh  Bhutan  India  Maldives  Nepal  Pakistan  Sri Lanka

*The bride's family gives expensive presents to the groom's family. This is called the dowry.*

*The groom is eleven years old. He is leading his bride to the marriage ceremony.*

### Floods in Bangladesh

Bangladesh is a very low, flat country, criss-crossed with rivers. After heavy rain, flooding can cause terrible damage. This farmer is helping to push a tricycle taxi, called a rickshaw, through a flooded village in northeastern Bangladesh.

### Women at the Top

Most people in Pakistan are Muslims. In 1988, Benazir Bhutto was voted the first female prime minister of a Muslim country.

### Climb Every Mountain

The Sherpa people of Nepal live high up in the Himalayas. Many Sherpas earn money by guiding tourists, trekkers and mountaineers up the steep and rocky paths.

### Red-Hot Spice

Curry is a very popular Indian dish, and is enjoyed all around the world. Spices are important ingredients in a curry.

Lentils
Coriander
Ginger

Naan bread

Spicy potatoes

Lamb curry

Brunei

Burma

# SOUTHEAST ASIA

It is hard to get away from water in most parts of Southeast Asia! The ten countries that make up the region are linked by waterways and surrounded by oceans. The hot, wet environment is ideal for farming rice, the staple crop of the region. It also supports large areas of tropical rainforests. Sadly, heavy logging has forced many forest people to move away to towns, where the way of life is very different.

**People Power**
The Penan people live in the rainforests of Sarawak. They have tried to stop the destruction of their forest home by blocking roads into the rainforest. Sarawak has the world's highest rate of logging.

**The Secret of Success**
The small island state of Singapore is a powerful trading nation. Singapore became successful because of its position. It was built up as a key trading post between the Far East and the West, and is now one of Asia's richest countries.

**Living with Water**
Many houses in Malaysia and Indonesia are built on stilts. This helps protect them from floods during torrential rainstorms.

*The houses are called 'long' houses. Behind each door is a large room, or 'bilik', where the family lives.*

*The houses are made both from natural and modern materials. Some roofs are made from palms, others from corrugated iron.*

Cambodia  East Timor  Indonesia  Laos  Malaysia  Palau  Philippines  Singapore  Thailand  Vietnam

## Floating Market
Much of Bangkok in Thailand is below sea level, and the city has a busy network of canals. Floating markets are colourful occasions – local traders bring their goods to market by boat, and shoppers paddle up to take a look at what is on offer.

## Bali Dancers
The Indonesian island of Bali is famous for its exciting dances. Historical tales of local princes and heroes are acted out in a masked dance called the Wayang Topeng. The dance is very entertaining, with lots of clowning about as well as serious storytelling.

*A Topeng dancer acts out the character of the mask.*

*Every movement is carefully controlled.*

## Doing Time
The vast majority of Thais are Buddhists. Every male Buddhist is expected to become a monk for a while, to study religious teachings and prepare for adult life.

## Pirates on the South Seas
Pirates are still terrorizing the seas of Southeast Asia, capturing boats and stealing their cargo. In March 1991, a big oil tanker disappeared off the Philippines. This was almost certainly the work of pirates.

*Boats are the main form of transport. Rivers provide links between small communities.*

*Notched tree trunks or ladders are used to get down to the water level.*

# AUSTRALASIA & OCEANIA

Most Australians live in big cities like Sydney, the capital of New South Wales. Both Australia and New Zealand are big economic powers, trading mainly with Asia and the United States. By contrast, many Pacific islanders of Oceania live in isolated communities that have little contact with the outside world.

**Emergency!**
The Royal Flying Doctor Service is a lifesaver for people living in remote parts of Australia. Few patients are more than a two-hour flight away from a hospital.

**Aboriginal Art**
Aboriginal peoples were the first to settle in Australia, over 40,000 years ago. They have strong artistic traditions, and Aboriginal art is now sold around the world, making much needed money for their communities.

**Australian Megamix**
British settlers first came to Australia about 200 years ago, but in the last 70 years there have been many new arrivals from other parts of Europe and Asia.

*Many Italians moved to Australia after the Second World War.*

*The majority of Australians share a love of the outdoors, and live by the sea.*

*A large number of Australians have British ancestors.*

*New European arrivals include many Greeks.*

Nauru

New Zealand

Papua New Guinea

Samoa

Solomon Islands

Tonga

Tuvalu

Vanuatu

**Teaching in Tonga**
Tonga is one of the independent nations among the Pacific islands of Oceania. English and Tongan are the two official languages for the small population of 105,000. In Tonga, children have to go to school between the ages of six and fourteen.

**First People**
These people were some of the first settlers in Australasia and Oceania.

Pacific islander

Papua New Guinea tribesman

Maori woman

*This boy has Vietnamese parents. English is his second language, just as it is for one in eight other Australians.*

**Stone Money**
Some Pacific island tribal traditions have not changed for thousands of years. The people of Yap island still use stones like this one as money when they make important property deals.

*This girl's parents are Chinese. Many Australians are of Asian descent.*

**Rugby Dance**
The Maoris settled in New Zealand about 1,000 years ago. The New Zealand rugby team, the All Blacks, has borrowed some Maori traditions. They use an old Maori war chant, called a haka, to get them in the mood for matches.

*Surfing is popular along the coast of Australia.*

Aboriginal tribesman

# CHAPTER 4

# SCIENCE AND TECHNOLOGY

Through the centuries, people's lives have changed enormously. Today, the way you live is completely dominated by technology, from the electric toaster that produces your breakfast to the bus that takes you to school, the computers you use for learning and playing games, and the television you watch in the evening.

Science and technology have helped us in lots of ways. Because of them, we can grow and distribute food cheaply, manufacture clothing and household goods in huge quantities, treat illnesses of all kinds, and travel from place to place quickly.

But we have to be very careful to use the technology we have in a responsible way. The same knowledge that saves lives and makes our world better can also lead to the development of powerful weapons and chemicals that can harm us and our planet.

**Science and Machines**
**Energy and Industry**
**Transport**

# SCIENCE AND MACHINES

You don't need to walk into a laboratory to see science in action. Science is all around you, every day of your life. There are three main kinds of science. The science of the natural world – plants and animals – is called biology. The study of what things are made of and what happens when they are mixed together is chemistry. The third science, physics, is about how everything in the universe works.

The world of physics includes the study of machines. Machines help us to perform tasks using less effort. For example, one of the first machines, the wheel, makes it easier to move things from place to place. From scissors to smoke detectors, machines are all around us, making our lives easier and safer.

Biology is all about living things.

The laws of flight are studied in physics.

When you heat eggs, a chemical reaction makes the runny part hard and white.

Tunnelling machine

Light bulb

The development of the wheel

Coloured image of nerve cells from the brain

Quartz clock

Portable video game

# LIVING THINGS

Cherries

You are a living thing. All living things are made up of cells, and your body is made up of many billions of cells. Your cells join together to make tissues, for example muscles. Tissues combine to make organs, like your heart.

Biologists are scientists who study living things. They have divided the world of living things into groups called 'kingdoms'. The study of plants is called botany, and the study of animals is called zoology.

Seaweed

Moss

Fly agaric fungus

### Bacteria and Fungi Kingdoms

Bacteria are so tiny they can't be seen without a microscope. They have a simple, one-cell structure. Bacteria and fungi feed on other living things and recycle the remains.

*A kitten grows up into a cat. All living things grow.*

### Splitting Up

Living things are made up of at least one cell. For a living thing to reproduce and grow, its cells must keep on splitting into identical pairs. This single-cell bacterium divides every 20 minutes. Look how many bacteria there are after one hour.

*Now*

*20 minutes later*

*40 minutes later*

*One hour later*

*All living things make copies of themselves. This is reproduction.*

*Living things all find some way of breathing. A cat breathes through its nose.*

*Living things need food to stay alive.*

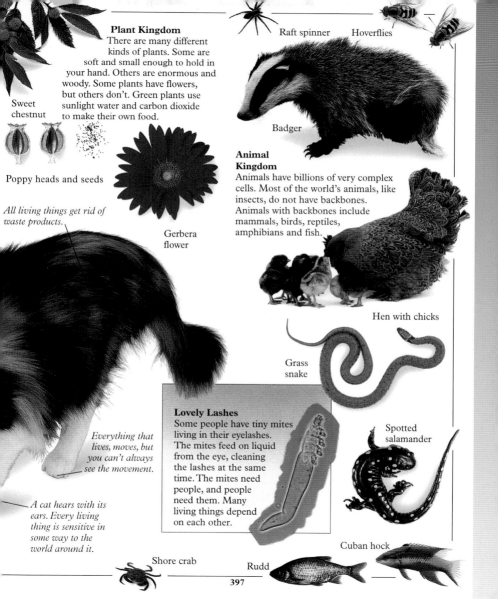

Raft spinner   Hoverflies

## Plant Kingdom
There are many different kinds of plants. Some are soft and small enough to hold in your hand. Others are enormous and woody. Some plants have flowers, but others don't. Green plants use sunlight water and carbon dioxide to make their own food.

Sweet chestnut

Poppy heads and seeds

*All living things get rid of waste products.*

Gerbera flower

Badger

## Animal Kingdom
Animals have billions of very complex cells. Most of the world's animals, like insects, do not have backbones. Animals with backbones include mammals, birds, reptiles, amphibians and fish.

Hen with chicks

Grass snake

*Everything that lives, moves, but you can't always see the movement.*

*A cat hears with its ears. Every living thing is sensitive in some way to the world around it.*

### Lovely Lashes
Some people have tiny mites living in their eyelashes. The mites feed on liquid from the eye, cleaning the lashes at the same time. The mites need people, and people need them. Many living things depend on each other.

Spotted salamander

Cuban hock

Shore crab

Rudd

# SOLIDS

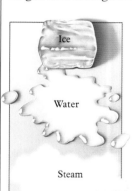

Everything is made up of matter. Molecules are the building blocks of matter. In solids, molecules are usually packed together in a regular way, so the solid keeps its shape without needing a container to hold it. Most matter is visible, like the pages of this book, but some matter is invisible, like air. Matter may be solid, liquid or gas and change from one state to another.

Hydrogen atom

Uranium atom

### Amazing Atoms
The smallest amount of a pure substance is called an atom. The simplest atom is hydrogen, but other atoms are more complex. Atoms are incredibly tiny – about 100,000 million atoms fit on this full stop.

Ice

Water

Steam

### In a State
Ice, water and steam are made up of the same molecules. They are not alike, because their molecules are spaced differently. Solid ice melts into liquid water. When water is boiled, it turns into a gas called steam.

### Molecules in a Solid
Each of these children is acting the part of a molecule in a solid.

*The children are all wearing red T-shirts, to show that the molecules are all the same.*

*The molecules in most solids make up a very regular pattern.*

### Solids on Show
You can tell these solids apart, because they do not look, feel, weigh or smell the same. They all have different properties.

A flower is soft and delicate.

A cake is crumbly and tasty.

**Making Molecules**
Atoms link up to make molecules. Two atoms of hydrogen join together to make one molecule of hydrogen gas.

*The molecules in a cool solid do not move about very fast. If a solid is heated, the molecules move about faster and faster.*

*There are strong links between the molecules in a solid. This means that solids have a fixed shape.*

**Larger than Life**
These long, thin wax molecules are shown about 3 million times larger than they are in real life. The tiny blue dots are atoms that have joined together to make up the wax molecules.

Sugar

**Crystal Clear**
Grains of sugar are solid crystals. Their atoms are close together and arranged in a regular pattern called a lattice. Many solids that look smooth actually have a crystal structure, like these vitamin C tablets.

Vitamin C crystals, seen through a microscope.

Vitamin C tablets

A shell is hard and brittle.

A spider's web is light and strong.

**Graphite and Diamond**
Graphite is soft and is used in pencils, and diamond is the hardest solid in the world. But diamond and graphite have a lot in common! They are two different forms of carbon. This means they have the same molecules, but they are arranged in different ways.

# LIQUIDS

If you spread some butter on hot toast, the butter melts. When a solid gets hot enough to melt it turns into a liquid. Liquids behave differently to solids. The heat that melts a solid breaks down some of the strong links between the molecules, so that the molecules can move about more freely. A liquid flows, because its molecules can't hold together strongly enough to form a solid shape.

Syrup flows slowly.

Car oil flows quite well.

Ink flows very easily.

**Sticky Spoonful**
Some liquids flow much more easily than others. Liquids that are viscous do not flow well.

**Molecules in a Liquid**
These children are behaving like molecules in a liquid.

**Fair Shares?**
Who has more milk to drink? It may not look like it, but these glasses hold the same amount. Containers of different shapes can hold the same volume, or amount, of liquid.

**Liquid Levels**
Liquids flow to fill containers of any shape or size. The surface of a liquid always stays level, however much you may tilt the container.

### Too Hot to Handle?

Ice creams melt very easily, but not all solids have such low melting points. Some only melt if they are heated to very high temperatures. The steel in this factory melts at 1,500°C.

### On the Boil

When a liquid is heated to a certain temperature, it turns into a gas. This temperature is called the boiling point. Different liquids have different boiling points. The water in this pan boils at 100°C.

*In a liquid, the molecules are separate from each other.*

*Moving molecules can get right into all the corners of a container. This is why liquids take up the shape of the container that holds them.*

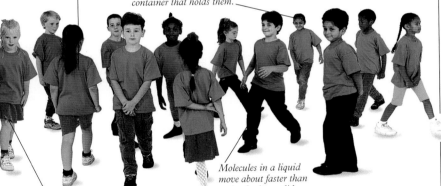

*Molecules in a liquid move about faster than molecules in a solid.*

*Molecules in a liquid are not arranged in a regular pattern, so they can move about freely.*

### On the Surface

Molecules near the surface of a liquid pull towards each other. A drop keeps its shape because of this surface tension. If some washing-up liquid is added to a water drop, the surface tension is made weaker, so the drop spreads out.

### Good Mixers

Blackcurrant juice mixes well with water. It dissolves completely.

### Bad Mixers

Some liquids do not mix at all. Oil does not dissolve in water.

# GASES

Gases are all around us and can't usually be seen or felt, but some can be smelt. All smells are molecules of gas mixed in the air. If you smell some tasty soup, you are actually sniffing in molecules of the soup. When you heat a liquid, it turns into a gas. The heat makes the molecules in the liquid move about faster and faster. The gas molecules fly off in all directions, spreading through the air.

**Lighter than Air**
When a gas gets hot, it takes up more room and gets lighter. A hot-air balloon rises up in the air, because the air inside it is hot and much lighter than the air outside.

**Molecules in a Gas**
Each child is acting like a molecule in a gas. Look how they are bumping into each other.

*There are no links between any of the molecules in a gas.*

**Dancing on Air**
When a shaft of light shines through a gap in the trees, specks of dust look like they are dancing in the sunlight. What is really happening is that the molecules in the air currents move about, flicking the dust in all directions.

*As a gas spreads, the molecules get farther and farther apart. Gases will always spread to fit the space they are in.*

Carbon dioxide
Other gases
Oxygen
Nitrogen

**In the Air**
There are a number of different gases in the air we breathe. 78 per cent of air is nitrogen gas. Oxygen makes up 21 per cent. Carbon dioxide and a variety of other gases make up just one per cent of the gases in the air.

### Pumping Air
It is easy to squash together, or compress, gas molecules. When you pump up a tyre, you compress air molecules into a small space. The more air molecules you pump in, the more they push against the inside of the tyre. The tyre gets harder, because pressure increases inside it.

### High Pressure
Air presses on everything on Earth. You can see air pressure at work. If you suck juice out of a carton, the carton buckles. This is because air pressure pushing on the carton is greater than air pressure inside the carton.

*Molecules in a gas move very quickly, darting about in all directions.*

### Night and Day
Plants help keep the balance of gases in the air. Night and day, they take in oxygen and 'breathe out' carbon dioxide, as we do. But by day, they also take in large amounts of carbon dioxide – which they need to make their food and give off oxygen.

### Out of Breath
Gases can dissolve in liquids, and oxygen from the air dissolves in water. Fish need oxygen to breathe, so they use the oxygen in water to survive under water. Humans also breathe oxygen, but unlike fish, we can't breathe under water without a supply of compressed air.

# ENERGY

Energy is needed for life and for every single movement in the whole universe. When you have run a race you may feel that you have used up all your energy. But your energy has not been lost, it has changed into different kinds of energy: movement and heat. When work is done, energy is never lost but it changes into other kinds of energy. Movement and heat energy are just two of the many different kinds of energy.

**Jumping Jack**
When the lid is closed, the puppet's spring is coiled up, ready to push the puppet out of the box. We say the spring has potential energy. When you open the lid, the spring's potential energy turns into movement energy.

**Energy Changes**
We can't make energy or destroy it. Instead, energy can change from one kind to another. This toy robot shows how energy may not stay in one form for very long!

**Eating Energy**
We get our energy from food, and we need to eat plants, or animals that have eaten plants, to stay alive. Plants get energy to grow from sunlight, so our energy really comes from the sun.

**Sun Power**
Living things that grew millions of years ago were buried under rock, where they slowly turned into coal, oil and gas. Energy from these fuels comes from the sun, shining long ago.

*1. When the robot is switched on, chemical energy stored in the batteries turns into electrical energy.*

Batteries

*2. As the robot moves, electrical energy turns into kinetic energy, which is another name for movement energy.*

*3. The flashing lights show that electrical energy has been changed into light energy.*

*4. The robot makes a noise as it moves. Electrical energy has been turned into sound energy.*

*5. The robot gets warm. Movement energy has changed into heat energy.*

**Running Out of Energy**
Most machines need energy to work. The energy from oil, coal and gas is in danger of running out altogether. Once these fuels, called fossil fuels, have been used up, there will be no way of replacing them.

**Everlasting Energy**
The sun's rays beat down on these solar panels. Heat is stored and used to make electricity. Energy from the wind and waves also provides power. Scientists are trying to find cheaper ways of capturing the endless supply of natural energy.

**Splitting the Atom**
Neutrons are tiny particles inside an atom. If a uranium atom takes in one extra neutron, it splits in half, releasing a huge amount of energy. Nuclear energy produces radioactive waste, which has to be handled and got rid of very carefully.

# HEAT

The sun's rays can make you very hot. The way heat rays move through air is called radiation. You feel warm because the radiation makes the molecules in your skin move about faster than usual. Heat comes from molecules moving around.

It moves through solids by conduction – the molecules in a solid vibrate, bumping the heat along. Heat travels through air and liquids in a circular movement called convection.

*Heat moves along the _____ wooden spoon by conduction. The spoon takes a long time to get hot, because wood is not a good conductor of heat.*

### Snug as a Bug?
Heat doesn't travel easily through air, so materials that trap air keep you warm. This polar explorer is wearing clothes made of materials that insulate his body. This means they keep his body heat close to his body, where he needs it.

### Tricky Fingers
If you dip one finger in hot water and another in cold, the hot water will feel hot and the cold water will feel cold. If you then dip both fingers in lukewarm water, your 'hot' finger is tricked into finding the water cold, and your 'cold' finger finds the water hot.

### Good Conductors

If you heat a solid, its molecules jostle about, passing the heat from molecule to molecule. Just as a whisper moves along a line of children, so the moving molecules pass, or conduct, the heat from one end of the solid to the other.

*As the water reaches its boiling point, it evaporates into steam.*

*When the water near the heat source gets hot, it rises up towards the surface.*

*The cooler water near the surface will sink to the bottom of the pan, where it is then warmed up by the heat source.*

### Building Bridges

When most solids are heated, they get bigger, or expand. This is because the heat speeds up the molecules and they get farther and farther apart as they move. Bridges are built with small gaps between the long pieces of metal, so there is room for the metal to expand on a hot day.

*The flames are a direct source of heat.*

*Metal is a good conductor of heat.*

#### Familiar Temperatures

100°C
Water boils

60°C
Cup of tea

37°C
Body temperature

30°C
Hot summer day

10°C
Cold drink

0°C
Water freezes

# LIGHT

You may need to wear sunglasses on a sunny day, because the bright light hurts your eyes. It is dangerous to look straight at the sun. The sun's light is not just blinding, it also travels to us very fast. In just one second, light travels 300,000 kilometres. If a straight beam of light has to pass through obstacles such as convex and concave lenses, it changes direction. This is called refraction.

*Concave lenses curve inwards in the middle.*

*This beam of light comes from a torch. A torch is a man-made light source.*

*Light bends outwards when it passes through a concave lens.*

*Convex lenses bulge in the middle.*

Retina

Pupil

Optic nerve

Lens

### How We See Light
Light enters your eye through your pupil. It passes through a lens, which focuses the object you are looking at onto the retina. Millions of tiny cells inside the retina turn this upside-down image into electrical messages. The optic nerve carries these messages to your brain, which 'sees' the image the right way up.

### Light for Life
Plants always grow towards the light, even if, like this plant, they have to grow round corners to reach it! Light is very important for life. Plants need light to grow and we need to eat plants, or animals that eat plants, to stay alive.

**The Big Bang**
Light travels faster than sound. When fireworks explode high in the sky, you see the lights before you hear the big bang. Light reaches your eyes more quickly than sound reaches your ears.

**Over the Rainbow**
Drops of rain act like tiny prisms. When light passes through rain drops, the colours of light are split up to form a rainbow.

*When a beam of light passes through a prism, the colours split apart because each wavelength is bent a different amount.*

*Light travels in tiny waves. Light has a mixture of different wavelengths.*

*A prism is a solid triangle-shaped piece of glass or plastic.*

*When light is reflected, the beams of light bounce off the mirror at the same angle as they hit it.*

*When light passes through a convex lens, it is bent, or refracted inwards.*

*When light hits an object that it can't travel through, like this mirror, a shadow forms behind the object where the light can't reach.*

**Busy Line**
When you talk on the telephone, your voice is turned into laser light signals and sent down very thin fibre glass tubes called optical fibres. Up to 150,000 different conversations can be sent down just one of these optical fibres.

# COLOUR

Imagine waking up in a world without colour. There would be no beautiful paintings or rainbows to look at and no bright shoes or clothes to wear. At night when you switch off the light, all the bright colours around you suddenly disappear. This is because you cannot see the colour of an object without light. White light can be split into all the colours of the rainbow – shades of red, orange, yellow, green, blue, indigo and violet. When all these colours are mixed back together, they make white light again.

**Colour Cones**
The inside of the back of your eye looks like this through a microscope. You have cells in the back of your eyes called cones, which send messages to your brain about the colours you see.

**Seeing in Colour**
If you don't have all the different types of cones in your eyes, you may find it hard to tell some colours apart. A colour-blind person may not be able to see the number on this colour blindness test.

*White is the only colour that can't be made by mixing together the primary colours of paint.*

**Seeing Red**
We see things because light bounces off them. Light is actually a mixture of all the colours of the rainbow. When light hits these shoes, all the colours sink in, except the red colour that is reflected back to your eyes.

**Light Mixing**
The colours of light behave differently to paint colours. When red, green and blue light are mixed together, they make white light. The same colours of paint mix to make a dark colour.

**Paint Mixing**
You can make new colours by mixing the primary colours of paint together.

*Blue, yellow and red are the primary colours of paint.*

*Red and yellow mix to make orange.*

*Blue and red mix to make purple.*

*Different shades can be made by adding more of one colour than another.*

*Blue and yellow mix to make green.*

**Tasty Morsels**
Which of these dinners do you fancy? Both meals would taste the same, but the food colouring in one puts you off before you start. Colour can change our feelings about things, especially food.

**Warning Colours**
Colours are often used as a warning. This moth is poisonous, and its bright wings warn hungry birds to leave it alone. We also use colours to warn us of danger. A red traffic light tells us to stop, but a green traffic light means that it is safe to go.

# SOUND

Astronauts talk to each other by radio, because their voices can't travel through empty space. Sound travels in waves. When these waves move through air, the air molecules move quickly, or vibrate. If there are no air molecules, no sound is made, because there is nothing to vibrate. When you shout, the vocal cords in your throat vibrate. These vibrations pass through your mouth into the air, making the air itself vibrate. Your ear picks up the vibrations and you can hear them as sound.

**Deafening Decibels**
The loudness of sounds is measured in decibels. When aeroplanes land, they reach a very high number of decibels. This ground controller is wearing ear protectors to stop himself being deafened by the noise.

*The bottle tops clink together when the jingling stick is shaken.*

*Lentils inside the shaker make a soft, rattling sound.*

*Strings vibrate as the instrument is plucked. The tighter the string, the higher the note.*

**Wailing Whales**
Whales communicate under water over huge distances. The sound of a great whale may travel hundreds of kilometres under water. Sound travels faster and further through liquids and solids than through air. This is because molecules in liquids and solids are more tightly packed.

### Seeing Sounds
You can show that sound vibrations exist by hitting a tray next to a drum sprinkled with rice. The rice bounces up and down with the vibrations that the sound makes.

*Hitting a tin plate makes it vibrate. You hear a loud and crashing noise.*

### Bouncing Sound
This pregnant woman can see her baby before it is born. High frequency sound waves are reflected as they reach the baby, making an image on the computer screen.

### What is Frequency?
The number of complete sound waves that pass by in a second gives us the 'frequency' of a sound. Frequency is measured in hertz. High notes have a high frequency. They make lots of vibrations and have a high number of hertz. Low notes have a low frequency.

### Hearing Sounds
We can not hear sounds of very high or low frequencies, but some animals can. It is impossible for us to hear these sounds, because they are outside our hearing range.

*When a wind instrument is played, the air inside the tube vibrates to make a sound.*

*Blowing into the pipe makes the air inside it vibrate all the way along to the funnel at the end.*

**Bat**
up to 120,000 hertz

**Mouse**
up to 100,000 hertz

**Dog**
up to 35,000 hertz

**Cat**
up to 25,000 hertz

**Young person**
up to 20,000 hertz

# FORCE AND MOVEMENT

A rocket can only take off because a blast of energy forces it to move. Things move if they are pushed or pulled, or if they are high up to start with. The movement they make has a speed in a particular direction. How quickly they speed up depends on how big the force is, and how heavy the moving thing is. Some forces make things move, but others stop things moving. Friction is the name for the force that stops movement.

Push it!

**Playing with Force**
Forces can act in lots of different directions to change the shape of something. Try this for yourself with a lump of modelling dough.

Pull it!

Squeeze it!

**Roll Apart**
If one girl pushes the other, both will start to roll away from each other. When a force pushes one way, it also pushes equally in the opposite direction.

*The go-cart wheels will keep moving until something stops them or slows them down.*

*If the passenger is heavy, it is hard to push the go-cart along and make it speed up.*

*Friction is a force that slows things down. The go-cart wheels rub against the ground, making friction.*

## Speed and Velocity

The time something takes to move a distance is called speed. Velocity is speed in a particular direction. A rocket's velocity is much greater than a snail's!

*A snail moves at about 0.0049 km per hour.*

*A fast sprinter runs at about 36 km per hour.*

*A racing car reaches speeds of up to 338 km per hour.*

*A rocket leaves the Earth's atmosphere at 40,000 km per hour.*

### Down to Earth

When you jump, a strong force called gravity pulls you back down to Earth. Earth's gravity gets weaker as you travel away from it. On the Moon gravity is much less strong, so astronauts can jump high with heavy packs on their backs before gravity pulls them back down again.

*Pushing is a kind of force. The harder the boy pushes, the bigger the force on the go-cart.*

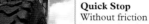

### Quick Stop

Without friction between its wheels and the ground, this truck would slip all over the road. The thick patterns on the tyres, called tread, help the truck get a grip on the ground.

*More pushing power is needed to start off the go-cart than to keep it moving.*

### Good Performance

At high speeds air rushes over the top of a racing car, pushing it down onto the track. This makes the wide tyres grip the track better, so the car can take bends faster than an ordinary car.

# MAGNETS

Magnets are pieces of special material which have an invisible force that can push things away or pull things towards them. The biggest magnet of all is the world itself. Scientists think that as the Earth turns round, electricity is made in the hot metal deep down in the centre. This electricity gives the Earth magnetic power. The Earth has two magnetic poles, called the magnetic North and South Poles. Compass needles always point to the magnetic North Pole.

## Magnetic Fields

A magnetic field is where a magnet has its power. If iron filings are sprinkled around a magnet, they gather together where the magnetic field is strongest. Two identical poles push each other away, so iron filings curve outwards.

Two different poles attract. The iron filings run straight between them.

N

S

## Left Out

Magnets only attract some kinds of material. Not all metals are attracted by magnets.

*Magnets are fun to play with! These magnets are called horseshoe magnets because of their curved shape.*

*The area where the magnet has its power is called the magnetic field.*

## What are Magnets?

Scientists think that atoms behave like tiny magnets. In a nonmagnetic material, the atoms face in different directions. In a magnet, all the atoms face the same way. Magnets lose their strength if they are hit, dropped or heated, as this makes the atoms face in different directions.

### Make a Magnet

If you stroke a needle about 50 times with a magnet, it will become magnetic. Stroking the needle in the same direction turns its atoms to face the same way.

### Simple Compass

Compasses are made with magnets – see for yourself! Tape your magnetic needle to a piece of cork and float the cork in some water. It points the same way as a real compass needle – towards the magnetic North Pole.

*The ends of a magnet are called its poles.*

**N**

**S**

**N**

**S**

*It is hard to push two identical poles together. The magnetic forces are pushing them apart.*

*Every magnet has two poles, a south pole (S) and a north pole (N).*

*It isn't easy to pull two different poles apart. The magnetic forces between them hold them close together.*

### Electricity and Magnets

Electricity is used to make magnets which can be switched on and off. This electromagnet is used to sort scrap metal. You can make an electromagnet by winding some wire around a nail and connecting it up to a battery. The nail becomes magnetic.

# MACHINES

When you do a difficult sum, you are working hard, but this is not what scientists call work! In science, work is only done when something is moved, for example, lifted or turned around. Machines make it easier to move things, so less effort is needed to do a job. Bicycles help us move quickly. Like most machines, bicycles are made up of a number of small, simple machines. Wheels, axles, pulleys, gears, levers, slopes and screws are all common simple machines.

**Forced Apart**
Wedges are simple machines that split things open. When a force hammers a wedge into a block of wood, the wood is pushed apart. A wedge is a kind of slope.

*Fulcrum*

**Easy Does It**
Levers make hard jobs easier. A seesaw is a kind of lever. The balancing point is called a fulcrum. The girl's weight is the force, and the box is the load.

**Saddle Sore?**
It is possible to ride a long way on a bike – between 1922 and 1973 a Scot called Tommy Chambers cycled 1,286,517 kilometres!

*Cables link the brake levers to the brake blocks. Pulling the brake levers makes the brake blocks stop the moving wheels.*

*Brake blocks press against the wheel. They use friction to stop it moving.*

**Wheel Genius**
The wheel is one of our most important machines. Two wheels can be joined together by a pole called an axle. A small movement of an axle makes a big turn of a wheel.

*The wheel spins, or rotates, round an axle.*

Difficult · Easy

## Get into Gear

A toothed wheel that turns another toothed wheel is called a gear. Gears change the speed or direction of the moving part of a machine. The small wheel spins round twice as fast as the big wheel, turning in the opposite direction.

## Uphill Climb

Slopes are simple machines. They make it easier to move things onto a higher or lower level. A screw is a kind of slope. If you could unwind the spiral grooves on a screw, they would flatten out as a slope.

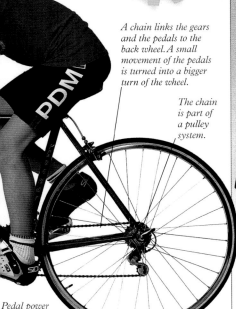

*A chain links the gears and the pedals to the back wheel. A small movement of the pedals is turned into a bigger turn of the wheel.*

*The chain is part of a pulley system.*

*Pedal power is the force that gets you started.*

## Light as a Feather?

Lifting up a weight with your bare hands is hard work. It is much easier to lift a weight by pulling down on the ropes of a pulley. If you double the number of pulley wheels, the same amount of effort will lift twice as many weights.

# ENGINES AND MOTORS

Engines and motors provide power to make things move. Motors usually run on electricity and drive small things, like hairdriers. Engines are usually more powerful and run on heat. In steam engines – the first real engines – heat boils water to make steam and the steam pushes the engine round, just as steam in a pan of boiling water pushes up the lid. Cars have 'internal combustion' engines. In these, the engine is pushed round by the gas produced from burning petrol inside the engine.

*A. DEAKIN & SONS. MODERN AMUSEMENTS*

*Boiler to make steam*

### Letting off Steam
Until about 40 years ago, brightly coloured steam traction engines like this one were often seen at fairgrounds. The traction engine drove the rides and made electricity for the lights.

### Electric Power
Electric motors work by magnetism. An electric current passing through a coil of wire turns the coil into a very powerful magnet. If the coil is set between another magnet, it is driven round at great speed to power your hairdrier.

*Magnet*

*Coil of wire spins round*

### Jet Power
Most modern aeroplanes have jet engines. These push a blast of hot air out at the back which drives the plane forwards at enormous speed.

## Petrol Engine

This is a model of an internal combustion engine, just like those used in most cars today. Fuel is constantly drawn into the engine's cylinder where it is set alight by an electric spark. The explosion pushes the piston down and turns the engine.

*Fuel is drawn into the engine through this inlet pipe.*

*This is the spark plug that lights the fuel.*

*This is the cylinder where the fuel is burned.*

*Old burnt fuel is pushed out through this exhaust pipe.*

*This is the piston. It has been pushed down by the burning fuel.*

*Cooling fins*

*This is the crankshaft. It turns round and round as the piston goes up and down.*

## Four Steps

In most cars, the engine works in four steps, which is why it is called a 4-stroke engine.

*Cylinder*

1. Fuel and air pass into the cylinder.

2. The fuel and air are squashed.

*Spark plug*

3. The spark sets fire to the fuel.

4. The burnt gases are pushed out.

## Spot the Engine

You can find a machine's engine in all sorts of places. The engines here are coloured green.

Electric car

Magnet-powered train

Propeller aircraft

Jet plane

# WAR MACHINES

An aircraft carrier

Hand grenade

Modern armies have all sorts of weapons, from rifles and grenades for fighting a single enemy, to bombs and missiles for attacking large targets. Soldiers can go into battle riding in a tank – a huge gun on wheels protected by heavy armour plating. But nothing can protect against nuclear bombs, the most powerful weapons of all.

**Going Bang!**

Gunpowder was first used in China about 1,000 years ago for making fireworks.

In 1605, Guy Fawkes tried to blow up the English Parliament with gunpowder.

In 1867, Alfred Nobel invented a very powerful explosive called dynamite.

*The main gun can fire powerful shells that will travel 3,000 metres.*

*This is the turret. It turns round so the gun can be aimed in any direction.*

*The tank can carry a huge amount of fuel – around 1,900 litres. But it is only enough to drive about 440 kilometres at 40 kilometres an hour.*

*The commander sits at the top.*

*The driver sits inside at the front and uses mirrors to see what is happening outside.*

*The gunner aims the main gun using a thermal imaging sight. This picks up the heat given out by enemy targets.*

*The loader loads the main gun with explosive shells. He also operates the radio.*

## Runway at Sea

Aircraft carriers are huge ships with flat decks which war planes use for taking off and landing. The carriers sail close to enemy coasts so the planes can launch attacks.

## Getting up Speed

Muskets were used by soldiers in the 17th century. They needed reloading after each shot.

*One of the crew uses a machine gun to defend the tank against enemy aircraft.*

*Heavy steel armour up to 13 cm thick protects the crew from enemy fire.*

Hand-guns like this Colt 45 were carried about 150 years ago by cowboys in the American west. They could fire six bullets without being reloaded.

Machine guns were invented in 1884 by Sir Hiram Maxim. They could fire dozens of bullets one after the other.

*The wheels run inside tough metal bands called caterpillar tracks. To steer, the driver makes one track run faster than the other.*

*Destruction caused by a nuclear bomb in Hiroshima, Japan, 1945.*

## Nuclear Weapons

A single nuclear bomb can destroy a whole city, and the radiation it leaves behind can kill people and animals years later. There are now enough nuclear weapons to destroy the world.

## A Nuclear Explosion

1. As the bomb explodes it makes a giant fireball.

2. The explosion shakes the city below.

3. The blast and fire destroy buildings.

4. Rubble and dust mushroom up high into the sky.

# COMPUTER MAGIC

Computers are the world's cleverest machines. Inside a computer are thousands of very tiny electronic switches, a bit like light switches. By switching them on and off in different combinations, computers can perform all kinds of tasks. They are used every day in car factories, hospitals, supermarkets and offices. Some guide aircraft, ships, submarines and spacecraft. Others are used just for fun, playing games and watching films.

**Keeping your Head Up**
A jet fighter pilot must not take his eyes off the view ahead, even for a second. All the information he needs to control the plane and fire at targets is fed to a computer and projected onto the pilot's face mask. This is called a 'head-up' display.

**Seeing Inside**
Doctors can use a CT (computed tomography) scanner to see inside a patient's body. A CT scanner uses X-rays to create images of 'slices' through the body. These are put together on a computer to create a 3-D image, which doctors use to see what needs treating.

**Bytes and Megabytes**
Computers can help with homework or get an astronaut to the Moon.

**Pocket Brain**
Fifty years ago, the first computers filled a large room. Now there are cleverer and faster computers that can be held in your hand, such as this smartphone.

**Shrinking Switches**
The switches in computers have got steadily smaller and more complicated.

*The first computers had big glass valves.*

*Computers now have tiny microprocessors.*

Laptop computer

Tablet computer

Global positioning system (GPS)

Gaming device

Data computer

# ROBOTS

*The camera in Asimo's head allows him to see objects, plan routes and even recognize faces.*

Robots are machines that 'think' with a computer brain that tells them what to do. Once they have been programmed, they can work entirely by themselves. Some people believe that one day we will be able to make robots that can do everything a human can – and they may even look like humans. At the moment, though, most robots in use today are nothing more than mechanical arms or cranes.

*Asimo automatically bends or twists his body to keep balanced while walking or running.*

### Mechanical Men
Automata are clever machines that move rather like humans or animals. This one was made for a fair in Victorian times.

### Factory Hand
A factory robot is often just a moving arm. But a robotic arm can hold things, screw them into place, weld them and check that they work. It can replace lots of human workers.

### Robots at Work and Play

Robot space probe

Robot dog

Bomb-disposal robot

Robotic arm

*There are force sensors in Asimo's wrists, so if someone shakes his hand, he can tell if he needs to move closer or step back.*

ASIMO

HONDA

HONDA

**Handy Robot**
Asimo has thumbs just like a real person, so he can grip objects, carry trays, open doors and even pour a drink!

**Amazing Asimo**
The first walking robots made by Honda in the 1980s have led to Asimo: a robot that interacts with humans and can help them in the home or office.

ASIMO

HONDA

Asimo can walk, run, and climb up and down stairs.

*The 'backpack' is Asimo's power source, which lasts for an hour on a single charge.*

**Robots in Space**
NASA have sent the first humanoid robot into space. Robonaut 2 is on the International Space Station, doing jobs that are too dangerous or mundane for humans to do.

# ENERGY AND INDUSTRY

In today's world there are thousands of different industries, and they are divided into three groups. Primary industries, such as farming and mining, take raw materials from the earth. Manufacturing industries make, or manufacture, useful things from the raw materials. Service industries are made up of people who sell these goods or supply skills such as nursing or teaching. All industry needs energy to work, so as the world becomes more industrial, it needs more and more energy.

Energy for industry comes mostly from fossil fuels – coal, oil, and gas. These are being used up quickly, and soon they may be gone.

Oil rig

Wind is a type of endless energy.

Oil

Coal

Natural gas

Nuclear energy

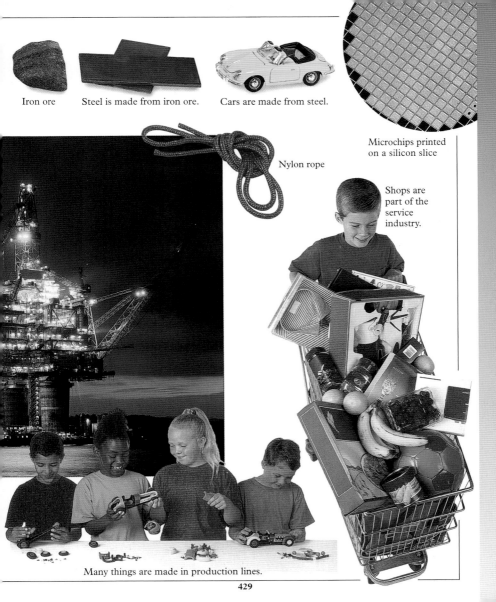

Iron ore

Steel is made from iron ore.

Cars are made from steel.

Microchips printed on a silicon slice

Nylon rope

Shops are part of the service industry.

Many things are made in production lines.

429

# COAL

Like layers of cream in a cake, there are bands, or seams, of coal in the rocks beneath the ground. Some seams are near enough to the surface to be scraped out with diggers. This is called opencast mining. But most seams are found deeper down and have to be dug up by miners using massive machines. About half of the 6,000 million tonnes of coal mined each year is burnt in power stations to generate electricity.

**Cooking Coke**
Coal is put into giant ovens and baked at more than 900°C. When the oven door is opened, coke topples out. Coke is needed to make steel.

*Coke is coal minus tar, oils and gases.*

*The tar that collects at the bottom of a coke oven is used to make soap!*

*Big wheels, called winding gear, lift the coal bucket to the surface.*

*Opencast mine*

*Fans suck stale air out of the mine shaft. This drags fresh air down the other shaft.*

**Cut It Out**
Each scoop on this coal-cutting machine is big enough to hold a car!

*Scoop*

*Roof supports*

**Face Facts**
The part of a seam where coal is being cut is called a face. The coal is ripped out by a spinning cutter with steel teeth.

*Coal face*

*A big bucket carries coal to the surface.*

*Water is sprayed onto the coal to cut down the coal dust.*

*Conveyor belt*

*Pumps take water from the bottom of the mine.*

Air in

Computer control room

The coal is washed and separated into different-sized lumps before it leaves the mine.

**Burning to Go**
Nonstop trains take coal straight to the power station.

Cages carry miners down a deep shaft.

The main shaft was blown out of the rock with explosives.

**All Aboard!**
Miners travel on trains to coal faces that are many kilometres away from the shaft.

Most of the coal in this seam has already been dug out.

A breeze can always be felt in the tunnel as the air moves through the mine.

Long tunnels are dug to reach new coal seams.

**Boring!**
Big machines chew through the rock to open up new tunnels.

Mine shafts can be 1,200 metres deep.

## Down to Earth

Not all coal is the same. Hard coals, which are found deeper underground, release more energy when they burn.

Half-squashed coal, or peat, is made into fuel bricks.

Soft, crumbly brown coal is burnt to make coke.

Black bituminous coal is burnt to generate electricity.

Anthracite coal is used in houses and factories.

Davy's safety lamp

**Seeing the Light**
Miners once worked by candlelight but the flames often set fire to the explosive gases that build up in tunnels. In 1815, a safety lamp was invented. Its flame was kept behind a wire mesh. Modern lamps are even safer as they are battery-powered.

431

# OIL

In the rocks under hot deserts, snowy plains and stormy seas there is buried treasure: a 'liquid gold' called oil. Most of this sticky, black fossil fuel is used for energy but twelve per cent of each barrel is turned into chemicals and plastics. All oil is brought to the surface by drilling deep holes called wells. On land this is fairly easy, but at sea platforms as tall as skyscrapers have to be built.

*Sandstone*

*Sandstone with oil*

### Solid 'Sponge'
Oil is found in the tiny spaces in rocks such as sandstone. This oily layer is often sandwiched between water and a layer of natural gas.

*Natural gas*

*Trapped oil*

*Water*

*Each marble stands for a grain of rock.*

### A Boring Bit
A sharp-toothed metal cutter, called a bit, bores through rock to reach oil. Drill bits are replaced twice a day as they wear out quickly.

*During drilling, chemicals are pumped around the bit to carry rubble up to the surface.*

*This is a model of an oil platform, called Brent C, in the North Sea.*

*Unwanted gas is burnt from the top of a tall tower.*

*Drilling pipes hang from a tower called a derrick.*

*Two hundred people live and work on this oil platform.*

*Helicopter*

*Lifeboat*

*Every day, one quarter of a million barrels of hot, freshly drilled oil are pumped into the hollow concrete legs to cool down.*

*Some oil is piped into a gigantic, underwater storage tank.*

*Cooled oil is piped ashore.*

*Explosives are used to make cracks in the rock so that oil can flow into the wells.*

*Gas*

*An arched layer of oil-proof rock, such as granite, traps oil underneath it.*

*Oil*

*Water*

*Wells fan out to reach the oil.*

**Only Way Out**
A 1,284-kilometre-long pipe snakes across the snowy wastes of Alaska. Oil takes a whole week to flow down the pipe to reach an ice-free port in the South.

**Oil at Sea**
Huge structures, called rigs, drill down to find oil. At sea, some rigs float on the surface but others stand on the sea bed.

*Huge tankers 'plug into' this oil store to take on oil.*

*Tankers can take oil all over the world.*

*Look how big this rig is compared to the Statue of Liberty!*

Jack-up rig

*Anchors keep the oil store on the sea bed.*

Drill ship

**Pump It Up**
Not all oil gushes to the surface naturally. Some is pumped up by machines called nodding donkeys! This 'donkey' has been painted to look like a grasshopper.

Semi-submersible rig

*This zigzag break in the picture is to show that oil is usually found under thousands of metres of rock.*

*Gas gushes out when the pressure is released.*

**Wildcat Wanted?**
Before a well is dug, geologists must be sure that the rocks below the ground are the right shape to trap oil. A test drill, or 'wildcat', is only started if the surveys and satellite pictures look good.

**Bubble Trouble**
Just like the fizz in a fizzy drink, bubbles of natural gas are trapped in oil. If there is enough gas, it is piped ashore. If not, the gas is just burnt.

# NATURAL GAS

**What a Whiff!**
Natural gas has no smell. Chemicals are added to it so that leaks can be smelt.

In 1918, a gas was discovered in an oilfield in Texas. It was named natural gas because it replaced a gas that was manufactured from coal. This new fuel is now used in factories and homes across the world. Natural gas travels a long way before it reaches the top of your stove, to burn as a bright blue flame. It has to be released from deep below the ground, cleaned, and piped countless kilometres.

*The journey begins at a gas rig.*

**Mostly Methane**
Natural gas contains three different gases. Butane and propane are taken out at a gas terminal. Methane, the part that burns best, is sent through pipes to houses and factories.

*Gas terminal*

*Giant fans waft natural gas along the pipes.*

*Butane gas camping stove*

*Pipe*

*'Pig'*

*Soil*

**Cool It**
Ships take methane to places that are not connected to pipelines. The gas is cooled into a liquid so that it takes up 600 times less room.

*If it is cooled into a liquid, a balloonful of methane gas can fit into a space the size of a pea.*

*Methane is cooled to -162°C to make it turn into a liquid.*

*Methane tank*

**Very Important Pig**
'Pigs', not people, check natural gas pipes! A 'pig' is a computer on wheels that whizzes down pipes to pinpoint cracks and other problems.

### On the Way Up
This big building, called a rig, gathers up gas that flows from deep under the sea bed. The drill to reach the pocket of gas may be six kilometres long.

*Some gas is stored near homes to supply sudden daily demands – such as at dinner time!*

*The roof floats on top of the gas. So the lower the roof is, the less gas is left.*

*Iron pipe*

*Gas is sent through pipes to homes and factories.*

*Pumping stations keep the gas moving.*

*The plastic gas pipe is dragged through the tunnel by the 'mole'.*

*Road*

*The 'mole' smashes through the earth like a pneumatic drill.*

*'Mole' hole*

### What Size Pipe?

You could stand up in the pipe that travels between the rig and the terminal.

A dog could fit into the pipe that links factory pipes to gas-terminal pipes.

It is roomy enough for a cat to sit inside the pipes that take gas to factories.

A mouse could fit into the small plastic pipe that goes into your home.

### Growing Gas
Farms off the coast of California grow a giant seaweed, called kelp. It is harvested three times a year by special ships and then put in tanks and left to rot. The decaying kelp gives off methane gas.

### Moles Beat Diggers
Small pipes can be laid without digging up streets using a rocket-like machine, called a 'mole'. Its route is guided by a computer.

# NUCLEAR ENERGY

**Super Fuel**
One handful of pure uranium can release as much energy as 72,000 barrels of oil!

Atoms are the tiny particles that make up the whole universe. Enormous amounts of energy are locked inside atoms. When billions of uranium atoms are torn apart in a nuclear power station the energy that is set free can boil water. Steam from this hot water is used to generate electricity. People worry about nuclear power because when the energy is released from an atom, deadly rays, called radiation, also escape.

**Not So Fast**
This drawing shows very simply how neutrons whizz around a nuclear reactor and crash into uranium atoms in fuel rods.

*2. The splitting uranium atoms inside the fuel rod 'shoot out' new neutrons which travel at 16,000 kilometres a second.*

*1. Energy is released when neutrons hit atoms in the fuel rods.*

*Water warms up*

Fuel rod

*A neutron collides with an atom.*

*The centre of the uranium atom splits in half.*

*Two or three new neutrons escape. Each one can collide with another atom and set free more energy.*

*Energy and radiation*

**Fission Division**
The heart of an atom, called a nucleus, is made up of neutrons and protons. These are held together by energy. When an atom is split, some of this energy is set free. Splitting an atom to release energy is called fission.

*Old fuel rods are radioactive 'rubbish'.*

*Cold water*

**Cool It**
Fuel rods are replaced every few years. Before the reusable uranium can be removed from them, the rods are cooled in a special pond.

Moderator

*Inside this building, a turning turbine generates electricity.*

*The nuclear reactor is in here.*

## A Powerful Building
The nuclear reactor is surrounded by thick concrete walls. These make sure that dangerous radiation does not escape.

*The reactor is under this red steel floor.*

*3. The neutrons collide with atoms in the moderator. This slows them down to just two kilometres a second!*

*If the neutrons travel too fast, they will just whizz past the uranium atoms in the fuel rod and not release any energy to heat up the water.*

*4. This metal rod is a neutron stopper! It is pulled in and out to let just the right number of neutrons through.*

Control rod

## Safe Deposit?
A typical nuclear power station produces about 20 bathfuls of very dangerous radioactive waste each year. It is made into a sort of glass and poured into steel tanks, which are coated in concrete and buried.

*Less dangerous waste is buried in barrels.*

*If too many neutrons pass the control rod, too much energy is released and the reactor could explode.*

*Hot water*

*5. Heat passes from the hot water inside the reactor to this flow of cold water. The cold water boils into steam.*

*Laser beam*

## Sunny Future
When super-hot atoms collide, they fuse together and set energy free. It is this fusion that makes the Sun shine. Scientists are trying to build 'Suns' on Earth by firing lasers at atoms.

*6. The powerful jet of steam turns a turbine to generate electricity.*

# ENDLESS ENERGY

When oil, gas and coal run out, people will need other sources of energy to fuel their cars and light their houses. Wind and water are already being put to work but the best hope for an endless supply of free energy is the Sun. Light and heat from the Sun pour down onto the Earth all the time. Today, sunshine runs calculators, watches and even power stations. One day scientists hope to collect sunlight in space and beam it back to Earth!

**What a Gas!**
In some countries manure is collected, tipped into containers and left to rot. The gas it gives off is piped to homes and used for cooking and heating.

**Falling for You**
The energy of the crashing water at Niagara Falls has been used since 1891. The cascading water forces huge paddles, called turbines, to move round. The spinning turbines turn a shaft to generate electricity.

*Spinning shaft*

*Whooshing water pushes the paddles round.*

**Trick of the Light**
This is the world's first solar power station. It was built in 1969 at Odeillo in France. Electricity is generated by using reflected sunlight to boil water into steam.

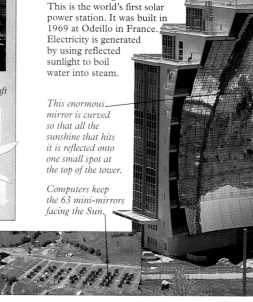

*This enormous mirror is curved so that all the sunshine that hits it is reflected onto one small spot at the top of the tower.*

*Computers keep the 63 mini-mirrors facing the Sun.*

**Not Alone**
The solar power station is faced by 63 small, flat mirrors. They reflect extra light onto the main mirror.

## Whizzing in the Wind

Strong, steady winds can be put to work turning windmill blades. As the blades spin, they turn a shaft that generates electricity. These modern windmills come in several shapes. Groups of them are called wind farms.

*Blades*

*Shafts*  *Electricity generators*

*Reflection of the ground*

*A solar power station does not need a chimney – there are no fumes or ash!*

*This mirror is 42 metres wide. It is built onto the side of a building.*

*Water inside this tower turns to steam.*

*It can get as hot as 3,800 °C inside this tower.*

## No Need for a Plug

Solar cells, made from slices of wafer-thin silicon, turn sunlight into electricity. This remote jungle telephone is powered by several solar cells.

*Sunlight knocks electrons from the top layer to the bottom layer of silicon. This generates an electric current that is collected by the metal layers.*

*Sunlight*  *Metal*

*Silicon*

*Metal*

# ELECTRICITY

Electricity is used as a way of moving energy from place to place. It can take energy from burning coal in a power station into your home to work your television. Most electricity is generated in machines. Small machines, called dynamos, light the lights on bikes. Huge generators in power stations light whole cities. Pedal power works a dynamo, but steam produces the electricity in a power station. This steam is made by using the heat from burning fossil fuels or splitting atoms. Sunshine, falling water and whirling windmills can also generate electricity.

*Dynamo*

**Mighty Machine**
The big blue generator inside this power station is about ten times as tall as you!

*This magnet spins round because it is fixed to a rod that touches the turning wheel.*

*Electricity is generated in this coil of wire by the spinning magnet.*

*Chimney*

*3. Steam surges from the boiler into the generator. It pushes round huge paddles, called turbines.*

*2. The burning coal makes water turn into steam.*

*1. Coal is crushed and then blown into the boiler to burn.*

*A pile of coal as heavy as 40 elephants is burnt each hour.*

*4. Turbines turn a massive magnet round 50 times a second.*

*5. The moving magnet creates an electric current in huge coils of wire.*

*First transformer*

*A condenser turns the hot steam into hot water.*

*The cooling tower cools the hot water so that it can be used again.*

**Choice of Fuels**
A power station uses just one sort of fuel to generate its electricity. This one burns coal, but other power stations use oil, natural gas or nuclear fuel.

Oil

Natural gas

Uranium

**In Charge**
Power stations can't be built near all the places that need electricity. So the electricity generated flows into a network of cables, called a grid. At the touch of a button, electricity is made to flow to wherever it is needed.

*Electricity is dangerous, so tall pylons hold the long cables high above the ground.*

*Second transformer*

*Electricity cables are laid under the ground in towns and cities.*

*A substation makes electricity safe for you to use in your home.*

*Aluminium cable*

*Energy travels down the cables at about 250,000 kilometres a second – almost as fast as the speed of light!*

**Going Up or Going Down?**
Machines, called transformers, change the strength of an electric current. The current that flows between pylons has to be decreased to stop the cables from melting.

*These children are pretending to be tiny parts of atoms, called electrons.*

*Each ball is a 'parcel' of electrical energy.*

**Pass the Parcel**
People once thought that electricity flowed like water, which is why it was called a current. In fact, energy moves along a cable more like balls being passed down a line!

**Watt is Power?**
The speed at which different machines use energy is measured in units called watts.

Electric clock
(10 watts)

Vacuum cleaner
(1,000 watts)

Welding machine
(10,000 watts)

# METALS

Metals are found in the ground, hidden in special rocks, called ores. Tin, copper and iron all have to be taken out of their ores before a factory can melt and shape them into a can, pan or car. Pure metals, however, are usually too weak to be used in industry and have to be mixed together to make better metals called alloys. Lead is soft and tin breaks easily. Together they can make a strong tough alloy known as pewter.

*Iron ore*

*Copper pan*

### Not Natural
Brass is an alloy, which means it can't be dug out of the ground. It is made by mixing two weaker metals, copper and zinc.

*Brass is stronger than zinc or copper.*

*Zinc-coated bucket and wire*

### Precious Metals
Gold and silver are used to make far more than just jewellery. Gold is sprayed onto an astronaut's visor to reflect sunlight. Silver mixtures are used to make photographic films as they are sensitive to light.

### Steel from Iron
Iron has a lot of carbon in it, which makes it crack easily. If some carbon is removed, iron turns into super-strong steel. This change starts in a blast furnace.

*Limestone*

*Crushed iron ore*

*Coke*

*Blast furnace*

*Hot air*

*Coke, limestone and iron ore heat up and turn into iron and a waste material called slag.*

*Slag*

*Iron*

### 1. Blasted Iron Ore
A stream of iron is flowing from this huge oven, called a blast furnace. It has been burned out of iron ore by blasts of hot air.

**Big Dipper**
Steel girders are dipped in a bath of melted zinc to stop them from going rusty. This process is known as galvanizing.

**Plane Wrapper**
Aluminium is a marvellous metal. Thin sheets are wrapped around chocolate to preserve its taste. Thick sheets are made into jumbo jets. Aluminium is used to make planes because it does not rust and it is very light. The aluminium is made as stiff as steel by adding a little copper.

*Iron waiting to be converted*

*Oxygen rushes down this tube.*

*Upright converter*

*Scrap iron can be put into the converter too.*

*In 40 minutes the converter can make 350 tonnes of steel.*

**Rust Buster**
You would not want to eat with rusty cutlery! So chromium is added to steel to make an alloy called stainless steel.

*Tipped-up converter*

*When the strips of steel are cold they can be squashed by rollers into flat slabs.*

*Hot steel*

**2. Iron In, Steel Out**
The liquid iron is poured into a converter. After a powerful jet of oxygen has burnt out the impurities and most of the carbon, the converter is tipped up to pour out steel.

**3. Taking Shape**
Hot, freshly made steel is poured into a big tray. When it has almost set, nozzles are opened and steel oozes out, like toothpaste out of a tube.

# MAKING A CAR

Model T

Every few seconds, somewhere in the world, a brand-new car rolls off a production line and out of a car factory. Each car is made from raw materials, such as iron ore, sulphur and sand, which have been shaped into more than 30,000 parts! Most of this 'jigsaw puzzle' is put together on a kind of giant conveyor belt. Each area of the factory puts on a few particular pieces, for example, the body shop adds the roof, but never the seats. The first car made like this was the Model T Ford.

**Stamp It Out**
Sheets of cold steel are stamped into shape by machines called presses. A press room can be the size of three football stadiums!

*Press*

*Steel*

*The start of the 'conveyor belt'.*

*Each car body is made from more than 20 pieces, or panels, of steel.*

*About 80 per cent of a car is made of iron and steel.*

**Start with Steel**
Steel is the most important ingredient for making cars. Rolling mills press hot steel into thin sheets. These are then rolled up and sent to car factories.

*A roller test is used to check that the car is working.*

*Apart from their colour, all the cars made on this production line are the same.*

*Cars are washed and polished before they leave the factory to be sold.*

**Ready to Go**
Cars were only invented about 120 years ago but there are now more than 700 million of them.

**Built to Bounce**
To make your journey smooth, tyres are made of rubber and filled with air.

*Strands of steel or nylon toughen the tyres.*

## Robots in Charge

The steel sides, roof and doors have to be joined together. This is done by welding – making the metal melt and stick together. Using more than 1,000 welds, robots can build a car body in just 42 seconds.

*Robot welder*

*The pressed steel panels form a rigid box to protect the passengers.*

*Robot painter*

## Mechanical Monets

Cars are painted by robots with sprays. The robots are not harmed by paint fumes and can put paint on quickly and accurately.

*Heavy cars use more fuel. So more and more metal parts, such as bumpers, are being made of plastic.*

*The doors are removed so that the inside can be reached more easily.*

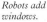

*Bare steel base*    *Top coat*

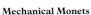

*Fifteen coats of paint are put on each panel.*

*The car is lowered onto an engine, which was built on a separate production line. This may have been in another country!*

*Robots add windows.*

*Each worker repeats the same job over and over again.*

## Pile Up

A new car may not be as new as you think. Up to 40 per cent of the steel may have come from old cars! Recycling scrap steel saves raw materials and energy.

## Together at Last

The engine is the heart of the car but it is not added to the body until near the end of the production line.

# CHEMICAL INDUSTRIES

Soap, fertilizer and glue are just a few of the useful products of the chemical industries. They are made by combining different substances. Crude oil is the main raw material for these industries. The carbon and hydrogen in oil can be made to join up in different ways to make more than half a million things, such as petrol, paint or pills! This manufacturing starts in special factories called refineries.

Oil refinery

**Made to Spread**
Runny vegetable oil is made into solid margarine by adding hydrogen atoms.

### Split It Up!
Crude oil is split into useful oils inside a distillation tower at a refinery. The oils are separated by being boiled into a gas and then cooled back into a liquid.

*Distillation tower*

*110 °C*

*Cooling oil drips from the edge of this 'saucer' into the tray below.*

### Liquid Again
If you put a saucer over a cup of steaming hot liquid, droplets collect on the saucer. The liquid has turned into steam and then cooled back into a liquid when it hit the cold saucer.

*Kerosene is the fuel used by aeroplanes.*

*180 °C*

*The cloud of crude oil gets cooler and cooler as it wafts up the tower.*

*Lubricating oil makes machines run smoothly.*

*At 385 °C, crude oil turns into a gas.*

*Very hot liquid turns into a gas.*    *Gas cools into a liquid.*

*Crude oil is pumped into a furnace to be boiled into a gas.*

### All Change

Chlorine keeps the water in swimming pools clean and safe to swim in. It is made in a factory by passing electricity through salty water. The electric current makes the atoms in the salt and water rearrange and produce chlorine.

*The gases that come out of the top of the tower are made into plastics.*

*One-fifth of each barrel of crude oil separates into petrol.*

*Petrol is the most common fuel used to power cars.*

*When the cloud of crude oil reaches this height, it is cool enough for diesel to turn into a liquid.*

*Diesel is the fuel used by many trains.*

*A different oil flows out of each pipe because all the oils in crude oil cool into liquids at different temperatures.*

*Dark industrial oil is burnt in factories and power stations.*

*Bitumen is the first oil to flow out of the tower.*

*Thick, sticky bitumen is spread on the surface of roads.*

### Cat Cracker

Oil is made up of long chains of carbon and hydrogen atoms. Useful chemicals, called petrochemicals, are made by breaking up these chains. This is done by heating the oil in tanks called cat crackers. The small chains can be used to make useful things such as shampoo.

*Carbon atom* — *Hydrogen atom*

Hydrogen atoms are forced between the carbon atoms to break up the chain.

Shampoo  Plastics
*Antiseptic liquid*
*Nail varnish*

### Sulphur So Good

About 150 million tonnes of sulphuric acid are used every year to help make things such as fertilizer, paper and explosives! This acid is made by heating a yellow rock called sulphur.

# PLASTICS

Plastics are amazing materials. They don't rot like wood or rust like some metals, and they are light and easy to shape. Plastic pens, shoes and even surfboards are all made from oil or coal. Chemicals are taken from these fossil fuels and turned into small, white pellets. These are then melted and blown to form bags or rolled flat to make floor tiles. Buckets, bowls and boxes are usually shaped by being injected into moulding machines.

### Get Set or Go?
Some plastics, such as Bakelite, are like bread! Once they have been 'baked' they cannot be reheated and made into new shapes. A melamine mug will not change shape when hot drinks are poured into it. Polystyrene and polythene are more like chocolate – they can be melted again and again. Each time the mixture cools, it sets into the shape of the mould it has been poured into.

*The two halves of the steel mould lock tightly together.*

### Bowled Out
Washing-up bowls are made by injecting melted plastic pellets into the space between two halves of a steel mould. The plastic cools inside the mould and sets into a bowl shape.

*Cold water cools down the plastic after it has been moulded.*

*Colouring and plastic pellets are poured in.*

*Heaters help to melt the pellets.*

*New bowl*

*Mould*

*A screw pushes the squashed, hot pellets into the mould.*

*Melted plastic*

*Each bowl needs this amount of colouring.*

*Two handfuls of polypropylene plastic pellets make each bowl.*

*Temperatures of 280 °C are needed to melt the pellets and make them flow into this mould.*

**Plastic Products**

*Nose cone*

A plane's nose cone is made from glass-reinforced plastic, not metal, so that radar waves can pass through it.

*Polystyrene is plastic too.*

Many electronic gadgets, such as personal stereos, are made of a tough plastic called ABS.

*Each half of this bowl mould weighs as much as twenty eight-year-old children!*

*This half of the mould moves back to let the warm, newly shaped bowl drop onto a conveyor belt.*

*Four bowls can be made in a minute.*

*Under the rim, you may see a line. This is where the two halves of the mould met.*

*Jets of air blow the bowl off the mould when it is finished.*

*Every bowl that comes out of this machine is exactly the same shape.*

Food slides off the slippery plastic, known as Teflon, used to coat the surface of nonstick pans.

Plastic packaging keeps food fresh for longer. For example, polythene bags stop bread from drying out.

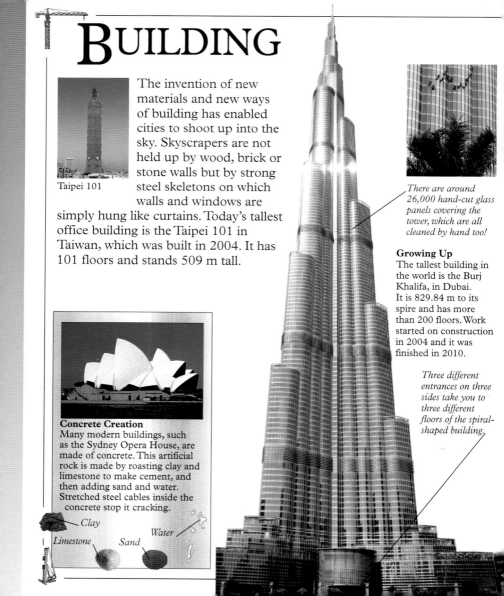

# BUILDING

Taipei 101

The invention of new materials and new ways of building has enabled cities to shoot up into the sky. Skyscrapers are not held up by wood, brick or stone walls but by strong steel skeletons on which walls and windows are simply hung like curtains. Today's tallest office building is the Taipei 101 in Taiwan, which was built in 2004. It has 101 floors and stands 509 m tall.

*There are around 26,000 hand-cut glass panels covering the tower, which are all cleaned by hand too!*

**Growing Up**
The tallest building in the world is the Burj Khalifa, in Dubai. It is 829.84 m to its spire and has more than 200 floors. Work started on construction in 2004 and it was finished in 2010.

*Three different entrances on three sides take you to three different floors of the spiral-shaped building.*

**Concrete Creation**
Many modern buildings, such as the Sydney Opera House, are made of concrete. This artificial rock is made by roasting clay and limestone to make cement, and then adding sand and water. Stretched steel cables inside the concrete stop it cracking.

Clay
Water
Limestone
Sand

*It took around 22 million man-hours to complete the tower.*

*There are 26 stages where the tower gets narrower as it gets taller.*

*There are 31,400 tons of reinforced steel bars in the tower – enough to reach more than a quarter of the way around the world.*

## Building Bridges
Simple beam bridges can span streams, but more complicated bridges are built across wider rivers.

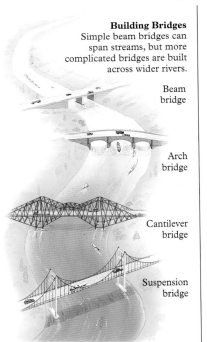

Beam bridge

Arch bridge

Cantilever bridge

Suspension bridge

*A team of more than 380 people worked on putting on the glass and metal cladding – as many as 175 panels a day.*

Steel frame

Concrete base

### Rock Steady
Buildings need a strong base, or foundation, to stop them sinking, slipping sideways or being blown over by the wind. Tall buildings are held down by long steel or cement piles.

*Piles are pushed into solid rock.*

*Soft rock*

# TRANSPORT

Transport is so much a part of our daily lives that most of us take it for granted. Without it, we would all grind to a halt. Millions of people would not get to work, many children would not get to school and no goods would be delivered to the shops. Even the letters we send would never reach their destinations.

Early people relied on animal transport, and this remained the only way of getting around until about 200 years ago, when the bicycle was invented. Cars didn't come into common use until the first part of the 20th century. Today, though, a jet plane can fly you across the world in hours, and huge spacecraft take astronauts on exploratory journeys into space. Before long, you may be able to book a ticket to Venus or Mars for your holiday!

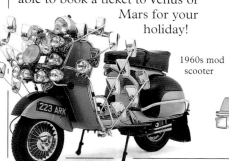

1960s mod scooter

223 ARK

1950s American car

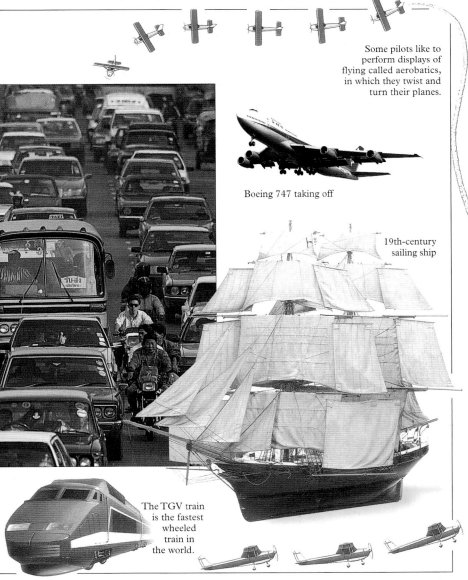

Some pilots like to perform displays of flying called aerobatics, in which they twist and turn their planes.

Boeing 747 taking off

19th-century sailing ship

The TGV train is the fastest wheeled train in the world.

# BIKES

Bicycles were invented in the late 1700s. But they have changed their shape so much over the years that some early bikes such as the 'ordinary' bicycle, also called the penny-farthing, look very strange to us today. Power for a bicycle comes from the rider but sometimes the rider simply runs out of energy! In 1885 a German, Gottlieb Daimler, added an engine to the bicycle and so the motorbike was invented. The very first motorbikes had tiny steam engines, but today they have petrol engines and can more than match cars for speed.

**Fix it Yourself**
Bicycles are simple machines and one of the cheapest forms of transport. Most faults with bicycles are quite simple, too, and can be repaired cheaply and easily by their owners.

**Pollution-Free Traffic**
There are around 500 million bicycles in China, and in the rush hour in Shanghai there is a crowd of bicycles as people ride home. Imagine the terrible fumes and the effect on the environment if all these cyclists drove cars instead of pollution-free bicycles.

*Protective helmet*

*Reflective strips help motorists see cyclists at night.*

*The pedals are linked to the back wheel by a chain.*

*The brakes are operated by levers on the handlebars.*

*Riding a motorbike can be dangerous and a rider should wear leather clothes and a special helmet for protection.*

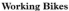

## Working Bikes

Scooters, which are motorbikes with small engines, are used for many jobs around the world. The Spanish Post Office uses yellow scooters for delivering much of its post. Bicycles can also be adapted for carrying all sorts of things – even pigs!

*There are storage compartments under the seat.*

*This part can be removed to make a seat for a passenger.*

## Hot Wheels

Motorbikes come in all shapes and sizes for different jobs and sports.

World War II
US Army motorbike

1966 police motorbike

1983 Racing motorbike

Motocross motorbike

*The panels of this motorbike are shaped so the bike will cut smoothly through the air. Its top speed is 238 kilometres an hour.*

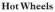

*The motorbike engine runs on petrol.*

*The exhaust carries waste fumes from the engine.*

# CARS TODAY

It is hard to imagine a world without cars. They are all around us and are always being improved to make them more comfortable, more reliable, faster and safer. And cars must continue to change. There are now so many cars in the world that they are one of the greatest threats to our environment. Experts are constantly thinking of new ways to make affordable cars that use less energy and produce less pollution.

**Safety First**
Engineers test all new car designs for safety by crashing the car and filming what happens to dummies inside. Some cars have airbags in the steering wheel that inflate in a fraction of a second in a crash.

*Lever for indicator lights*

*Speedometer*

*Steering wheel*

*The windscreen is made of special glass that stays in one piece if it is broken.*

*Aerial*

*The clutch is used for changing gear.*

*Gear lever*

*Handbrake*

*Brake pedal*

*Accelerator*

*The bonnet lifts to show the engine.*

*Headlamp*

*Bumper*

*Wing mirror*

**Models for Motoring**
Cars are designed to suit the needs of many different people.

Mini car    Saloon car    Sports car    Family car

### Record Breaker
Cars like this are the fastest on land. In 1997 ThrustSSC made a new Supersonic World Land Speed Record, travelling at 1228.49 km/h.

### Sticking to the Road
Racing cars have low bodies, an aerofoil or 'wing' at the back that pushes the car down, and wide, gripping tyres. These are all designed to keep the car firmly on the road at speeds of up to 370 kilometres an hour.

*The bodywork is strengthened to act like a protective 'cage'.*

*This door opens wide so that luggage can be stored in the back.*

### Cars of the Future?
Most petrol engines are quite noisy and give off harmful fumes. Electric cars are quieter and cleaner, although their batteries need charging. Some futuristic cars, such as the Fun-Vii concept car (above), can even display pictures on their outsides.

*Filling up with petrol*

*These lights are used to tell the driver behind if the car is going to turn, brake or reverse. They also show where the car is in the dark.*

*Knobbly tyres grip the road in all weathers.*

Pick-up truck

Stretch limousine

Camper van

זהירות! מטען חורג

# TRUCKS

Trucks come in all shapes and sizes and do very different jobs. Some trucks are very specialized and are used for essential services like collecting rubbish and fighting fires. Most trucks, however, are used for transporting goods. Trucks are ideal for this job as they can deliver right to the door. Even things carried by trains, planes and boats usually need trucks to take them on the last stage of their journey.

**Tight Corners**
Long trucks are often made up of two parts that are hinged so they can turn tight corners. The front part is called the tractor and it pulls a semi-trailer.

*Semi-trailer*

*Tractor*

*Floodlight for night emergencies*

*Warning light*

*Hose storage rack*

*This area is for storing equipment such as extinguishers, axes, buckets and sand.*

*Torch*

*This gauge shows how much water is left in the fire engine.*

*Pump for the fire engine's internal water supply*

**Trains Without Tracks**
Some of the world's biggest trucks are used to transport goods across the desert in Australia. They are called roadtrains because one truck pulls many trailers.

## Big Trucks

Amphibious truck

Cement truck

Earth mover

Car transporter

*The equipment for cutting people out of crashed cars is stored in here.*

*The ladder can be raised automatically to a height of 13.5 metres.*

*Blue flashing lights*

Air deflector       Container

### A Working Arrangement

The same tractor can hook on semi-trailers of many different types, so no journey is wasted. Air deflectors make some loads more streamlined to save fuel.

Tanker

*Five crew members can sit in the front and rear of the cab.*

*This reflective strip makes the fire engine easy to see.*

### Over the Top

Trucks are not just used for work. People often race them and perform crazy stunts with them, too. This Big Foot truck is demonstrating how to flatten a row of parked cars!

### Cab Comforts

At night, long-distance truck drivers usually sleep in their cabs, in an area behind the seats. Some have only bunks, but others have televisions, fridges and even ovens.

# ELECTRIC AND DIESEL TRAINS

In 1964 the Japanese opened the first high-speed electric railway. These 'bullet' passenger trains reached speeds of 210 kilometres an hour, a world record at that time. But railway companies earn most of their money by moving goods, called freight. Freight trains are often pulled by diesel locomotives and they keep a lot of traffic off the roads. The world's longest freight train, in South Africa, had 660 wagons and was over seven kilometres long!

**Round the Bend**
Most trains only travel at top speeds on straight tracks. But in Italy they have designed a train that tilts inwards on curves. This means it doesn't need to slow down much on bends.

*On electric trains, the section that pulls the carriages is called a power car.*

*Pantographs pick up electricity from overhead wires to power the train.*

*The Inter-City Express, or ICE, is an electric train from Germany.*

**Diesel Power**
Like this long Canadian railway convoy, many passengers and goods still travel by cheaper, diesel-powered trains.

*The French electric high-speed train is called the TGV. On its regular route it has a top speed of 300 km/h.*

*High-speed train routes are expensive to set up because they need a special track that has gentle curves.*

## At the Controls

The control centre for TGVs in Paris is in contact with the driver of every train. Controllers can warn the driver about any problems ahead, such as hold-ups, signal failures and electrification faults. In this way, the control centre keeps the rail network running as smoothly as possible.

## Grand Central Station

The largest railway station in the world is Grand Central Station in New York. It has two levels with 41 tracks on the upper level and 26 tracks on the lower one.

*An ICE has two power cars and can carry up to 500 passengers in twelve carriages.*

## On the Tracks

A great variety of engines and wagons use the railway tracks of the world today.

Breakdown train

Snow plough

Passenger train

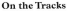

## Coast to Coast

One of the great railway journeys of the world crosses Australia, from Sydney to Perth. The route covers 3,968 kilometres in three days and along the way includes a world record – 478 kilometres of completely straight track!

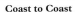

*The streamlined shape of electric trains helps them speed along. In tests the ICE has reached 345 km/h.*

Freight train

# UNDERGROUND AND OVERGROUND

As a city grows busier, the traffic on the roads becomes heavier and slower. This problem can often be solved by building a railway across the city, either over it, on tracks raised above the roads, or under it! There are underground railways all over the world, from London, which has the longest with 408 kilometres of route, to Moscow, where stations are like palaces. But they all do the same job – keep people moving.

**No Smoking**
The first underground railway opened in London in 1863. It used steam trains but the smoke often made it impossible to see in the tunnels. The answer was electric trains, which were introduced in 1890.

**A Tight Squeeze**
So many people travel on the underground railway in Tokyo, Japan, during the rush hour, that special 'shovers' are employed to squeeze passengers into the trains.

*The London Underground is also called the 'tube' because the deep tunnels are built using steel tubing. Tunnels near the surface are dug like ditches and then covered over.*

*Underground trains are powered by electricity picked up from special rails.*

Emergency stairs

*Signs tell people where there is an underground station.*

Ticket machines

Ticket office

*Automatic gates open when a ticket is put in the slot.*

*The escalator is taking passengers towards the platform. A different route will take people from the trains out of the station.*

*Staff in the control room check the progress of the trains and watch the platform on special television screens.*

Route map

### Riding a Single Rail
It is not always possible to build an expensive underground railway system, so some railways run overground. In Sydney, Australia, some trains run on top of a single rail, called a monorail.

### Hanging On
Not all trains run on top of the rail. The first monorail was built in Wuppertal, Germany, and the electric trains hang from the line.

### Going Up!
Special types of transport are needed for getting people up steep slopes.

Rack railway

Cable car

Funicular railway

# SAILING SHIPS

Nearly three-quarters of the Earth's surface is covered by water, most of it in the seas and oceans. For thousands of years people have been finding ways to cross this water. At first they built rafts, and boats with oars, but around 2900 BCE the Egyptians began to use sails. From then on, sailing ships ruled the seas until a century ago. Today, big ships have engines, but small sailing ships are used for sport, fishing and local trade.

**A Quick Tea**
A ship's speed is measured in knots – one knot is about 1.85 km/h. The fastest sailing ships were clippers, like the Cutty Sark, which had a top speed of 17 knots (31 km/h). It transported tea from China to England in about 100 days.

China tea bundles

*Using a sextant, sailors can find their way when they are in the middle of the ocean from the position of the Sun or the stars.*

**Sea Charts**
The sea often hides dangers, like shallow waters or shipwrecks, so sailors must find their way using sea maps, called charts. These also show other information, like the route a ship must take to avoid other ships.

**Tall Ships**
Many of the great ships of the past have been restored and are used today for special 'Tall Ships' races.

**Across the Ocean**
For hundreds of years sailing ships have travelled the oceans of the world for exploration, trade and war.

15th-century Portuguese caravel

16th-century Spanish galleon

17th-century merchant ship

This ship is called a junk. It has square sails, called lugsails, and comes from China.

The masts hold the sails in a good position for catching the wind.

Bamboo rods keep the sails flat and stiff and make a good ladder, too!

**Sailing to Work**
Many countries, such as Sri Lanka, still rely on small sailing ships for coastal fishing.

When the sails are full of wind the ship will move forwards.

Big ships carry a small boat for getting to land because they anchor in deep water a little way from the shore.

The rudder is used for steering the ship.

**Old Junks**
The junk, which can still be seen in harbours such as Hong Kong, in the Far East, was one of the earliest types of boat. It is also one of the most sturdy sailing ships.

18th-century man-of-war

19th-century iron-hulled trading ship

# SHIPS WITH ENGINES

Wind is not a very reliable form of power – sometimes it blows from the wrong direction and sometimes it does not blow at all! But from around 1800, steam engines were used to turn paddle wheels or propellers. Steam power moved ships faster and was a more reliable way of transporting people and goods. Today, ships use mainly diesel engines and their most important job is carrying cargo.

**Propeller Power**
The ship's engine turns a propeller at the back of the ship. This pushes the ship forwards. On a big ship these propellers can be enormous.

*The ship is steered from the wheelhouse.*

*Living quarters*

*This part of the ship is called the bridge.*

*The cruising speed of a ship like this is around 15 knots or 28 km/h.*

**In the Dock**
In modern ports, like Singapore, most cargo arrives on trucks and trains and is already packed in containers. These are stored on the dockside and can then be neatly loaded onto the ships using cranes.

**Pull and Tug**
Big ships are difficult to control and from full speed can take several kilometres just to stop. So in ports and harbours small, powerful boats, called tugs, help push and pull big ships safely into position.

### A Holiday at Sea
Cruise ships offer passengers a luxury holiday as they travel. The biggest cruiser today is the *Allure of the Seas*. It can hold 6,318 passengers and 2,100 crew.

### A Loading Line
On the side of a ship is a row of marks called a Plimsoll line. A certain one of these marks must always be above water or the ship may sink. There are several marks, as ships float at different levels in salt or fresh water, in summer or winter, and in the tropics or the North Atlantic.

*Plimsoll line*

*Containers are stacked in racks on the deck.*

*The front of the ship is marked with a sighting mast. Otherwise it would be hidden from the crew in the bridge by the cargo on the deck.*

GRACECHURCH CROWN

### Save Our Souls
In an emergency at sea, passengers and crew put on life jackets and send an SOS signal. Rescue is carried out by a lifeboat crew.

### Ship Shapes
The seaways of the world are busy with ships of all shapes and sizes.

Naval frigate

Roll-on/roll-off ferry

Oil tanker

# SKIMMING OVER THE WATER

Most water travel is not very fast because the water itself slows the boat down. But hovercraft and hydrofoils just skim across the water, so they can travel at great speed. A hovercraft is not really a boat because it hovers above the surface of the water. It is also amphibious, which means that it can travel on both land and water.

**Water Rafting**
People get around the reed beds and watery forests of the Everglades in Florida, in the USA, using flat-bottomed rafts. These have raised fan motors that do not get caught in the weeds.

Propellers push the vehicle forwards.

*The car deck will hold up to 60 cars.*

*This hovercraft can travel at a speed of 60 knots (111 kilometres an hour) in calm waters.*

**What a Drag!**
Water-skiers can speed over the water, but will slow right down if they fall in. This is because water is over 800 times denser than air.

Control cabin

The cars drive out of this door.

**Up and Away**
Hovercraft are also known as air-cushion vehicles because they float on a cushion of air.

*When the hovercraft is sitting still on the tarmac the skirt is flat and empty.*

*The engines start and the skirt fills with air to become a thick cushion.*

*Hovering just above the surface of the water, the vehicle speeds on its way.*

*The cars drive in through the doors at the back.*

**Thin Fins**
Fins under a hydrofoil lift it out of the water so that it can skim over the surface at great speed.

**Riding High**
Catamarans have two thin hulls so there is very little of the boat in the water to slow it down.

*The rudders twist to turn the vehicle.*

*Inflatable skirt*

*Air is sucked into inlets where fans push it into the skirt to lift the hovercraft.*

*A hovercraft like this can carry over 400 passengers.*

**Super Speedy**
Superboats have very powerful engines. They race at speeds of around 250 kilometres an hour – so fast that their hulls rise right out of the water.

# PLANES WITH PROPELLERS

For hundreds of years people tried in all sorts of crazy ways to fly like birds and insects. But it was not until 1903, when the Wright brothers fixed a propeller to a small petrol engine, that people first managed to control a plane's take-off and landing. Today, huge jet planes can fly hundreds of people around the world, but smaller, cheaper planes with propellers are still the best form of transport for many jobs.

*These propellers have three blades. As they spin round, they move the plane forwards.*

*Skis have been fixed to the wheels so the plane can land and take off from the snow.*

**Fresh Air!**
In 1927 Charles Lindbergh made the first nonstop solo flight across the Atlantic in the *Spirit of St Louis*. Like all pilots at that time, Lindbergh had to wear warm leather flying gear such as a helmet, gloves, a coat and boots to protect himself from the cold.

*Open cockpit*

**To the Rescue**
Light aircraft are relatively cheap to run and are ideal for transport in large remote areas. In parts of Africa, for example, the only way doctors can get to their patients quickly is by plane.

### Short Take-Off
Small planes only need short runways. This means they can go to places where larger planes could not land, like this grassy airstrip on a mountainside in Nepal.

### War and Peace
Over the years, there have been many types of propeller-driven aircraft.

*This plane can seat up to 19 passengers.*

*The rudder moves the plane to the left or the right.*

World War I triplane

*This tailplane keeps the plane stable. Hinged flaps at the back of it move up and down to make the plane climb or dive.*

World War II Spitfire

*This twin-engined 'Otter' can take off and land in a small space.*

Cessna light plane

### Fighting Flames
This Canadair plane is specially designed for fighting forest fires.

*The pilot prepares to lower two pipes to scoop up water into the body of the plane.*

*Flying slowly and quite low, the pilot opens a hatch to release the water.*

*As the plane skims the surface, up to 6,400 litres of water are forced into the tanks in 10 seconds.*

Floatplane

# PASSENGER PLANES

The biggest airliner today is the Airbus A380, which can carry 555 passengers and enough fuel to fly 14,800 km – as far as England to Australia. Big planes have made flying much cheaper, and millions of people pass through the world's airports each year. The passengers simply step onto a waiting plane, but many jobs must be done to ensure every flight takes off and lands safely.

**Join the Queue**
The busiest airport in the world is Hartsfield–Jackson Atlanta International Airport, Georgia, USA. More than 92 million passengers pass through it every year, as well as 950,000 planes.

**A Job for Batman**
Once a plane has landed, a marshaller helps to park it by signalling instructions to the pilot with brightly coloured bats.

*Special trucks pump fuel from underground tanks into the plane.*

*Aeroplane movement on the ground is directed from this control tower.*

*All sorts of vehicles are needed to take luggage, supplies and freight from the plane to the terminal.*

*This plane can carry up to 116 passengers.*

BRITISH AIRWAYS

G-BGDI

## Top Speed

The fastest passenger plane in the skies today is the Boeing 747, also known as the jumbo jet. The average 747-400 plane takes off at 290 km/h, cruises at 910 km/h, and lands at 260 km/h.

## A Room with a View

At peak hours in major international airports planes are landing almost every 60 seconds, while other planes wait to take off. The take-off and landing of these planes is carefully supervised from the control tower.

## Curious Cargo

Goods may be loaded onto a plane with a scissor-action crane or a conveyor belt. Some cargo simply walks in and out of the hold!

## A Good Check Up

Before each journey the ground crew give the plane a good clean, inside and sometimes outside! Engineers check that the plane is in perfect working order.

*A loading tunnel links the plane to the terminal.*

*From this control tower, staff direct take-offs and landings.*

*Service vehicle*

*Passengers check in for their flights in the airport terminal.*

# Index

## A
abacus 293
Aboriginals 301, 390, 391
ABS plastic 449
acacia 63, 79
Achilles tendon 241
Africa 15, 325, 348, 360-3
    animals 192, 193, 194,
        199, 208, 210
    birds 173, 174, 182
Afrikaners 289, 363
afterlife 258
agave 62
air 402-3, 412
    pollution 357, 456
Airbus A380 aircraft 472
aircraft carrier 422-3
air-cushion vehicles 468-9
airports 472-3
Alaska, USA 351
albatross, Royal 158
Albertosaurus 149
algae 57
Algeria 360, 361
All Blacks rugby team 391
allium 73
Allosaurus 149
alloys 442
Allure of the Seas (ship) 467
alpaca 213
alpine plants 71
aluminium 443, 451
American civil war 290-1
Amerindians 251, 276-7,
    352-3, 356, 359
amphibians 57, 151, 397
Amsterdam, Holland 370
Amundsen, Roald 351
Andes mountains, South
    America 273, 359
angler fish 85
animals 57, 87, 259, 396
    breathing 232-3, 402, 403
    See also individual species
Antarctica 25, 178-9, 350-1
antelopes 187, 214
anther 72, 74
anthracite coal 431
ants 108, 120-1
apartheid 363
Apatosaurus 142
apes 198-9
Apollo space program 36-9,
    40-1
apple 60
arachnids 108
Arctic 25, 58, 160-1, 350-1,
    366-7
Arizona, USA 51, 151
Armstrong, Neil 40
'Arnolfini Marriage,
    The' (J. van Eyck) 310-11
artists 271, 310-11, 383, 390
    Cook's voyages 282-3
Ashanti kingdom 278-9
Asia 325, 326, 380-1
    animals 192, 193, 194

*See also* individual
    countries
Asimo (robot) 426-7
ass 208-9
Astaire, Fred 305
asteroids 35, 50, 51, 150-1
astrolabe 267
astronomy 52-3
athletics 260-1
atoms 398, 436-7
aubergine 343
Australia 11, 79, 288, 390-1
    animals 175, 188-9
    food production 336, 346
Austria 376-7
automata 426
avocado 77, 273
Ayers Rock, Australia 11

## B
baby development 246-7
bacteria 57, 396
badger 174, 397
bagpipes 301
Bakelite 448
baleen whales 102-3
Bali, dancers 389
ballet 295, 306-7
bamboo 69, 451
Bangkok, Thailand 389
Bangladesh 31, 386, 387
banjo 301
banyan 68
baobab 69
barley 322-3
Barosaurus 133, 140, 142-3
bats 75, 154, 187, 202-3, 413
batteries 405, 417
Bavarisaurus 146
bazaar, Istanbul 364
beans 273, 343
bears 196-7
Beauchamps (ballet teacher)
    306
beaver 206, 207
bedouin Arabs 364-5
bee-eaters 157, 175
beef 330-1
bees 74, 108, 124-5
beetles 109, 112-13
beetroot 340
Belgium 370
Berbers 360
Bering Strait 350
Bhutan 386
Bhutto, Benazir 387
Bible, Gutenberg 270
bicycles 418-19, 454-5
Billund, Denmark 367
biology 394, 396
birch 63, 82
bird of paradise flower 75
birds 57, 86, 151, 152-85, 221,
    225, 397
birds of paradise 173
birds of prey 160, 180-1
birth 247
bison 214-15, 253
bitumen 447
bivalves 88-9
black holes 55
blackberry 58

blackbuck 215
blood 224, 230-1
blood gun 319
blue tits 152, 159, 164
blue whale 84
Boeing 747 aircraft 472
boiling points 401
Bolivia 358, 359
bombs, nuclear 422-3
bones 242, 243, 244-5
books 267, 270
botany 396
bovids 214-15
Brachiosaurus 140-1, 142
Brahmaputra River, India 31
braille 226
brain 224-5, 226, 240
brass 442
Brazil 201, 346, 358, 359
breathing 96, 232-3, 396,
    402-3
bridges 451
British Isles 286-7, 368-9
Bronzino, Il 310
bubble shells 88
Buddhism 274, 383, 389
budgerigar 152
buffalo, African 215
buildings 450-1
Bunyols festival, Spain 372
Burj Khalifa, Dubai 450-1
bushmaster snake 346
Bushmen, Kalahari 362
bustard, Kori 175
butane 434
butterflies 74, 109, 114-17
butterfly fish 283
butterwort 67

## C
cable car 463
cactus 58, 61, 69
calcite 22, 23
California, USA 435
camels 212-13, 268-9, 330,
    364
Camarasaurus 132, 142
cameras 314-15
Canada 288, 346, 352-3
    animals 194, 197, 215
Canadair plane 471
'canaphone' 220
capsicum 342
capybara 206
car transporter 459
caravans 269
carbohydrates 238, 239
Caribbean 356-7
carnivores 194-5, 196
carnivorous plants 66-7
carnosaurs 149
carrot 340
cars 355, 444-5, 456-7
cartilage 97, 100, 245
cassava 341
cassowary 183
castles 266, 376, 379
cat cracker 447
Cat on a Hot Tin Roof
    (play) 298
Çatal Hüyük, Turkey 255
catamarans 469

caterpillars 109, 114-15, 116
Catherine II, Empress of
    Russia 280-1
catkins 74
cats 192-3, 225, 259, 263, 413
cattle 212, 214, 254, 330-1, 358
caves 22-3, 26
    paintings 252-3, 310
cavy, rock 206
Central America 272-3, 325,
    356-7
cephalopods 89
Ceratosaurus 135, 149
cereals 254, 256, 322-7
Cessna light plane 471
Chambers, Tommy 418
Chaplin, Charlie 316
cheetah 192-3
chemical industries 432, 446-9
chemistry 394
chillies 273, 343
chimpanzee 198-9
China 36, 310, 382-3, 422,
    454, 465
    Marco Polo 268-9
    plays 299
    sugar production 346
chinchilla 206
chipmunk 206
chiton 89
chlorine 447
chlorophyll 64-5
chocolate 272, 344, 370
Christ statue, Rio de Janeiro,
    Brazil 358
Christians 266, 365
chromium 443
chrysalis 116
circulatory system 219, 230-1
citrus fruits 336-7
clam 89
clementine 337
cliffs 23, 26-7, 171
clippers 464
clock, astronomical 283
clothes 253, 332, 361
    protective 406, 455
coal 286, 287, 404, 405, 428,
    430-1
coastlines 26-7
cobra lily 59, 66
cocido 373
cockatoos 141
cocoa 272, 344-5, 361
coconut 78-9, 328
cocoyam 341
Coelophysis 149
coffee 78, 344-5
coke 287, 430, 431
Collins, Michael 40
Colorado River, USA 31
colour 410-11
Columbus, Christopher 272
comedies 300-1
comets 50-1
compass 417
Compsognathus 135, 146
computers 424-5, 434
conduction 406-7
Congreve rockets 36
conifers 83, 143, 162

# PICTURE CREDITS

The publisher would like to thank the following for their kind permission to reproduce their photographs:

**A.F.P. Photo, Paris:** Mufti Munir 387cra; **Air France:** 473tl; **Alamy Images:** Chad Ehlers 366clb; **Doug Allan:** 179cr, c; **Allsport:** Russell Cheyne 391cr, Yann Guichaoua/Agence Vandystadt 404tl, D.Klutho 459bl, S.Powell 261br, Pascal Rondeau 415br; **Ancient Art & Architecture Collection:** 256tl, 260, 261c, 268bl; **Aquila Photographics:** C.Greaves 167tl; **Archiv Fur Kunst und Geschichte, Berlin:** Musee du Louvre, Paris 310bcr; **Ardea:** G.K.Brown 177l, D.Parer & E.Parer-Cook 13t, K.W.Fink 209cra, F.Gohier 102b, 103t, 105tc, 213cb, C.Haagner 13b, J.M.Labat 188c, Mike Osmond/Auscape Int.102-3, J.Swedberg 170c, R.&V.Taylor 98b, A.Warren 203cr, 199b, A.Wearing 239tr; **Art Directors:** 352c, 375tc; **ASAP:** Y.Mazur 365tl; **Australia House:** 461bc; **Australian Picture Library:** 371r; **Aviation Picture Library:** Austin J.Brown 449tr, 472tr, 473tcl; **Hans Banziger:** 119cl; Barnaby's Picture Library: 349br; **Michael Benton:** 137clb; **BFI Stills, Posters & Designs:** courtesy Productions La Fete Inc., Montreal, Canada 378tr; **Bibliotheque Nationale, Paris:** 267c; **Biofotos:** Heather Angel 29cr, 62br, 68br, 71tl, 78c, 78clb, 81tc, 106tr, 344cb, Bryn Campbell 25, Brian Rogers 29cra; **Birmingham Museum:** 349cb; **Black Hills Institute of Geological Research:** Ed Gerken 138bl, 139tc; **BNFL:** 437crb; **Bridgeman Art Library:** Bibliotheque National, Paris 310cl, Christies, London ©1993. Pollock-Krasner Foundation 311cr, Forbes Magazine Collection 287tc, Galleria del'Academia, Florence 313l, Galleria degli Uffizi, Florence 310bcl, Giraudon 306tl, 310tl, 310bl, Giraudon/Louvre 303br, National Palace, Mexico City 272br, Guildhall Library 462c, Musee Rodin, Paris 295br, National Gallery, London 311tl, Phillips 311bc, Private Collection ©ADAGP, Paris & DACS, London 1993 311bl, Private Collection ©DACS 1993 310br, Tretyakov Gallery 280bl; **British Aerospace:** 424bl; **British Coal:** 430tl, cr, 431tc, cl, bl; **British Gas:** 434br, 435c; **Courtesy Trustees of the British Museum:** 250bl, 251bl, br, 258tl, 258-9c&b, 259r, 260t, 260-1t, 278-9t, 357cra; **British Steel:** 430cl, 442br, 443bl; **John Brown:** 447bra. **J.Allan Cash:** 433c; **Christie's Colour Library:** 293bc; **Bruce Coleman Ltd.:** 170-1, D.Austen 212c, Jan & Des Bartlett 176cl, 182b, Erwin & Peggy Bauer 141tc, 175cr, M.N.Boulton 81tr, Mr.J.Brackenbury 122t, J.Burton 67bl, 78cla, 113bl, 194-5t, 204cr, J.Cancalosi 325cl, G.Cappelli 339cr, D. Chouston 180tr, A.Compost 198-9t, E. Crichton 114b, 145bl, 402cl, G.Cubitt 66tr, 69cr, P.Davey 216cl, A.Davies 200c, F.Erize 107d, 178tr, 206tr, Dr.I.Everson 102t, MPL Fogden 75tl, 118tr, Jeff Foott 61cl, 104-5b, 176r, 209ca, C.B. & D.W. Frith 64cl, F.Furlong 170tl, J.Grayson 109tr, D.Green 158tr, F.Greenaway 171tc, U.Hirsch 72br, M.P.Kahl 65tr, S.C.Kaufman 67br, 201br, 347bc,

S.J.Krasemann 115cb, 202-3b, 331bc, F.Labhardt 126cb, H.Lange 61tr, G. Langsbury 171cl, F.Lanting 116br, L.Lee Rue 66br, 329tr, 363bl, M.Timothy O'Keefe 70bl, 336bc, W.S.Paton 193tr, M.R.Phicton 137cra, 210cr, D.& M.Plage 10b, 217cr, Dr.E.Pott 74cr, 329br, Dr.Sandro Prato 66-7c, 115cr, M.P.Price 58-9c, A.J.Purcell 74bl, 109tc, M.Read 130t, H.Reinhard 60bl, 71tr, 106bl, 210tr, 215tc, F.Sauer 123b, J.Shaw 162-3, 151tl, K.Taylor 117bl, 123br, 127tl, 258bl, N.Tomalin 192cr, M.Viard 335crb, J.Visser 205cr, R.William 119tl, 141c, K.Wothe 69bc, 201tl; **Bruce Coleman Inc.:** 115cla; **Colorsport:** 375crb, Inga Sport 469cr; **Comstock Inc.:** George Lepp 159cl; **Corbis:** Astier/BSIP 424cb, Dave Bartruff 367ftl, Blue Jean Images 424-5, Tami Chappell/Reuters 472tr, Nikolai Golovanoff 425cra, Leo Mason 472tl, Charlie Nucci 425fcr, Markku Ojala/EPA 467tl, Tom Sibley 425bre; **James Davis Worldwide:** 388cla; **Derngate Theatre, Northampton:** 389tr; **DLP:** D.Heald 342-3c, D.Phillips 301tc; **Dorling Kindersley:** Kate Howey and Elgan Loane of Kentree Ltd, Ireland 426br, David Leffman/Rough Guides 367cr, John Rigg/The Robot Hut 426bl, Shutterstick 425ftlr. **Ebenezer Pictures:** J.Browne 383crb; **Ecoscene:** 449tc; **E.T.Archive:** 288bc, 464tr, National Maritime Museum 282tl, bl,V.&A. Museum 251cr; **Mary Evans Picture Library:** 284l, 285tr&b, 287b, 314tr, 357cl, 376clb, 422clb. **Gary Farr:** Photo appears courtesy of New Line Cinema Corp. 317crb; **Chris Fairclough:** 313tr, 330bl, 447tc; **Ffotograff:** Patricia Athie 369crb; **Fine Art Photographic:** 286bl; **Focus, Argentina:** 358-9c; **Michael & Patricia Fogden:** 77br; **Foods from Spain:** 337bl; **Ford Motor Co.Ltd.:** 456tr; **Werner Forman Archive:** Asantehene of Kumase 279crb, Statens Historiska Museum, Stockholm 264tl, Plains Indian Museum, Buffalo Bill Historical Centre,Wyoming 276; **French Railways Ltd.:** 461tr; **Fullwood:** 331c. **Christina Gaiscoigne:** 265tr; **John Paul Getty Museum:** 262cr; **David Gillette, PhD:** 137tl; **Getty Images:** Gianluca Colla/Bloomberg 426clb, Charles Crowell/Bloomberg 451bl, E+/Mie Ahmt 366tr, Gallo Images/Motivate Publishing 451cla, Sean Gallup 425fcra, The Image Bank/Martin Child 450c, Johner Images 366c, Jason Kempin/WireImage 426-7, Kimimasa Mayama/Bloomberg 457cra, Photographer's Choice RF/Franz Aberham 367tc, Pictorial Parade/Archive Photos 425tc, Robert Harding World Imagery/Eurasia 450ftl, Joel Sagel/AFP 450ftr, Sankei 427tr, Stone/Arnulf Husmo 366-7, Yoshikazu Tsuno/AFP 427c, Universal Images Group/Environment Images/UIG 424clb; **Giraudon:** 285tc; **Ronald Grant Archive:** 316bc, 317br; EMI Film Productions Ltd.: 306c, © Saul Zaentz Co., all rights reserved, Francois Duhamel: 318bl; **S.&R.Greenhill:** 220cl, 236cl; **Geoscience Features:** 16c, 17, 23tr, 151cl. **Rafn Hafnfjord:** 15; **Robert Harding Picture Library:** 23tl, 27b, 248-9, 252tr, 256br, 266bl, 271cl, 282-3b, 316tr, 333tc, 342tl, br, 347tr, 353cl, 362cla, 366tr, 372cla, 374tr, 386clb, 387crb, 434cl, 439cr, 444cl, bl, 445tc, 451br, 455tc, 463cr, 496tl, tc, tr, Bildagentur Schuster/Meier 379bl, M.J. Bramwell 470-1c, P.Craven 380-1, G. Heller 385bc, J.Green 471cl, D.Maxwell 232cl, C.Rennie 328bl, 381c, 455tr,

W.Rawlings 370cb, V.Southwell 257tr, G.M.Wilkins 469cra, A.Wolf 460bc, A.Woolfitt 370-11bc, 386cla; **Holt Studios International:** R. Anthony 325bl, D.Donne Bryant 327tr, cr, Nigel Cattlin 68cl, 78cr, bc, 323cb, 326-7t, 333cla, 334bl, 340br, 343cla, 344c, 345br, Jurgen Dielenschneider 329bc, Primrose Peacock 341c, Inga Spence 320-11c, 338-9tc, 339clb; **House of Marbles:** 292tl,tr; **Dianne R. Hughes:** Biological Sciences, Macquarie University, NSW Australia 99tc; **Hulton-Deutsch Collection Ltd.:** 304c, 470bl; **Robert Hunt Library:** 423br; **Hunterian Museum, Glasgow:** Malcolm McCleod 278b; **Hutchison Picture Library:** 296clb, 361tl, Sarah Errington 363tl, V.Lamont 325c, L.McIntyre 325tl, M.MacIntyre 302bl, Stephen Pern 381cl, John Ryle 358cl. **The Image Bank:** 444tr, S.Allen 457crb, D.Berwin 366c, I.Block 390cl, J.Carrier 407tr, A. Caulfield 450tl, 371cl, G.M.Corian 137cla, A.Choisnet 308cr, M.Coyne 450cl, G.V.Faint 280-1r, 460bla, D.Fisher 412tr, Fotoworld 377cl, Di Giacomo 332-3, T.King 468bl, R.Lockyer 308tl, N.Mascardi 392-3, R.Phillips 301tr, Andrea Pistolesi - 356b, Barrie Rokeach 354br, Marc Romanelli 301c, Guido Alberto Rossi 212tr, 288tl, Schloter 445br, H.Schoenbeck 460-1bc, M.Skaryd 472cl, J.Smith 443tr, Harald Sund 288-9, 383cb, Dag Sundberg 367c, Jack Ward 209br, Frank Wing 338c; **Images:** 2tr, 229cl, 234cla, 244cr, 287cr, 370cl, 390cla, 396tc, 404bl, 466tr, 467tr, cr, 472bl; **Impact:** Sergio Dorantes 357tl, M.McQueen 422cla, G.Mendel 363br, M. Mirecki 373tc, B.Rybolt 298tr. **Jacana:** A.Le Garsmeur 382tr, Jean-Michel Labat 157tc, Jean-Philippe Varin 159t. **Kobal Collection:** 305tr, 316cl, 317cra, tr, Warner Bros. 318br. **Ian Lambot:** 451tl,cl,bl; **Frank Lane Picture Agency:** E.&D.Hosking 191tl, S.McCutcheon 268clb, M.Newman 160-1, R.Van Nostrand 124tcr, Fritz Polking 174bl, Len Robinson 185t; **La Vie Du Rail:** 460tr; **Legoland:** 367cl; **Courtesy of Lucasfilms Ltd.:** 'Jedi' TM&©. Lucasfilm Ltd. (LFL) 1983 all rights reserved 319cl. **Magnum:** Abbas 360tr, 387c, Eve Arnold 382-3c, Bruno Barbey 294-5c, 373c, Fred Mayer 373bl, James Nachtwey 357cr, Chris Steele Perkins 359c, Raghu Rai 3c, 386-7c; **MARS:** U.S.Navy 422tr; **Marshall Cavendish Picture Library:** 267tr, 292tc, bc, Palazzo Tursi di Genoa, Servizio Beni Culturali 268tl; **Michelin:** 415cr; **Massey-Ferguson Ltd.:** 321br; **Michel Muller:** ©Henry Moore Foundation (1993) reproduction by kind permission of the Henry Moore Foundation 312br; **Museum of Automata:** York © 426cl; **Museum of London:** 250br, 262b, 263; **Museum of the Rockies:** Bruce Selyem 136b, 137br. **NASA:** 37tl, 39br, 40, 42br, 43t, 45t, 46tr, 47tl, br, 49c, 51br, 53cr, 150cr, 415tr, 427bc; **©National Geographic Society:** Wilbur E.Garrett 350cl; **National**

128tl; **Quadrant:** 473cr, A.Dalton 446-7c. **©John Reader 1994:** 359cra, 360clb, 362cr, b, 364bc, 364-5c, 373tl, 386cb, c, 389tr, 391c; **Renault:** 457cr; **Retna Pictures:** J.Welsby 375c; **Rex Features Ltd.:** M.Friedel 374cl, Stevens/Zihnioglu/ Sipa Press 375cla, Stills/Pat/Arnal 370cr; **Ludwig Richter:** Guttenberg Museum 270c, bl, br; **Royal Botanic Gardens, Kew:** David Cutler 70br; **Royal Collection, St.James' Palace ©Her Majesty The Queen:** 280tl; **Royal Geographical Society:** 351tc; **Royal Museums of Scotland:** 250bcr. **Scala:** 253tr, Iraq Museum, Baghdad 257tl, Museo della Scienza, Firenze 271tr, Museo Vaticano, Vinci 271cb; **Science Museum:** 36c, 39bl, 42cr, 44-45; **Science Photo Library:** 53tr, A.Bartel 422bl, 438cl, 440-1tc, Dr. Jeremy Burgess 399cr, CNRI 243tr, 394-5c, T.Craddock 430tr, 438-9bc, Dr.Martin N.England 55br, Fred Espanak 34-5c, 55cr, European Space Agency 8b, 10tl, Dr.G.Feldman/ NASA/GSFC 87tr, S.Fraser 1c, 447tr, D.A.Hardy 55c, 150bc, Adam Hart-Davies 410cr, Kapteyn Laboratorium 52b, Dr.J.Lorre 55cra, M.Marten 437tl, J.Mason 437tr, A.McClenaghan 411br, P.Menzel 424bc, 460tlb, Prof.Motta/Dept. of Anatomy, University 'La Sapienza', Rome 235br, 238tl, 410tr, Prof.E. Mueller 151c, NASA 10-1c, 37r, 49t, 50b, 151b, 412tl, 414, 442bl, NOAO 54b, Claude Nuridsany & Marie Perennou 286l, cla, bl, D.Parker 18, Max Planck Institute 52t, E.Pritchard 452-3c, R. Ressmeyer, Starlight 436bc, 437bc, R.Royer 54-5, J.Sanford 51t, c, 53tl, Dr.R.Schild/Smithsonian Astrophysical Observatory 54t, Dr.E.Spicer 150cl, S.Terry 21r, 42bc, A.Tsiaras 413tr, U.S.Dept.of Energy 427br, 436tl, 437cr, U.S.Naval Observatory 55tr, Tom Van Sant/ Geosphere, Santa Monica 40l, 11crb, bc, D.Vaughan 351c, V.Vick 351cr, E.Viktor 150bl; **Schwangau/ Ostallgau, Germany:** Tanner Nesselwang 376bh; **Sea Containers:** 469crb; **Survival Anglia:** Jeff Foott 211tr, 435bl, J.&J.Palmer 324c, J.M.Pearson 194bl, Alan Root 189cr, J.Root 211c; **Shell:** 434-5c; **Harry Smith Collection:** 337cr, 341cl; **Smithsonian Institute, Washington D.C.:** 113br; **Society for Co-operation in Russian & Soviet Studies:** 281bl, br; **Frank Spooner Pictures/Gamma:** Graham 370cla, T.Mackie 314cr, Rotolo 461cl, V.Shone 380clb, 381bc, W.Volz 313br; **Staatliche Museen zu Berlin, PK Antikensammlung/ BPK:** 260b; **Standard Fireworks:** 409tl; **Steel Can Recycling Information Bureau:** 419tl; **Still Pictures:** B.&C. Alexander 367c, N.Dickinson 388c, J.Schytte 438tr; **Tony Stone Images:** 264-5b, 348-9c, 352cr, 355cr, 356cla, cr, 368cl, 377cra, 405bc, 428-9c, 433tc, Glen Allison 5cr, 439tl, Chris Baker 186-7c, P.Berger 389cla, K.Biggs 405tr, Bryn Campbell 349bl, Paul Chesley 348cl, 345cra, 349cl, 462bl, B. Chittock 390tr, P.Correz 468c, R. Frerck 372cla, Roy Giles 465cr, M. Gowan 382c, D.Hanson 354bc, D.Hiser 348bl, 357bc, 391tc, A. Husmo 367b, 404cl, A.Le Garsmeur

382cb, J.Murphy 466bc, S.Proehl 385tl, R.Smyth 463tr, Olaf Soot 357bl, N.Turner 365cr; **Swift Picture Library:** 252-3c; **Sygma:** J.Andanson 371tl, T.H.Barbier-Proken 470br, A.Grace 379cla, A.Gyori 378cl, J.Jones 363cl, A.Nogues 369c. **Telegraph Colour Library:** 304cl, 402br, Colorific!/Ken Haas 116tl,/ Claus Meyer, Camara Tres 358bl,/ Roger Ressmeyer, Wheeler 355tl, Masterfile/H.Blohm 351bl, 353cla,/ John Foster 353tl, /J.A.Kraulis 352cla, /V.C.L. 374br; **Topham Picture Source:** 271bc; **Truck Magazine:** 459br, bc. **University of Bristol:** Dr.Mervyn Miles 399t; **Jack Vartoogian:** Christina Garcia Rodero 372cr; Max Whitaker: 328cl; **Windsor Castle Royal Library, ©1992 Her Majesty The Queen:** 27tl. **ZEFA:** 65bra, c, 182cr, 198bl, 229tr, 289b, 295tc, 312bl, 323cl, 329cra, 335cra, 355bl, 359ca, 364cl, 402tr, 406bl, tr, 438bc, 441c, 459br, 462tl, 465tr, Damm 30, 374cla, Davies 368tr, G.Deichmann/ Transglobe 33b, T.Dimock 399bc, W.Eastep 466bl, J.Feingersch 409br, Freitag 160tr, Goebel 351tl, R.Halin 401tr, Heintgel 168cl, bc, c, Knight & Hunt 33t, Maroon 355crb, W. McIntyre/Allstock 21l, NASA 408tr, R.Nicholas 473tr, Rossenbach 27t, Schlenker 358cla, Schroeter 409tc, B.Simmons 312tl, M.Tortoli 123c, A.Von Humboldt 464cr, T.J.Zhejiang 344bl; **Zinc Galvanising Association:** 443tl.

All other images © Dorling Kindersley

For further information see www. dkimages.com

tl - top left
clb - centre left below
tr - top right
crb - centre right below
cla - centre left above
bl - bottom left
cra - centre right above
br - bottom right
cr - centre right
tc - top centre
c - centre
cb - centre below
cl - centre left
bc - bottom centre
f - far